Forming the Early Chinese Court

Forming the Early Chinese Court

RITUALS, SPACES, ROLES

Luke Habberstad

UNIVERSITY OF WASHINGTON PRESS
Seattle and London

THIS BOOK IS MADE POSSIBLE BY A COLLABORATIVE GRANT FROM THE ANDREW W. MELLON FOUNDATION.

Publication of this book was also supported by grants from the Association for Asian Studies First Book Subvention Program and the Center for Asian and Pacific Studies at the University of Oregon.

Printed and bound in the United States of America

21 20 19 18 17 5 4 3 2 1

University of Washington Press
www.washington.edu/uwpress

Library of Congress Cataloging-in-Publication Data on file

ISBN (hc) 978-0-295-74239-7
ISBN (pb) 978-0-295-74260-1
ISBN (ebook) 978-0-295-74240-3

CONTENTS

ACKNOWLEDGMENTS

This book has no dedicatee, an omission that has nothing to do with lack of candidates and everything to do with a personal inability to settle on a single person or even a group of people. My indecision, if frustrating and a bit embarrassing, is a heartening testament to the many forms of assistance that I have received over the years as this book took its circuitous path to completion. Unending thanks are due above all to Michael Nylan. Since I first conceived of researching the imperial court, she was game for a risky undertaking that even I had to admit did not always sound so promising. From the project's overall significance to the subtleties of my translations and lexical choices, Michael's comments, not to mention her friendship and personal support, have proven endlessly helpful. I know they will continue to inspire me in the years to come.

Many others offered suggestions and critiques. At UC Berkeley, Mark Csikszentmihalyi, Nicholas Tackett, Mary Elizabeth Berry, Paula Varsano, and Gene Irschick all provided helpful criticism that moved the project along. At Princeton, Robert Bagley offered me his insightful eyes and ears and provided one inspiring observation that I am still pondering: that material evidence for China's pre-imperial royal courts differs so much from descriptions in texts that we can justifiably wonder how often their authors even entered a court! I am grateful to Griet Vankeerberghen and Michael Loewe for reading and commenting on different portions of my work. Though the final book is quite a bit different from what they read, their comments continue to be helpful. I am fortunate to have many colleagues at the University of Oregon who helped me get this book across the finish line. Special thanks go to Maram Epstein and Roy Chan, both of whom read my manuscript and helped me in shaping the final book. Patricia Ebrey and Jonathan Lipman also kindly read and commented on an entire draft of the manuscript. Many other people, whom I cannot possibly thank individually, offered their reactions and comments, particularly in response to presentations of different portions of my research that I gave at conferences and workshops.

Everybody at the University of Washington Press has done exemplary work, for which I am profoundly grateful. I am happy to give special thanks to Lorri Hagman, who gave feedback on everything from the content to the format and the book cover. The fact that the publication process has gone so smoothly is entirely due to Lorri's intelligence and professionalism. The anonymous reviewers she arranged to referee the manuscript offered immensely helpful critiques, for which I am pleased to thank them here. My only regret is that, despite my efforts, I have doubtless been unable to address all of their comments. Support from many other institutions made possible both this book and the research from which it developed. The Center for Chinese Studies at UC Berkeley, Blakemore Foundation, Mellon Foundation, American Council of Learned Societies, the Oregon Humanities Center at the University of Oregon, UO's Center for Asia Pacific Studies, and the Association for Asian Studies all offered assistance at critical stages of research, writing, and publication. Chapter 2 and chapter 4 are revised versions of articles published, respectively, in the *Journal of the Economic and Social History of the Orient* and in an edited volume published by UW Press. I thank both for giving me permission to include them here. In Taiwan, Liu Tseng-kuei and Hsing I-t'ien welcomed me and provided me with numerous resources at Academia Sinica. I must also thank the libraries and librarians of UC Berkeley and the University of Oregon, especially He Jianye at Berkeley and Wang Xiaotong at Oregon. Both provided constant (and cheerful) assistance at all stages of this project.

I am blessed to have many smart and encouraging colleagues and friends. To name them all individually and point out the help they provided would require a separate chapter or book, one I will happily write if I can find a willing publisher. Until that happens, I can only single out a few people whose support was indispensable. Thanks are due above all to April Hughes, who read and commented on many different versions and portions of the manuscript. Without her constant encouragement and friendship, I could not have finished. Sarah Anne Minkin literally stood next to me as we wrote together in various Oakland coffee bars and cafés, and she continues to inspire me today. Sarah Cowan and Rebecca Weinstein were always available to help me through the tough moments and remind me to celebrate milestones.

As potential dedicatees of this book, my family members are probably the strongest contenders. My sister and brother have always cheered me on, while it is to my parents that I owe my interest in learning, politics, and distant places and cultures. I have always been inspired by their kindness, curiosity, and integrity. Finally, my husband, Ethan, has provided me with endless love and support. To even speak of appreciation or gratitude seems absurd. Our life together is an endless adventure, which regularly has me considering a question that I think concerned many Han officials who pondered their good fortune: Why am I so lucky?

CHRONOLOGY OF DYNASTIES AND HAN REIGN PERIODS

Five Lords . . . . Legendary; traditionally third millennium BCE
Xia . . . . Traditionally 2205–1766 BCE
Shang. . . . . Traditionally 1600–ca. 1050 BCE
Western Zhou . . . . ca. 1050–771 BCE
Chunqiu . . . . 770–481 BCE
Zhanguo . . . . 475–222 BCE
Qin . . . . 221–210 BCE
Western Han . . . . 206 BCE–9 CE
Reign periods
Gaodi (Gaozu) . . . . 206–195 BCE
Huidi. . . . . 195–188 BCE
Shaodi Gong . . . . 188–184 BCE
Shaodi Hong . . . . 184–180 BCE
Wendi . . . . 180–157 BCE
Jingdi. . . . . 157–141 BCE
Wudi . . . . 141–87 BCE
Zhaodi . . . . 87–74 BCE
Xuandi . . . . 74–48 BCE
Yuandi . . . . 48–33 BCE
Chengdi . . . . 33–7 BCE
Aidi . . . . 7–1 BCE
Pingdi . . . . 1 BCE–6 CE
(Liu Ying) . . . . 6–23 CE
Xin dynasty. . . . . 9–23 CE (Wang Mang Interregnum)
Eastern Han . . . . 25–220 CE
Reign periods
Guangwudi. . . . . 25–57 CE
Mingdi . . . . 57–75 CE

Zhangdi . . . . 75–88 CE
Hedi . . . . 88–105 CE
Shangdi. . . . . 105–106 CE
Andi . . . . 106–125 CE
Shundi . . . . 125–144 CE
Zhidi . . . . 144–146 CE
Huandi. . . . . 146–168 CE
Lingdi . . . . 168–189 CE
Xiandi . . . . 189–220 CE
Sanguo . . . . 220–65 CE
Jin . . . . 265–420 CE
Western . . . . 265–316 CE
Eastern. . . . . 317–420 CE
Nanbeichao (a.k.a. Six Dynasties) . 420–589 CE
Sui . . . . 589–617 CE
Tang . . . . 618–907 CE
Song . . . . 960–1279 CE
Northern . . . . 960–1126 CE
Southern . . . . 1126–1279 CE
Yuan . . . . 1279–1368 CE
Ming . . . . 1368–1644 CE
Qing . . . . 1644–1911 CE

Forming the Early Chinese Court

Introduction

Forming the Early Chinese Court

Around 142 BCE, in a region of what is now modern Hubei Province, a man serving as a local official died. He was interred with ceramics, lacquers, and a bound manuscript, composed of some 478 bamboo strips, that had been wrapped in silk and deposited in the northeast corner of the tomb's outer coffin.[1] This "daybook" (*rishu**) details methods for determining auspicious and inauspicious times for different activities (e.g., travel, marriage, construction), similar to daybook manuscripts recovered from several other Qin (221–210 BCE) and Western Han (206 BCE–9 CE) tombs.[2] Our 142 BCE manuscript, however, contains one unique element: a diagram, absent from other excavated daybooks, that might be one of the earliest board games ever discovered in East Asia. The diagram takes players through the ups and downs of their careers, with success partially gauged by money earned, features that have striking parallels with modern board games, particularly the game Life. There are differences, of course, especially between the final goals of the two games: instead of the wealthy retirement enjoyed by winners of Life, those who played the Western Han board game aimed to reach or even replace a ruler residing at the heart of the realm.

The diagram hardly appears game-like to modern eyes, being nothing more than a series of concentric circles containing all sixty combinations of "stems and branches" (*ganzhi*), a cyclical counting system that marked time and delineated space. A text written directly below, meanwhile, provides an explanation (see figure I.1). Archaeologists published a line drawing of the diagram, reproduced here along with a duplicate that replaces the sixty stems and branches with their Arabic numeral equivalents of 1 through 60 (see figure I.2). As figure I.2 shows, the sixty stem-branch combinations chart a path through five concentric circles, repeatedly taking us toward and then away from the diagram's center. Starting from number 1 in the lower right corner, we travel up and then in toward number 14 in the fourth concentric circle, before moving back to the outer, upper right position at number 15. From 15, we repeat this movement toward the center, ending with number 29 in the middle. Number 30 starts back at the outer edge, this time in the upper left corner, the position opposite number 1. The sequence again moves in, then out, and then back in again, stopping at number 59 in the center before moving once more to the outer circle with number 60 at the lower right. The stem-branch combinations have thus returned us to the beginning: the starting position at number 1 is just one space to the right of number 60. In this fashion, the diagram moves in regular patterns from the fifth, outermost circle across the fourth, third, and second circles, before finally arriving in the center, at which point the whole cycle begins again.

This looped path, then, takes players across the diagram's concentric circles in a manner not too different from the road traveling across the Life game board. The text below the diagram, however, reveals even more striking similarities between the two games. Keyed to the diagram's five concentric circles, it explains the significance of moving from one circle to another.[3] The text thus might be one of our earliest examples of board game instructions, and like games played today they reveal much about the values and concerns of the players:

> These are the heaven-sent punishments: The first is called dismissal; the second is called fines; the third is called shaving the beard; the fourth is called mutilating punishment; the fifth is called death.
>
> Holding office and serving the emperor: The first is called promotion, a big take; the second is called further advancement, but do not. . . .[4] The fourth is called entering deeper, increasing your take. The fifth is called the vassal replaces his ruler.[5]

The text thus describes two paths through the diagram: one of criminal punishment and the other of recommendation, promotion, and material gain in office. The details of play remain unknowable, however, and we can only speculate how players moved through the diagram. Perhaps they rolled dice, using the text as a guide for determining what players won or lost as they moved from one concentric circle to another.[6] Players no doubt followed countless variations in

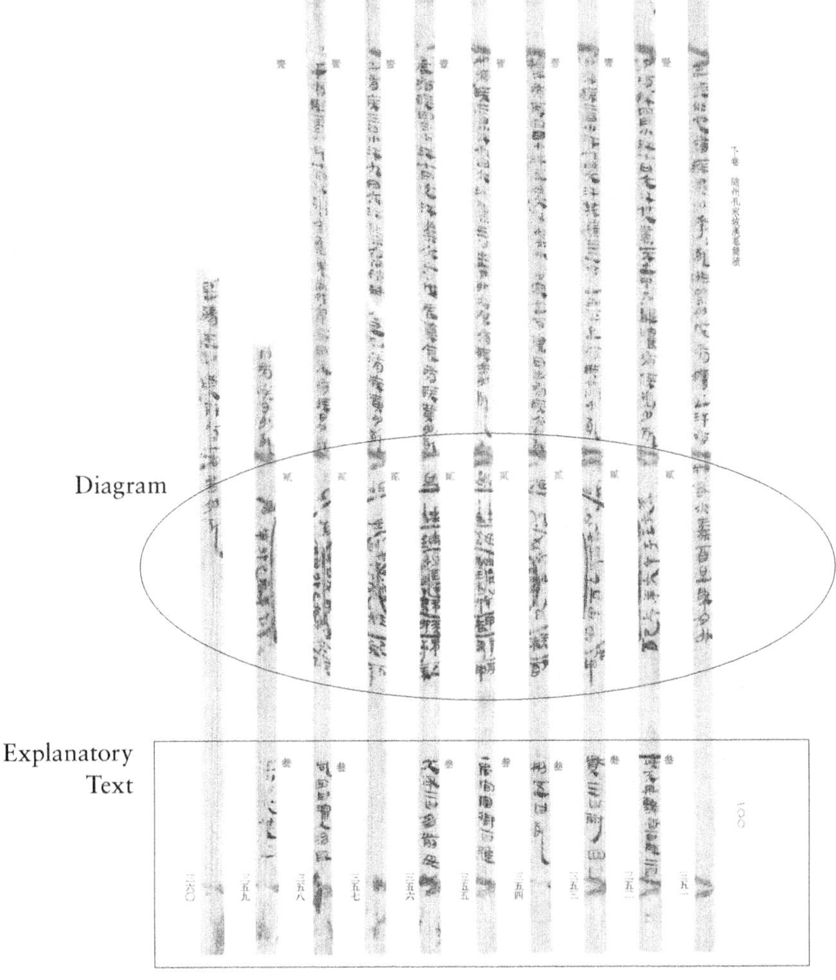

Figure I.1. Diagram from 148 BCE daybook. After Hubei Sheng Wenwu Kaogu Yanjiusuo and Suizhou Shi Kaogu Duibian 2006, 100. English text and graphics added by author.

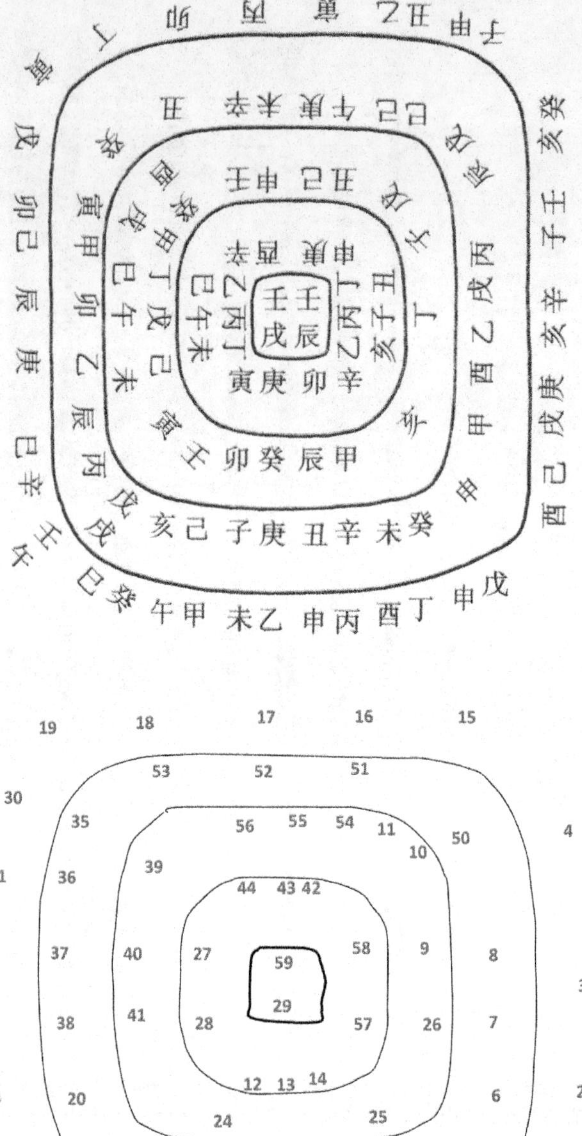

Figure I.2. Drawings of 148 BCE diagram. Top image with stem-branch graphs from Hubei Sheng Wenwu Kaogu Yanjiusuo and Suizhou Shi Kaogu Duibian 2006, 174. Bottom image author's own design.

play, and the relationship between the punishment and promotion cycles of the game remains unclear. Nonetheless, the text and diagram together strongly indicate that the game moved toward either the most intense form of punishment (death) or the most exalted form of promotion (replacing the ruler).

This game might have been a very early precursor of the "promotion games" (*sheng guan tu*) that became widespread in late imperial China, many centuries after the Han. Without denying affinities between the two, however, the differences between our early imperial, Western Han diagram and the promotion games are more striking. Indeed, such differences reveal changing conceptions of official service and even shifting visions of the entire government. Promotion games emerged perhaps as early as the ninth century CE, though most extant examples of actual game boards come from late imperial times, when they were quite popular. The boards contained elaborate charts with finely articulated boxes, each of them representing government posts, from county-level offices to the highest positions at the capital.[7] As the version in figure I.3 from the Qing (1644–1911 CE) period shows, promotion in the late imperial games entailed movement through discrete offices, with the titles and ranks of each carefully noted. Players began in the lower left corner before proceeding in spiral fashion toward the center. Unlike our Western Han game, the center square, representing the capital, does not explicitly mention or depict the emperor, let alone the possibility of replacing him. We see instead only the three top officials of the bureaucracy. The pattern is not particular to this example. Other late imperial promotion games depict in the center square either offices or a building, presumably a building in the capital or imperial palace.

The two games, to be sure, are not without similarities. Both players of the Western Han game and players of the late imperial game moved toward the center. Moreover, chance and fate were equally important in both: the mention of Heaven in the Western Han instructions probably refers to nothing more than run-of-the-mill luck. It is the worlds in which chance and fate operated that distinguish the early game from its late imperial successors. Note, for instance, that in contrast to the late imperial promotion games, players of the Western Han game could be punished as much as rewarded. More important, while the ruler receives explicit mention, not a word is offered regarding offices or official duties. At least in the case of the promotion path, players "enter deeper and increase their take" before finally

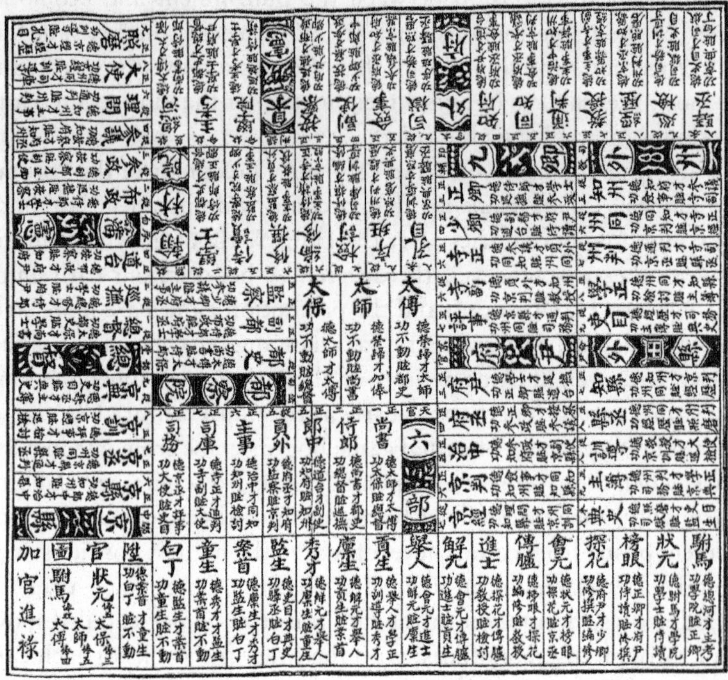

Figure I.3. Ming dynasty "promotion game" (*shengguan tu*). Image from Song Bingren 2005, 71.

"replacing the ruler." "Promotion" was thus not a journey through discrete offices or levels of the imperial bureaucracy, as in the late imperial games. Rather, it was a recommendation-propelled ascent up the rungs of a ladder of material wealth and political power, one that brought players progressively closer to the ruler and, ultimately, to replacing the ruler at court. The highly materialist career of the Western Han game, then, was determined by luck, human connections, and relationships that were largely beyond the control of the players. The ruler, ensconced in the center, rested at the heart of this mysterious cycle of wealth and punishment.

This division between punitive measures and promotion recalls formulations in many early texts that emphasize "punishments and rewards" (often, *xingde* or *shangfa*). The twin concepts could be understood as political, legal, divine, or even cosmological forces, but they always supported models of proper rulership and the "principle of good government."[8] For instance, the *Xunzi* (ca. early third century BCE) and the *Han Feizi* (ca. mid-third century BCE), both being texts that outline comprehensive programs for statecraft, emphasized in slightly different terms the importance for rulers of penalizing bad or illegal behavior and rewarding proper actions that conformed to either ritual practices or legal regulations.[9] Our Western Han game board, however, reversed the perspective from ruler to official, providing a graphic and interactive means for officials to contemplate (playfully or not) the role played by imperially disbursed rewards and punishments in their own lives. The game board, as noted earlier, is the only diagram of this precise type thus far known from excavated manuscripts. At least one other diagram from an earlier tomb, however, appears to be a graphic representation of portions of a text entitled "The Way to Act as a Good Official" (Wei li zhi dao*). That text, included in a manuscript recovered from yet a third tomb, articulated a series of aphorisms, all describing the principles by which officials could serve successfully in their posts.[10] These sources hint at lively and complex interactions between literature about government service, on the one hand, and a rich body of writings and diagrams detailing auspicious activities relevant for local officials, on the other. They also remind us that even if texts such as the *Xunzi* and *Han Feizi* conceptualized ideal forms of government with the ruler in mind, similar concepts circulated among and were refashioned by a broader population of officials for other, sometimes unexpected purposes. In other words, models and understandings of the government in general and the imperial court in particular were just as much rooted in the concerns and anxieties of officials and advisers as they were in the aspirational designs of the ruler.

The diachronic contrast highlighted here as a gap between our excavated board game and later imperial promotion games points us toward an important change in normative understandings of imperial order. This change occurred at some point during and after Western Han, the dynasty that succeeded the short-lived Qin and maintained a unified empire for over two centuries. While people in later eras imagined government as a hierarchical collection of defined offices slotted into categories, early imperial subjects saw not categories but relationships, which were centered around the imperial court and regulated by rewards and punishments. How and why did this change occur? This book is a study of these questions. It is also, however, something more. The synchronic social and intellectual worlds of the Western Han diagram (e.g., discussions of "punishments and rewards" in the *Xunzi* and *Han Feizi*) remind us that establishing a government was not solely a process of creating institutions and asserting political and military power. Nor was it limited to promulgating an "ideology," even one that might have changed over time. The excavated game demonstrates rather that early imperial subjects, in myriad ways, also actively sought to make sense of, and thus come to agreements and understandings about, the institutions they inhabited on a daily basis.[11] In other words, transformations in early imperial institutions and political culture were due not solely to the adoption or rejection of an ideology.[12] They were rooted in the development of new practices and conventions, especially at the early imperial court, by people who sought to articulate their own status in a wealthy and politically treacherous world.

This book thus attempts to understand institutional change not merely as a search for more effective means of exerting power (though this is certainly part of the story) but also for making meaning. The terms *normative understanding* and *model* are key here, for the story of the early Chinese court goes beyond greater institutional articulation or bureaucratic creep in a classic Weberian sense.[13] To be sure, growth and expansion are inevitably central to any history of early imperial China. Correspondingly, close attention must be paid to the details (scant as they often are) of institutional change during Western Han, the first sustained period of unified imperial rule in Chinese history. At the same time, early imperial institutions can be understood as products of literary and rhetorical representations. Such an understanding, however, need not deny the relationship between rhetoric and political, social, and economic processes. Indeed, underlining many of the arguments in this book is not only the idea that politics and literature in the Western Han were mutually constitutive and cannot be understood separately from each other but also that even positing such a divide potentially confuses the nature of early texts and imperial institutions alike.

Let us linger for a moment on the "literary" and the "institutional," since studies of both subjects have advanced in enlightening ways over the past few decades, even while they have tended to reify the two categories in ways that can be historically and ontologically misleading. Recent research on early literary texts has greatly deepened our understanding of what has been broadly termed "court literature." Studies of the "rhapsodies" (*fu*), the long prose poems that became the dominant literary form during the two Han dynasties, are particularly important in this regard. Translations of the rhapsodies have revealed myriad aspects of court life, from minute details of palace architecture to rhetorical practices at court.[14] Scholars have also begun to emphasize the ritual and performance contexts of many literary texts, the rhapsodies among them. Most of the Western Han rhapsodies, for instance, were probably initially written as or on the basis of elaborate performance pieces,[15] and the importance of court ritual performances hardly abated for most of the Han period. Moreover, claims of adherence to authoritative models were often the basis of authority for any "patterned" (*wen*) ritual performance or written text.[16] The late emergence of literary genre categories, most of which did not begin to be defined in any detail until after the fall of Eastern Han (25–220 CE), lends further support to our picture of a literary world in which text, ritual, and performance were all intimately intertwined at the imperial court. But what, precisely, was the institutional life of this "court literature"? The question has usually not received serious attention in histories of early literature, which tend to assume the institutional particulars of the imperial court as a backdrop.

Scholars interested in institutions, then, must turn to works on "institutional history" (Chinese: *zhidu shi*; Japanese: *seido shi*), a rich scholarly tradition examining everything from the management of official documents to the selection and promotion of officials to the precise duties of individual offices.[17] Most studies have focused on government structure: How was the imperial bureaucracy organized? How did government bureaus operate? How did people gain office and promotion? The seminal work in this vein, a classic of twentieth-century Sinology, is *The Bureaucracy of Han Times* (1980) by Hans Bielenstein. The book presented a staggeringly detailed and still indispensable overview of Han officialdom based on exhaustive analysis of relevant treatises in the *History of the Han* (Hanshu, compiled ca. 92 CE) and *History of the Latter [Eastern] Han* (Hou Hanshu, compiled ca. early fifth century CE),[18] supplemented by reference to *Records of the Grand Archivist* (Shiji, compiled ca. 87 BCE) and descriptions of offices from now-fragmented treatises written in the Han and post-Han periods. Our understanding of early imperial administrative operations has advanced considerably since Bielenstein wrote his book. Importantly, we now know that to even speak of a single, unchanging government structure throughout the Han period is misleading, since imperial administrative practices experienced numerous important changes between their establishment during the brief Qin dynasty and the early years of Western Han to their collapse at the end of Eastern Han some four centuries later.[19] Administrative and legal texts excavated over the past few decades have shed further light on many government practices. Most of these documents, however, have been recovered from wells or abandoned military outposts on the fringes of the empire, so their relevance for other regions, including the capital, is not always clear. As Michael Loewe observed decades ago in a statement still relevant today, the site-specific nature of excavated administrative texts means that conclusions reached on their basis may not be applicable to conditions in the interior.[20] Much of our most important information about the administration of the empire as a whole, then, still comes from the *Shiji*, *Hanshu*, *Hou Hanshu*, and other documents written and compiled at the imperial court.

As a result, our histories of the "literary" and the "institutional" in the first centuries of imperial rule converge on the court. It stands to reason that changing court practices of many different kinds must be central to any history of early literature or early imperial institutions, a fact that has begun to receive some attention in recent scholarship.[21] Nonetheless, most scholarship on the early Chinese empires has rarely stopped to ask what, precisely, the court *was*. A reticence among institutional historians to discuss the early court as a category is understandable, since our sources are so limited that detailed studies, perhaps akin to those focusing on late imperial court institutions, are simply not possible for the early imperial court.[22] Perhaps more important, venturing into the subject immediately puts us on shaky ontological ground, for whether treated as an institution or a cultural phenomenon, the boundaries of "the court" are perhaps necessarily ill-defined. This opinion, at least, seems to have been shared by an adviser to King Henry II of England (r. 1154–1189) named Walter Map (1140–ca. 1208–1210), who offered the following musings on the nebulous nature of the court: "In the court I exist and of the court I speak / But what the court is, God knows. I know not."[23] Map's quote, much loved by scholars of premodern courts, is significant not just because it handily illustrates a shared confusion that seems to permeate all discussions of the court, regardless of cultural or historical context. It also reveals that such confusion is exacerbated by the very term itself, which is just as slippery in European languages as it is in Chinese. On the one hand, as Map indicated, the "court" is a physical space ("in the court I exist") and a social or institutional entity ("of the court I speak"). He missed, or at least did not foreground, a third meaning: the rituals, etiquette, and refined conduct that constituted proper courtly behavior. In any case, Map importantly cast the court as a category conjured up but not fully understood by personal experience: he lives in and speaks of the court but cannot fathom its contours. Indeed, Map can only verify its existence (even if in jest) by reference to the divine.

In Map's formulation, then, the court is just as much a question of belief and symbolic rhetoric as it is one of space and institutions.[24] This fact has not been lost on specialists in court studies.[25] The field, however, whether focused on early China or other periods and places, continues to wrestle with the problem. Witness some recent calls for greater attention to the institutions and practices of power, as opposed to "rhetoric," that characterized premodern courts.[26] Most ancient courts, however, have left us little if any information free of complex rhetorical patterns.[27] In a recent essay regarding the imperial court in the latter centuries of the Roman Empire, for instance, one historian emphasized precisely this point: "The 'late Roman court' is a convenient shorthand expression for a complex historical category: the underlying subject at issue is a distinctively configured field of collective human activity and social experience, and the terms in which late Romans understood and represented it are themselves an aspect of the subject."[28] The same is equally true for the early Chinese imperial court. Indeed, questions of terminology get precisely to the problem, as I have experienced again and again, often to my bewilderment, when trying to explain this book's subject matter in modern Mandarin Chinese. After all, to even say that one is studying the "Western Han court" (*Xi Han chao* or *chaoting*) is confusing, almost nonsensical, for in Chinese *Han chao* is roughly equivalent to "Han dynasty" in English. The term is therefore impossibly and confusingly broad, somewhat akin to "the French Empire." It necessarily requires further specification and elaboration.

This moment of bewilderment constitutes the very heart of this book and the starting point of its analysis. Perhaps in earlier times, centuries before unification under Qin and Han, such confusion would not have arisen, since the available terms for *court* did not regularly carry such a global connotation. Some of our oldest sources, such as the poems of the *Odes* (Shijing) and the earliest strata of the

Documents (Shangshu), do not even contain *chaoting* 朝廷, a general term for "the court" found regularly in Zhanguo (475–221 BCE) and early imperial texts. Rather, *chao* or *ting* appear separately, both indicating either (a) physical spaces, whether in capital cities or local jurisdictions, in which rulers, nobles, and officials conducted all manner of ceremonies and government affairs; or (b) a particular ceremony, usually involving subordinate officials or vassals paying a ritual visit to a ruler (e.g., *lai chao*, "come for a court audience"; *bu ting*, "did not visit the court").[29] We occasionally encounter broader, symbolic references to the "royal court" (*wang ting*),[30] but such usage was relatively uncommon and not highly developed.

By contrast, late Zhanguo and early imperial texts are bursting with references to a basket of terms and concepts, many of them related to palaces and temples and different aspects of their architecture, that regularly connote meanings more social and symbolic than spatial or ceremonial. For instance, *langmiao*, literally referring to the halls of a temple or palace, occasionally can be understood as something more like the "corridors of power" from which plans and policies issued.[31] *Chao* and *ting*, meanwhile, hardly diminished in importance, and not only because the two terms combined as *chaoting* in texts from the last few centuries BCE. Equally if not more important is that during or after mid–Western Han both words could refer to the court's collection of people and institutions, if not the whole empire. For instance, both the *Shiji* and *Hanshu* mention a *Han ting* (Han court), often as a specific space but in some cases as a broad reference to the people and institutions of the court.[32] Only the later *Hanshu* uses *Han chao* to generally indicate the Han court as a social and institutional collective. Other Eastern Han texts use *chaoting* and *Han chao* as terms decoupled from specific places, denoting wherever the emperor happened to be, the empire as a whole, or even the Han as a historical period.[33] Notable too is that early imperial texts speak of "vassals of the court" (*chao chen* and *ting chen*), a category that, even if not fully or clearly defined, was almost entirely absent even from Zhanguo texts.

In other words, *ting* and especially *chao* eventually indicated practically everything: all the rituals, spaces, institutions, and people that composed the court and, by extension, the empire.[34] This book attempts to trace that highly significant semantic shift and follow the huge amount of cultural work that took place in order to imbue "the court" with so many layers of meaning. Along the way, it argues that the formation of the imperial court and, by extension, its surrounding empire, was just as much a process of people debating, depicting, and embodying proper models as it was the exertion of centralized imperial power.[35] The people who inhabited and directed imperial institutions wondered about their own proper place and status in the larger empire to which they belonged. To put the problem, and this book's entire argument, in the terms of our excavated diagram: the players had to discuss and come to agreement about the rules, however tentative and contested, before they could play the game.

This book thus places rhetoric and representation at the center of its analysis: it does not present a social or institutional history of the early Chinese imperial court but rather focuses on the emergence of different categories and ways of talking and writing about the court. Neither, however, does it deny the importance of careful study of groups and institutional structures: as emphasized earlier and explained in the chapters that follow, it can, after all, be difficult to separate rhetorical flourishes from institutional realities. Nonetheless, if understood as the apex of elite Han politics and "social structure," to borrow the title of a famous book on the subject,[36] then in fact we do know quite a bit about the imperial court and the different people participating in court life. Of course, often we do not have sufficient information to detail very basic facts. To take but one, albeit very important, problem: even if we can probably assume significant population growth in and around Chang'an over the course of Western Han, we know little about the pace and nature of this demographic change and the relationship between population increases in the capital at large and the growth of the imperial court.[37] Due to these limits in our sources, not to mention the problems of definition that rest at the heart of this book (i.e., what, exactly, was the court, and who could be defined as a "member"?), we simply cannot offer a population figure for the court itself. Nonetheless, with such caveats in mind, since many of the key terms and players described here will reappear in the chapters to come, the following summary of the social and institutional history of the Western Han court is meant to provide some context. Readers more familiar with early imperial history might choose to skip ahead.

The Han realm was led by an emperor (*huangdi*) who, at least in theory if not always in practice, stood at the very top of all social and political hierarchies. Han rulers, however, did not invent the title.

That honor goes to the king of Qin, Ying Zheng (260–210 BCE), who assumed the title of "First Emperor" (Shi huangdi) after defeating all of his rivals and establishing a politically unified Qin Empire. The title confirmed the ruler's status as the highest and most powerful figure in the realm, with all edicts and official appointments issued in his name. Qin and Han emperors alike were furthermore responsible for maintaining and making decisions about the state and ancestral sacrifices, all of which were understood as supremely important to the continued viability of the imperial household and the realm as a whole. If anything, even while the nature of these ceremonies changed significantly over time, the emperor's sacrificial responsibilities became more important over the course of Western and Eastern Han.[38]

Despite continued claims to the contrary, however, the emperor was no all-powerful autocrat, being subject to the demands of many different people as well as institutionalized checks on his power.[39] These included the emperor's mother, the empress dowager (*huang taihou*), whom the emperor could not openly contradict and whose permission was often required before the emperor or high officials could institute certain policies.[40] At times the empress dowager also issued edicts. On several occasions, she and male members of her family directed the government, a fact that is openly acknowledged, if at times with unease, in the *Shiji* and *Hanshu*. This prominent stature of the empress dowager was even reflected in Han palace architecture, for she and her staff resided in Changle Palace in Chang'an, an enormous complex directly connected to the emperor's Weiyang Palace via an elevated walkway (for the positions of the palaces, see figure I.4).[41] The consorts of the emperor also composed an important group: some of them resided within Weiyang Palace, and those who enjoyed the emperor's favor could at times command significant power, which only strengthened if they managed to provide the emperor a son.

Just below the emperor in status were the regional kings (*zhuhou wang*), who, even if not regularly resident in the capital, were required to visit regularly to participate in court audiences. One of the central dramas in Liu Bang's rise to power as founding Han emperor Gaozu (r. 206–195 BCE) was the basic fact that he was not strong enough to subdue his military rivals unilaterally. A low-level local official with no aristocratic pedigree, Gaozu relied on a network of allies to prevail in the civil war that followed the Qin's collapse. Since these allies naturally expected rewards for their assistance, Gaozu was obliged to reaffirm the title of "king" (*wang*) that ten of his most powerful

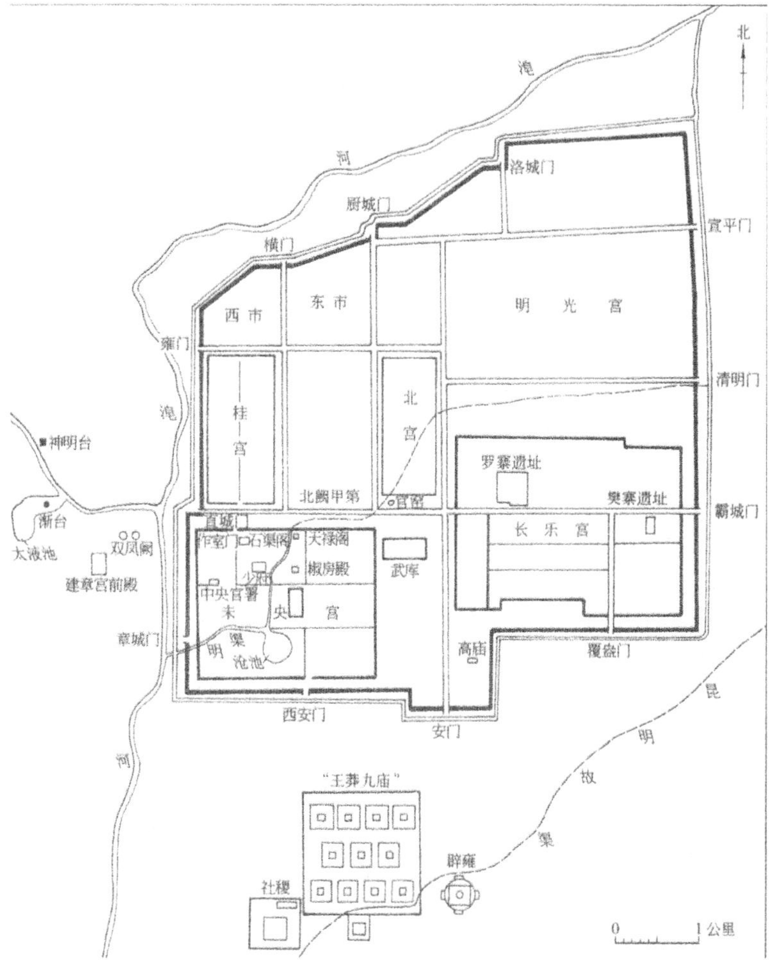

Figure I.4. Map of Chang'an, based on archaeological surveys and excavations. After Zhongguo Shehui Kexue Yuan Kaogu Yanjiusuo 2010, 177, fig. 5-1.

confederates had assumed during the civil war. Collectively, Gaozu ceded some two-thirds of the old Qin Empire to these kings, who ruled from kingdoms (*guo*) over which they maintained autonomous control. By adopting the title *huangdi*, Gaozu followed the Qin model, even while his establishment of the kingdoms resurrected a political pattern of independent realms that characterized the Zhanguo period prior to imperial unification.[42] The kings appointed senior officials, collected all taxes, mustered their own armies, and even employed laws that seem to have operated independently of the Han realm.[43]

Before the end of his reign, however, Gaozu managed to replace all of these kings with his sons and brothers, and Liu family control over the kingdoms continued as an unchallenged principle throughout Western and Eastern Han.[44] The kingdoms themselves, however, hardly remained unchanged, since political relations between the imperial household and the royal lineages became increasingly tense as family ties attenuated. After a major rebellion of several kingdoms in 154 BCE, which Jingdi (r. 157–141 BCE) and his supporters only barely managed to suppress, the kingdoms lost most of their autonomy. While they no longer enjoyed significant administrative and political power, the kingdoms were by no means rendered completely inconsequential. Indeed, the threat of royal rebellion lived on in debates and discussions at the imperial court, even late into Western Han.[45] At the same time, the kingdoms continued to hold important symbolic value, and, significantly, kings served as potential candidates for emperor when there was no viable heir at the capital.[46]

The kings were not the only group to benefit as Gaozu's allies at the outset of Western Han. He also endowed 137 important generals and military officials, men who had achieved military "merit" (*gong*[b]), with the order of "noble" (*chehou*, later *liehou*).[47] This noble title was the highest of twenty "orders of honor" (*jue*), which were regularly conferred by emperors both as rewards to individual recipients and as benevolent gifts to large swaths of the population, in the latter case often in order to mark special occasions and promote loyalty to the realm. The title "noble" was particularly coveted, since it was the only fully heritable rank available to people outside of the imperial family and bestowed title holders with income from a specified number of households. After Gaozu died, nobles were charged with supporting the temples to deceased emperors located throughout the empire.[48] As with the kings, the composition of the nobles changed significantly over the course of Western Han. Most important, whereas Gaozu gave out the first nobilities primarily for military valor, later emperors disbursed noble titles to sons of kings or to close associates for reasons of "favoritism" (*enze*). These at least are the categories used in the *Hanshu* tables (*biao*) that summarize the Western Han nobilities and provide some sense of shifts over time in those who held the title.

Changes in the numbers and makeup of kings and nobles during Western Han are summarized in table I.1.[49] As the table shows, the

TABLE I.1. NUMBER OF KINGS AND NOBLES APPOINTED BY REIGN

Emperor	Kings	Nobles				Total kings and nobles appointed
		Royal Sons	For merit	Favor-itism	Total	
Gaozu (202–195 BCE)	11	3	137	3	143	154
Huidi (195–188 BCE)	8		3		3	11
Empress Lü (188–180 BCE)	3 (11)	3	12	10	25	28
Wendi (180–157 BCE)	16 (20)	14	10	3	27	43
Jingdi (157–141 BCE)	25 (29)	7	18	4	29	54
Wudi (141–87 BCE)	9 (33)	178	75	9	262	271
Zhaodi (87–74 BCE)	(19)	11	8	6	25	44
Xuandi (74–48 BCE)	5 (22)	63	11	20	94	99
Yuandi (48–33 BCE)	6 (21)	48	1	2	51	57
Chengdi (33–7 BCE)	4 (22)	43	5	10	58	62
Aidi (7–1 BCE)	1 (19)	9		13	22	23
Pingdi (1 BCE–6 CE)	4 (22)	27		22	49	53

Note: Numbers in parentheses indicate the total number of kingdoms that existed during each reign.

biggest changes came during the reigns of Jingdi and Wudi (r. 141–87 BCE). Jingdi appointed twenty-five new kings, most of them his sons, while Wudi during his long reign appointed 262 new nobles, more even than the large number of nobles created by Gaozu. Many of Jingdi's royal appointees replaced kingdoms that had been eliminated in the wake of the 154 BCE rebellions. Wudi's nobles, meanwhile, were primarily sons of kings and men who had distinguished themselves in military campaigns that expanded the borders of the empire to the west and south. Moreover, forty of Wudi's seventy-five nobles appointed for merit were members of foreign groups who had surrendered to Han suzerainty. At the same time, we know that Wudi in 112 BCE eliminated a total of 106 nobilities. Other important changes include a more than double increase during the reign of Xuandi (r. 74–49 BCE) in the number of nobles appointed for reasons of favoritism.

Nonetheless, for reigns after Wudi, table I.1 tells a story of relative stability in the overall figures for kings and nobles. For instance, from the reign of Zhaodi (r. 87–74 BCE) the number of kingdoms remained more or less constant, at around twenty. Patterns in the nobilities are more difficult to discern, partly because we do not have complete records for when all nobilities were closed. Nonetheless, we can see from the table that after Wudi no emperor greatly increased the number of nobilities across all three categories. Rather, only one or two categories at most saw a significant increase. Though Xuandi gave out many nobilities, the overall numbers are balanced out by the fact that his predecessor Zhaodi gave only a quarter of Xuandi's number. Most striking, the number of nobilities bestowed for merit decreased significantly and then stabilized in late Western Han. As Loewe showed in his detailed study of the nobilities, from 90 BCE to the end of the Western Han the number of existing nobilities bestowed for merit hardly fluctuated at all: in 90 BCE, there were twenty-seven such nobilities, while in 10 CE there were twenty-five.[50]

This relative stability in the numbers of nobilities possibly reflects the fact that from the reign of Wudi on new means for recruiting officials emerged, with imperial edicts soliciting recommendations from the highest officials for candidates for lower level office. In Chang'an and the imperial palaces such high officials had always included the executive-level posts of chancellor (*chengxiang*) and imperial counselor (*yushi dafu*). They also included the ministers in charge of different government bureaus (agriculture, ceremonial, etc), some of which were quite large and employed many subordinate officials.[51] By the late Western Han, we know that roughly thirty thousand officials worked in the capital area. Surely, this number represented an increase from early Western Han, though we cannot say by how much or determine the rate of population increase.[52] Certainly, the population of officials might have increased with the addition of new recommendation and recruitment practices, even if these practices were never organized into a regular "system," and the criteria for recommendations remain unclear.[53]

Of course, not all of these officials can be understood as belonging to "the court" by any definition, not least because many lower level officials in a central government ministry probably never set foot within the walls of an imperial palace. Nonetheless, many recommended candidates for official posts were first installed as "gentlemen-at-arms" (*lang*), serving as imperial bodyguards in the Chang'an palaces. The number of such gentlemen-at-arms posts reportedly reached as many as one thousand.[54] These were hardly the only guards or attendants, however. Ministries headed by the commandant of guards (*weiwei*), superintendent of the Imperial Household (*langzhong ling*; later *guangluxun*), director of the Lesser Treasury (*shaofu*), and the director of the Household (*zhanshi*) all commanded large staffs charged with attending to the material and security needs of imperial family members. Their duties included maintaining and regulating access to the palaces and parks surrounding Chang'an.[55]

Emperors, empress dowagers, empresses and consorts, kings, nobles, and many different officials, advisers, attendants, and guards: this overview of the social and institutional structure of the Western Han court is not meant to be exhaustive, and there is much that we do not understand. It nonetheless manages to outline the demographic and architectural growth of the imperial court, both trends that provide critical background for the stories and arguments presented in this book. Important to keep in mind in this regard is that after the Qin's collapse, invading armies almost completely destroyed the palaces of Xianyang, the Qin capital located in the Wei River Valley, near what would become Chang'an (see map I.1). While there does not appear to have been a general massacre of the Qin population, the region in and around Xianyang did suffer significant damage. Perhaps partially as a result, Gaozu encouraged people to resettle around the capital.[56] Over the course of Western Han, the population and wealth of Han Chang'an and the capital region, not to mention the number of imperial palaces, continued to expand.

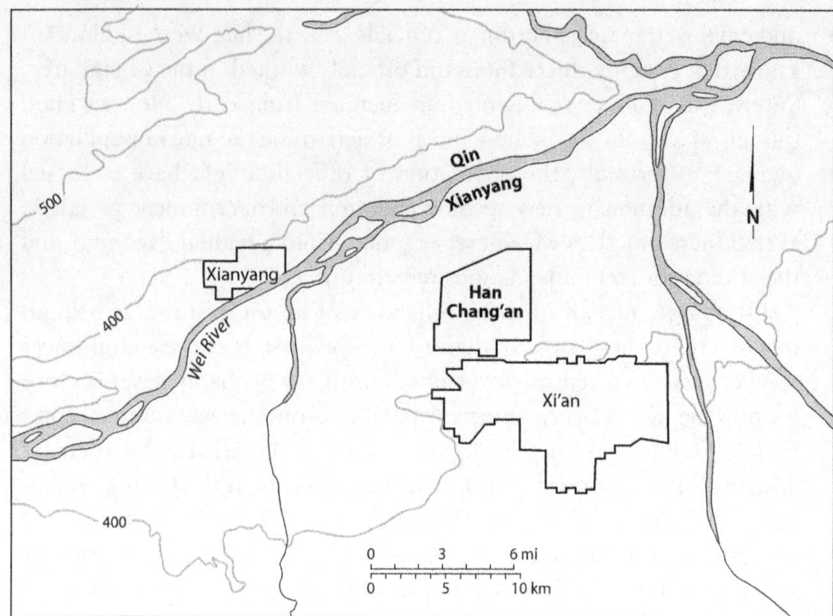

Map I.1. Location of Qin Xianyang and Han Chang'an. Map redrawn based on Zhongguo Shehui Kexue Yuan Kaogu Yanjiusuo 2010, 33, fig. 1-1.

This fact was not lost on many premodern scholars and exegetes, who spent considerable effort combing through received sources to reconstruct the architectural environment of the palaces of Chang'an.[57] Even though some of these efforts yielded remarkably accurate pictures of the city, excavations of Chang'an over the past fifty years have given us an infinitely more detailed vision of the capital.[58] In their reports and studies, archaeologists usually offer a map that indicates all of the structures that have thus far been excavated (some much more thoroughly than others). An example of such a map is shown in figure I.4, which indicates the peripheral city walls as well as the palaces, markets, and temples found both inside and in the immediate environs outside of the city. While helpful, such maps are historically deceptive. Just as Rome did not start out as a marbled and pillared city, Chang'an's structures built up over time, with particularly active construction programs during the reigns of Gaozu, Huidi, and Wudi.[59]

Changes in the built environment over the centuries of Western Han rule rendered the late Western Han version of the city practically unrecognizable from its earlier counterpart (see figure I.5). For most of the dynasty there was no "plan" when it came to constructing the city. Many of Chang'an's most important palaces, even those built by Wudi, were constructed on top of pounded earth foundations that had previously supported Qin structures, a logical move given the huge amount of money and manpower required for these building projects. It was not until the latter years of Western Han, and especially with Wang Mang's relocation of many temples and ritual sites to the immediate environs of the city, that any kind of urban "axis" emerged.[60] Only in this later period did the capital as a *whole* (rather than individual palaces or roadways and temples, located inside or outside the city) function together as a symbol of imperial power.

In sum, even the limited information available to us from received and excavated texts paints a picture of growth as well as increasing differentiation and articulation in institutional and spatial terms. The chapters that follow explore the connections between this growth and the elaboration of new understandings of the imperial court, particularly in the last century of Western Han rule. They also attempt to think through many of our received sources, emphasizing throughout that almost all of the extant sources available for the Western Han court were written within Chang'an palaces and bureaus, even if they were composed for complicated reasons that often had little to do with institutional operations or even straightforward commemoration and celebration of imperial power. There are correspondingly precious few "external" takes on the imperial court that we can check against the rhetorical complexities of our sources, which rarely, if ever, stopped to define the court world from which they emerged.[61]

Even if our ability to define the court is thereby limited, we cannot deny the impact that changing institutional practices and policies at court had on literary production. Recent scholarship on early imperial politics and literature has underscored this point from many different perspectives. For instance, as several scholars have emphasized, the well-known rise of "classical techniques" (*ru shu*) in the late Western Han was not a hermetically sealed process of ideological and generic development that resulted in a "victory of Han Confucianism" and firmly established an "orthodox" canon of texts.[62] Rather, a growing vogue for classicism was intimately related to interlinked processes of imperial expansion, literary innovation, political struggles, and competition between different realms of technical knowledge over the last

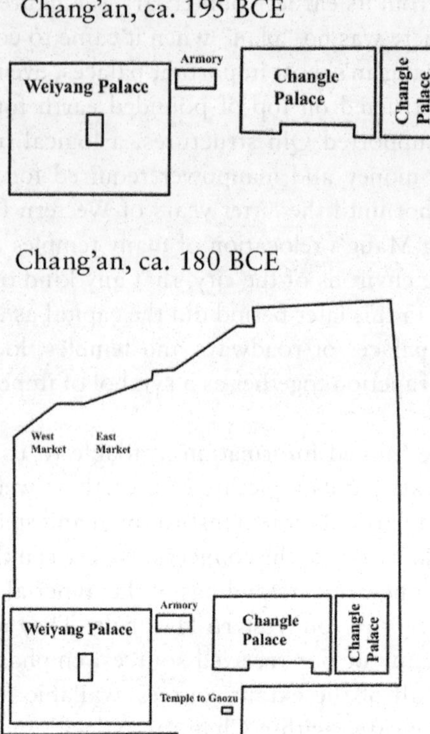

Figure I.5. (this page and opposite page) Western Han Chang'an through the centuries. The location of Mingguang Palace follows arguments in Liu Rui 2007 and 2011 (see n.61).

century of Western Han rule.[63] This book contends that a similar dynamic drove larger understandings about the court itself, which in turn influenced the depiction of imperial court institutions. In this sense, just as we must pause to consider the contexts from which archaeologically excavated documents were unearthed and delimit our conclusions appropriately, so too must we attempt to contextualize the sources produced at the imperial court and their interrelated discussions of the ritual, spatial, and institutional worlds from which they emerged.

Many of these sources are so famous that they scarcely require an introduction. By far the most important are the *Shiji* and *Hanshu*. The complex compilation histories of these texts create both pitfalls

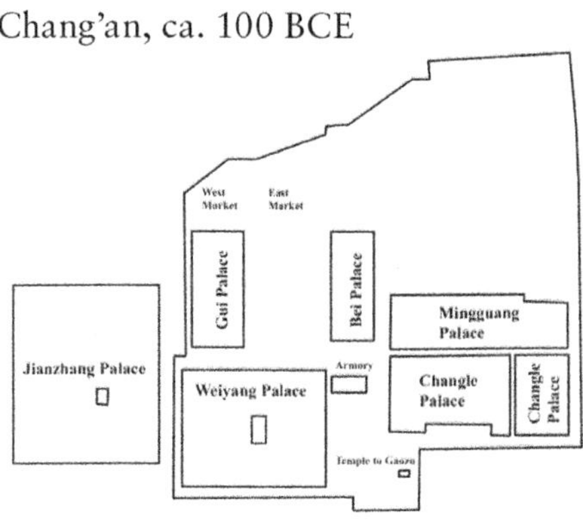

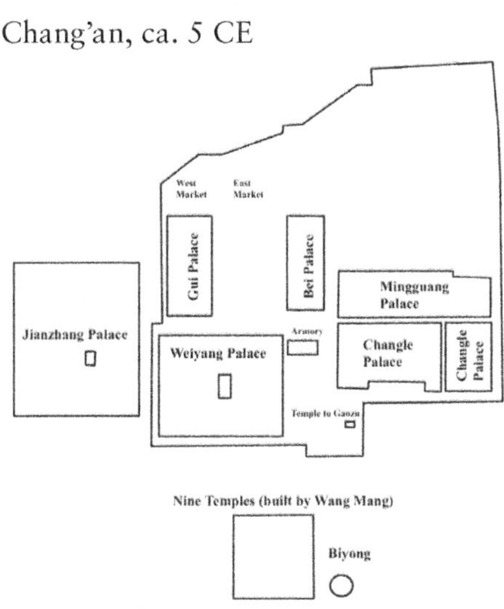

and rich opportunities for any student of the early imperial court. Portions of the *Shiji* were compiled by Sima Tan (d. 110 BCE) and his son Sima Qian (145?–86? BCE). Commentators have long pointed out, however, that father and son could not have composed many of the chapters eventually included in the *Shiji*, an insight that contemporary scholars have confirmed from different perspectives. This study does not necessarily shy away from these textual problems. In fact, at times I call attention to the later composition date of some sections, including additions by Chu Shaosun (104?–30? BCE) and others. I will not wade into long-standing and detailed debates about the authorship of chapters or passages written after Sima Qian's death.[64] At the same time, I do not hesitate to emphasize that Sima Qian could not have written these later portions, which, when contrasted with earlier chapters and passages, help highlight changing practices at and understandings of the court.

Similarly, juxtaposing many *Shiji* chapters with corresponding sections in the *Hanshu* can suggest further important changes. The *Hanshu* was largely compiled in the early Eastern Han by Ban Gu (32–92) on the basis of work initiated by his father, with the eight tables (*biao*) and a treatise (*zhi*[a]) completed by his sister, Ban Zhao (48?–116?), and Ma Xu (fl. 141).[65] In one hundred chapters—including imperial annals (*ji*), tables, treatises, and seventy accounts (*zhuan*)—the *Hanshu* details the history of the Western Han from the life and times of the imperial founder, Gaozu, to the death of Wang Mang (45 BCE–23 CE) and the collapse of his interregnum Xin (9–23) dynasty more than two centuries later. The relationship between the *Shiji* and the *Hanshu* is highly complicated: some portions of our current *Shiji* seem to be later reconstructions based on *Hanshu* chapters, so we cannot assume that all sections of the *Shiji* were written before the *Hanshu*. Nonetheless, in many cases profitable comparisons can be made between portions of the *Shiji* and the *Hanshu* that detail the same period or historical figure, for in some instances major differences between the two texts shed light on changes at court, particularly in the last century of Western Han rule. Even comparisons made within the confines of either text can yield important insights.

Archaeologically excavated documents are also important if highly complicated sources of information, fraught with methodological difficulties.[66] Because this study is concerned less with bureaucratic processes than with normative understandings and the terms by which the court itself was depicted, many of the Western Han administrative documents recovered from sites in the arid northwestern regions of China will not be consulted. Other sources, however, particularly legal texts dating to 186 BCE, recovered from a tomb near Zhangjiashan, Hubei, will provide important points of comparison with information in the *Shiji* and *Hanshu*. I will also occasionally refer to archaeological excavations completed in and around the capital of Chang'an. Interestingly, with two significant but highly specific exceptions, we have no major cache of excavated texts from Chang'an, despite the fact that the palaces, bureaus, and archives of the capital must have housed thousands if not tens of thousands of documents of many different sorts.[67]

As discussed earlier, the words *chao* and *ting* could refer equally to rituals, spaces, or social and institutional collectives as broad as the entire empire, though this final meaning developed only over the course of the Han period. While the chapters of this book focus on each of these three definitions of the court in early imperial China, all of them will touch in different ways upon the third and final meaning. Readers will also notice that my analysis continually turns back to the late Western Han, since this period saw serious and protracted reform efforts at the imperial court that attempted to match actual institutional organization and practice with normative visions of how an ideal court should operate.[68] I begin, however, with a discussion of ritual and sumptuary regulations in the opening decades of Western Han, when the central government focused on maintaining and consolidating its still tenuous hold on power, with scarcely any alteration of Qin institutions and practices. Though these institutions included bureaucratic offices, excavated legal statutes dating to 186 BCE indicate that salary ranks (*zhi*[b]) and orders of honor (*jue*) garnered more attention, since they provided a framework for disbursing gifts from the central government. Even though giving "imperial goods" (*yu wu*) symbolized the court's power, such gifts also helped organize the court internally and assert its supremacy externally, particularly against the rebellious regional kingdoms.

By mid– and late Western Han, however, this process of giving gifts and asserting sumptuary power, according to social and institutional categories worked out at court, was more or less established, since the Han had subdued the kingdoms and asserted itself as the empire's indisputable center of power. Concerns about ritual regulation experienced a parallel shift, demonstrated by a debate about one particular ceremony: the New Year's court audience (*chao* or *chaohui*) of 51 BCE. As the first audience to feature a leader from the foreign, nomadic Xiongnu, the ceremony signified the fracturing of a once powerful confederation that had threatened the Han since its founding. Less recognized is that the 51 BCE audience invited a debate about the nature of Han imperial power and the proper organization of a court that had no serious challengers. In three subtly different treatments of the audience in the *Hanshu* these questions continued to resonate long after 51 BCE, with Ban Gu eventually rewriting the history of the audience as a clash between classically minded officials and an autocratic emperor who had no interest in upholding the principles of classical ritual. As both chapter 1 and 2 demonstrate, the *Hanshu* retrospectively cast discussions of court ritual not as evidence of Han success, let alone supremacy, but as indications of the need to reform ritual along classical lines. Such calls for reform, however, could occur only as a result of complex institutional shifts that raised questions hardly imaginable in the opening decades of Western Han. If that early period required the formulation of ritual and sumptuary categories, by the late Western and early Eastern Han people began to ask how those categories were to be properly filled.

While ritual categories seem to have changed from early to late Western Han, the same could also be said of court space, and not only because the number of buildings increased. Palaces and parks of the capital began to be arranged into hierarchies and endowed with new symbolic meanings. Even from early Western Han palaces had been understood as symbols of imperial power. Later in the dynasty, however, some began to claim that *not* building palaces better demonstrated the court's might and moral perfection. At the same time, different spaces attained more nuanced symbolism and became associated with particular people: parks such as Shanglin were not places for the "grand vassals" (*da chen*) of the court; Weiyang Palace (and not other palaces) was the proper residence of the emperor; and the "forbidden zones" (*jinzhong*) and "inspection zones" (*xingzhong*) accommodated the most privileged groups of people in the empire. The notion of Chang'an's imperial palaces as the center of imperial power, then, is not only or even primarily the result of court rhetoric designed to bolster that power. Rather, it emerged from the complicated interaction of ritual practices, legal regulations, social patterns, and rhetorical representations that, above all, gave capital residents a stake in the notion of Chang'an as the center of the empire.

Offices at the imperial court, as well as their larger organizational structure and hierarchy, were also transformed at the hands of officials and imperial family members seeking new institutional arrangements. A reform of court offices in 8 BCE, for instance, was no minor event, for it was the first to formally establish the supposedly hoary executive council (*sangong*) model of a government headed by a tripartite group of offices, at equal rank, reporting to the emperor. The stakes of the 8 BCE reforms expanded beyond the court itself, since they also changed the ranks and duties of offices in the kingdoms and commanderies. At the same time, they extended deep into the imperial palaces, involving complex political alliances between and against the emperor and his family, even while emphasizing the importance of offices with clearly defined, "discrete duties" (*fen zhi*). Indeed, this notion of "discrete duties" appears to have gained political urgency as well as widespread rhetorical traction, for the idea pops up in a range of texts and literary forms that began to develop at the late Western Han court. The development was by no means uniformly expressed, nor was it entirely "classical," as demonstrated by the diversity of texts that reflect or extol "discrete duties" and their importance: biographies of high office holders, tables of officials in the *Shiji* and *Hanshu*, and a collection of poems called "admonitions" (*zhen*) that describe court offices. All of these sources follow different conventions but still support the same point: that the court, indeed the entire empire was composed of depersonalized and articulated *offices*, not officials, and that the substance of these offices endured beyond the vicissitudes of history and politics. This vision is not too distant from the boxed, clearly delineated diagrams in the late imperial board games, discussed earlier. Forming the imperial court and the exploration of new political, institutional, and literary conventions thus held important implications for transforming larger understandings of the empire itself.

PART I

Rituals

CHAPTER 1

Sumptuary Regulations and the Rhetoric of Equivalency

Late in the reign of Jingdi (r. 156–141 BCE), the son of Zhou Yafu (d. 143 BCE), a powerful retired chancellor (*chengxiang*), started making preparations for his elderly father's tomb and funeral ceremony. Among the items the son planned to inter were five hundred sets of armor paired with shields. He had arranged to purchase the armor sets from an official working at the Imperial Workshop (Shangfang), a bureau located within Weiyang Palace that manufactured items for use at the imperial court.[1] Unfortunately, Zhou's son was delinquent in paying a hired hand who, perhaps in retaliation, reported that the son was guilty of "illicitly purchasing" items belonging to the central government.[2] By the time the matter came to the attention of the emperor, Zhou Yafu himself had become implicated in his son's alleged offense. After Jingdi ordered an investigation, the superintendent of trials (*tingwei*), the top legal official in the empire, joined with other officials in questioning the former chancellor. The *Shiji* recorded a version of their interrogation:

> The superintendent of trials charged: "My lord wishes to rebel, does he not?"
>
> Zhou Yafu said: "The items I purchased were merely funerary goods. How can you speak of rebellion?"
>
> An official said: "Even if you have not rebelled on earth, you certainly desire to rebel below the earth."[3]

Zhou's questioners were probably not primarily concerned with a posthumous insurrection, let alone resurrection, from the grave.[4]

Rather, they implied that by breaking regulations governing burial items, Zhou had revealed his sinister and treasonous intentions. Political motivations possibly drove the interrogation: the *Shiji* records that investigating officials were merely doing the bidding of Jingdi, who wanted to eliminate the powerful head of the Zhou clan.[5] According to the *Shiji*, then, the insinuation that Zhou Yafu wished to rebel was part of a larger smear campaign.

If true, the architects of Zhou's downfall were clever indeed, since elite audiences in early Western Han would have immediately understood the connection between purchasing burial items and rebellion. The funerary ceremonies of wealthy and powerful people, after all, were some of the most visible events in the capital.[6] Moreover, funerals were among several practices governed by imperial sumptuary regulations. Such rules, promulgated in the early decades of Western Han, privileged the status and power of the imperial court, even as they helped solidify allegiance to the new government by providing Han subjects with real benefits. However, the regulations had another, equally important purpose: they provided a logic and process for the organization of the court, since they established social and institutional categories for the disbursement of an array of material goods.

More to the point of the insurrection accusations in the Zhou Yafu story, these sorts of sumptuary regulations had come into play less than a decade earlier, in 154 BCE. That year several kingdoms launched a rebellion that almost toppled the Liu imperial household. In an edict issued in response, Jingdi listed the crimes of the insurgent kings and called on Han generals to execute clients who supported the royal rebellion. The edict began by describing Gaozu's (r. 206–195 BCE) establishment of the kingdoms and Wendi's (r. 180–157 BCE) subsequent move to preserve royal lines, and then condemned several actions of the kings: "Now Liu Ang [king of Jiaoxi] and others have furthermore acted with grave impudence, burning imperial temples and plundering imperial goods. We are greatly pained by these acts and, donning white robes, have avoided the main hall of Weiyang Palace."[7] Significant for our purposes is the reference to kings plundering "imperial goods" (*yu wu*). The term, rare in early texts, sometimes refers to items associated with the imperial ancestral shrines established throughout the empire, as in this edict.[8] Elsewhere, however, it carries a more general meaning, as demonstrated by one late Western Han story describing empresses offering imperial goods as bribes.[9]

We need not necessarily go to stories from late Western Han, however, to find this broader usage, which in some texts seems to refer to gifts from the imperial household. Indeed, in early Western Han "imperial goods" were already important not merely as luxury items to be enjoyed but as items to be distributed at the imperial court's discretion. Such gifts had concrete implications for the organization of imperial institutions. A passage from *New Sayings* (Xin yu), by the early Western Han adviser Lu Jia (ca. 250–170 BCE), reflects this institutional significance of imperial gift-giving. It begins with a description of the procurement, transport, and finishing of precious wood, before a concluding statement that places the superlatively fine product into the system of imperial sumptuary privileges and bestowals: "When [the finished wood] is placed up high it is soft and supple; when inserted into the earth, hard and strong. Without any oils a bright sheen comes forth, and without carving any designs its refined patterns are complete. Above, it serves as an imperial good for emperors and kings, while below it is given as gifts to lords and ministers. Commoners are not allowed to use it when crafting their implements."[10] "Imperial goods" here is ambiguous: it could fit the narrower definition of items used in imperial shrines or refer more broadly to luxury goods enjoyed in the imperial palaces and residences. The important point is that even while such goods were made and explicitly reserved for the sumptuary pleasure of the ruler, the ruler could also give them to defined groups, in this case the "lords and ministers" (*gong qing*). Evidence from excavated legal texts dating to the early Western Han shows that such gifts were not just given to people populating preexisting social and institutional categories. Rather, the very constitution of such categories was predicated on the bestowal of gifts. In other words, "imperial goods" simultaneously symbolized the imperial court's power and, through bestowals of such goods as gifts, helped create the institutional framework by which the imperial court itself was organized and its power activated. As we shall see, hazy as the connection between gift-giving and institutional structure might appear, a shared language of drawing "equivalencies" both for giving gifts and for establishing salary ranks used at court—the so-called equivalent ranks (*bi zhi*)—show that such a connection was indeed present.

Externalized discussions of imperial regalia also drew upon a rich rhetoric of equivalency and comparison. After all, establishing and enforcing a sumptuary regime could not be done in a vacuum, for privileged consumption at the imperial court acquired meaning only if other groups were adequately defined, categorized, and given comparatively meager consumptive rights. A chariot with a "yellow carriage," to invoke an image found in many stories and texts, indicated the emperor only if the emperor could clearly delimit those forbidden from using such a chariot. This rhetoric of equivalencies reached a critical point prior to and immediately after the royal rebellions of 154 BCE, which saw the institution of several sumptuary reforms designed to ensure that no other realm could possibly "equal" the Han imperial court (*Han chao*). "Equivalency," then, was as important for external assertions of the court's power as it was for its internal organization. In a sort of perpetual feedback loop, the expansion and proclamation of imperial power provided the impetus for categorizing and signifying the status of the imperial court itself, a process that arguably continued until the reign of Xuandi at least. This chapter thus focuses less on whether or not sumptuary regulations were consistently enforced or effectively enacted and more on the role that such regulations and talk of sumptuary privileges played in the organization and articulation of imperial power.[11]

On this point, comparison of the *Shiji* and *Hanshu* is instructive, for even though both texts were compiled well after 154 BCE, they provided rather different descriptions and explanations of both the uprising of that year and subsequent insubordinate behavior by the kings. Specifically, the *Hanshu* went out of its way to pair the failure of sumptuary violations with the personal character failings of the kings. In other words, it shifted attention away from the capacity of sumptuary regulations to display power and enforce order, focusing instead on their impotence in preventing moral corruption.[12] By implication, the regulations of equivalency that had buttressed Western Han imperial power for centuries and provided a framework for institutional organization had to be completely reorganized.

INSTITUTIONAL DEFINITIONS AND SUMPTUARY REGULATIONS

Jingdi's 154 BCE edict, one portion of which was discussed earlier, concludes with a stern description of the strategy to be followed in quelling the rebellion of the kings and punishing their supporters: "The generals should urge their soldiers to attack rebels and take them prisoner. When attacking rebels and capturing them, deep incursions and large numbers killed will be held as meritorious. As for executing captives, those equivalent to officials at the rank of three hundred bushels or higher are all to be killed. There are no grounds for releasing them. Those who dare to dispute this edict and those who do not accord with it shall all be chopped in two at the waist."[13] In articulating the crimes of the kings and demands for retribution, the decree clarified both the severity of the rebellion as well as the incentives and means by which it would be suppressed: brutal, unsparing punishment. Hard as it may be to read beyond the violent punitive measures expressed in the edict, more important for our purposes is its mention of prisoners "equivalent to officials at the rank of three hundred bushels or higher." Commentators ignored the phrase, but it follows a common pattern used to categorize people both within and, in this case, outside the Han realm.[14] As we shall see, the salary ranks (*zhi*) and the orders of honor (*jue*) provided a means to organize people, some of them holding neither rank nor order, into different groups. These groups and categories, however, were primarily constituted for purposes of giving gifts, not punishments, and such category-based bestowals of gifts had significant institutional consequences for the imperial court itself.

A word on the salary ranks and orders is necessary before proceeding. We encountered the latter in the introduction, which detailed the reasons for conferring the order of noble (*chehou*, later *liehou*) as well as the privileges and benefits nobles received. The noble order, however, even if the highest, was just one of twenty orders given to imperial subjects. Individuals could receive orders in recognition of exemplary service, but Han sources also record general bestowals of the orders, probably to household heads, to mark important occasions or demonstrate imperial largesse.[15] Recipients of orders enjoyed legal privileges and material benefits, which might have included bestowals of land and housing. The salary ranks, meanwhile, were limited to people holding government posts, from low-level county officials to the highest ministers at the imperial court. The ranks were expressed in bushels (*shi*), which perhaps originally referred to the amounts of in-kind payments, probably of grain, given to officials. By the Han period, however, the bushels functioned only as a rank scale to which salaries were set. We have precious little information regarding the nature and actual amounts of salaries, especially for Western Han.[16]

The Twenty Orders of Honor (*Jue*)

gongshi
shangzao
zanniao
bu geng
dafu
guan dafu
gong dafu
gongcheng
wu dafu
zuo shuzhang
you shuzhang
zuo geng
zhonggeng
you geng
shao shangzao
da shangzao
si ju shuzhang
da shuzhang
guannei hou
chehou (later, *liehou*)

The orders and particularly the salary ranks have received little emphasis in English-language scholarship, perhaps not least because a list of ranks does not make for inspiring reading material. They merit our attention, however, as bread-and-butter systems for determining status at the imperial court and also because they experienced significant change during Western Han. On this point, Jingdi's edict proves enlightening with regard to the salary ranks, for its reference to "officials at the rank of three hundred bushels or more" provides a different perspective on the entire salary scale itself. As scholars of Han history are well aware, one of the more curious features of the scale are the so-called equivalent (*bi*) ranks.[17] According to the *Hanshu* "Table of the Many Offices and Ministerial Posts" (Bai guan gong qing biao), which importantly was not compiled until the first century CE, these were set at each level of the scale, from the highest rank of 2,000 bushels (highest until 8 BCE, when a new rank of 10,000 bushels was established) on down to the rank of 100 bushels. As Jingdi's edict makes clear, however, the term *equivalent* was not only understood as a fixed description of a particular kind of rank; it also indicated an act of equating particular ranks to other ranks outside of the Han bushel salary scale. Recall that Jingdi's edict asked generals and soldiers to perform precisely this kind of comparison, applying Han ranks to prisoners of war hailing from the rebellious kingdoms. At least in early Western Han, then, to call a rank "equivalent" was not to invoke an existing category but to describe a process of comparison between different systems of rank and groups of people.

Legal manuscripts excavated from the early Western Han tomb at Zhangjiashan, sealed in 186 BCE, suggest that this process of comparison was rooted in the gift-giving practices of the imperial court. Of course, because the systems of salary ranks and orders of honor dated to long before 186 BCE, the Zhangjiashan legal manuscripts do not "prove" that the ranks and honors themselves were the result of gift-giving practices. Indeed, one section of the manuscripts, entitled "Statutes on Salary Ranks" (Zhi lü), shows in some detail that at this early date in Western Han the salary ranks already existed and were applied to posts at all levels of officialdom. The "Statutes on Salary Ranks" are essentially a long list of official posts, starting with the imperial counselor (*yushi dafu*) at the imperial court in Chang'an, with a salary rank at 2,000 bushels, and ending with county-level military and security officials, ranked at 160 or 120 bushels.[18] The offices described in the statutes are thus organized not primarily according to type of work or even place or bureau of service but rather by salary rank. We correspondingly read, for instance, a long list of magistrates for different localities, followed in unbroken fashion by titles for offices in the capital and in the imperial palaces. All of these posts, the statute informs us, ranked at a salary grade of 600 bushels.[19] In this manner, the "Statutes on Salary Ranks" present Han officialdom (no doubt most of it, though we cannot assume all) in a hierarchical fashion determined entirely by salary rank, with no reference to or discussion of the significance of these ranks or their aim. The statutes thus underscore one rather unambiguous purpose for the salary ranks: they organized offices into a hierarchy.

Note, however, that the Zhangjiashan "Statutes on Salary Ranks" make no mention of "equivalent" ranks. The word *equivalent* only surfaces in other regulations regarding gift-giving, suggesting that gifts were an important part of putting the rank hierarchy into practice and had important ramifications for the organization of the imperial court and officialdom more broadly. Such a pattern, at least, is apparent from the "Statutes on Bestowals" (Ci lü), which set out regulations on gifts by the central government. One set of rules, for instance, describes the length and quality of cloth to be used in the manufacture of robes bestowed upon the death of officials or holders of an order of honor:

> When officials at the salary grade of 2,000 bushels do not rise from their sickbeds, they are to be given a robe and short undercoat, an inner coffin, and the robes and skirts of their office.[20] Commandery commandants are to be given robes, inner coffins, and the skirts of their office. When officials at the salary grades of 1,000 bushels to 600 bushels die in office, the county where they serve is to provide an inner coffin and the robes of their office.[21]

The statute concludes by saying that officials at the rank of 500 bushels are to receive an inner coffin only. In this manner, the salary ranks provided a regulatory framework for sumptuary privileges and the hierarchical distribution of funerary goods and honors. This hierarchy is even reflected in the language of the statute itself, since it refers to the death of officials at 2,000 bushels by the euphemism "do not rise from their sickbeds." Officials ranked between 600 and 1,000 bushels, meanwhile, are described in more direct fashion as "dying in office."[22]

At least one set of regulations included in the "Statutes on Bestowals," however, articulates a framework for distributing gifts according to the orders of honor. These rules set the amounts of cash to be awarded to people holding different orders of honor who wanted to receive money in place of the inner and outer coffins that were their due: "For somebody who is to be given an inner or outer coffin but wants to receive money instead: for orders of *qing* or higher, give 1,000 cash per order for inner coffins; give 600 cash per order for outer coffins. For orders of *wu dafu* or lower, give 600 cash per order for inner coffins; give 300 cash per order for outer coffins. Those without an order of honor shall receive inner coffin cash in the amount of 300."[23] The regulations raise several questions: When and according to what criteria would the central government be disposed to accommodate requests for cash instead of coffins? Could officeholders also make such requests? If so, why not use the salary ranks instead of the orders of honor? This final question raises a further problem: How did the system of salary ranks correspond with the orders of honor, and vice versa? Since the two systems of rank paralleled each other and simultaneously regulated sumptuary privileges, an explanation of their relationship seems necessary.

The compilers of the statutes apparently agreed, for some of the regulations included in the "Statutes on Bestowals" directly addressed this problem by describing the link between orders of honor and the salary ranks as a relationship of "equivalency" (*bi*). As the following equivalencies from the statutes make clear, the salary ranks provided the primary framework, with the orders of honor matched to them: "When bestowing to those not serving as officials as well as those serving the emperor: those at the order of *guanneihou* and above shall be equivalent to officials at the salary rank of 2,000 bushels; those holding an order of honor at the ministerial level shall be equivalent to officials of 1,000 bushels; *wu dafu* shall be equivalent to officials of 800 bushels; *gongcheng* shall be equivalent to officials of 600 bushels."[24] The statute proceeds in similar fashion all the way down to the lowest of the orders of honor. Scholars investigating this passage have focused in particular on the meaning of "those serving the emperor" (*huan huangdi zhe*). Some have advocated a tight definition of the term as referring to imperial court posts that did not draw a regular salary, while others have argued for a more capacious understanding that includes within the group all people who had served the emperor.[25]

Regardless of their precise identity, the important point is that the "Statute on Bestowals" uses the orders of honor to link "those serving the emperor" to the hierarchy of salary ranks. By connecting the orders to the salary ranks, the statutes allowed people who had rendered service to the imperial household, but did not hold an official position, to nonetheless receive gifts and rewards in a regularized fashion. In so doing, the statutes drew equivalencies between officials and people whose institutional identities were unclear, at least based on our sources. The "Statutes on Bestowals" established other equivalencies between official salary ranks and a group of people who were indisputably part of the ruling household: imperial princesses, the daughters or sisters of the emperor.[26] The statute, even if fragmented, clearly stipulates that princesses were to receive bestowals as if they were "equivalent" to officials ranked at 2,000 bushels.[27] The "Statute on Bestowals" thus linked members of the imperial family and the imperial household to the hierarchies of both the salary rank and the orders of honor that could be applied much more broadly to all imperial subjects.

Such rules point us toward later, more formalized systems of rank within the imperial court that were made equivalent to salary ranks and orders of honor. Even if there is a clear relationship between the two, however, the contrast suggests differences between the imperial court in the opening decades of the Western Han and the harder, more defined institutional patterns of late Western Han. For instance, the *Hanshu* "Account of the Imperial Distaff Clans" (Wai qi zhuan) describes the consort ranks used at the imperial court, noting that during the reign of Wudi four consort ranks were added to the six in use during the early Western Han. Yuandi later added the highest rank of Zhaoyi, so that by late Western Han imperial consorts were organized into fourteen ranks. The *Hanshu* "Account" also describes the equivalencies between these ranks and the salary ranks and orders of honor: "Zhaoyi, as a court position [*wei*[a]], looked to [*shi*] the chancellor, while its order of honor was equivalent [*bi*] to the regional kings; Jieyu looked to the high ministers, while its order of honor was equivalent to the nobles; Xing'e looked to fully 2,000 bushels, while its order of honor was equivalent to *guanneihou*."[28] The translation assumes a concrete meaning for the "positions" (*wei*[a]) of the consorts, for other discussions demonstrate that an "order of positions" (*wei*[a] *ci*) was used to physically situate participants in court ceremonies. The literal translation of *shi* as "look" is meant to evoke that ceremonial context; at least one account of Western Han court ceremonial, for instance, clearly described different groups situated on opposite sides of the emperor's dais.[29] Such ceremonial positions were understood more broadly to refer to the rank of the consorts and other groups within the imperial household outside of a court ceremony.[30] At the same time, the passage shows continued use of the word *equivalent* (*bi*), which in this case linked the consort ranks to the orders of honor, clarifying the benefits and privileges that the different levels of consort ranks enjoyed. The consort ranks thus represented a fusion that drew upon three different hierarchies: ceremonial position, office, and orders of honor. We cannot be sure when this system came into being, though perhaps it was not finalized until after Yuandi established the highest rank of Zhaoyi. The important point is that they represent a clear difference with the equivalencies articulated in the "Statute on Bounties," even if they show how the articulation of rules for gift-giving could provide the basis for much more concrete institutional definitions.

The point is demonstrated more clearly in a series of orders, described in the *Hanshu* "Annals of Huidi" (Huidi ji), issued when Huidi (r. 195–188 BCE) assumed the imperial throne at the tender age of seventeen. The summary of the orders (hardly a transcription of the original document) stipulated different groups that were to receive three different types of gifts: orders of honor, money for mourning ceremonies and tomb construction, and reductions in punishment.[31] The following translation is of the first category only, since it suggests the possible relationship among gift-giving, equivalencies, and institutional categories:

> Palace Gentlemen [*zhonglang*] and Gentlemen of the Palace [*langzhong*] who have served fully six years shall have orders of honor increased by three ranks; for those who have served four years, two ranks.[32] Outer Gentlemen [*wailang*] who have served fully six years shall have orders of honor increased by two ranks. Gentlemen of the Palace who have not served fully one year shall have their orders of honor increased by one rank. Outer Gentlemen who have not served fully two years shall be given cash in the amount of 10,000.
>
> Attending officials and the director of the kitchens shall be treated as equivalent to the Gentlemen of the Palace.[33] Imperial messengers, shield guards, halberd guards, martial soldiers, and cavalrymen shall be treated as equivalent to the Outer Gentlemen.[34]

The translation is only tentative, since some of the office titles listed are otherwise unknown. Significantly, these unattested titles include the Outer Gentlemen (*wailang*), which is found nowhere else in the *Shiji* or *Hanshu*, not even in the *Hanshu* "Table of the Many Offices." Without denying the possibility that an Outer Gentlemen office existed, in this particular summary the Palace Gentlemen and Outer Gentlemen emerge as inner and outer poles around which other offices are organized. They provided an organizational framework for the distribution of the orders of honor, with offices categorized as being equivalent (*bi*) to either Palace Gentlemen or Outer Gentlemen, and the former category receiving comparatively higher orders than the latter. In other words, this example demonstrates the means by which gift-giving helped establish institutional divisions between different kinds of offices at the imperial court.

This pattern of applying equivalent categories became more common as the population of the imperial court and all of its guards, attendants, and gentlemen-at-arms (*lang*) expanded in size. At least, this is the picture painted in the first section of the *Hanshu* "Table of the Many Offices and Ministerial Posts" (Bai guan gong qing biao).

For instance, the *Hanshu* "Table" describes the superintendent of the palace (*langzhong ling*), in charge of palace security, along with its subordinate offices. The entry on the superintendent gives a relatively detailed accounting of each of these offices, including their rank, with the following descriptions of the counselor (*dafu*) positions serving as an example:

> The counselors [*dafu*] were charged with debates and included the grand counselor of the palace [*taizhong dafu*], counselor of the palace [*zhong dafu*], and advisory counsel [*jian dafu*]. None of them had any personnel. The number installed in these positions could total into the several tens of people. The office of advisory counsel was first established in the fifth year of the period Yuanshou (118 BCE), during the reign of Wudi (r. 141–87 BCE).[35] Its rank was set as equivalent to 800 bushels. In the first year of the period Taichu [104 BCE], the title counselor of the palace was changed from *zhong dafu* to *guanglu dafu*, with a salary rank set as equivalent to 2,000 bushels. The grand counselor of the palace's salary rank was set as equivalent to 1,000 bushels in the same manner as before.[36]

Such entries hardly make for exhilarating reading. They are notable, however, because sections describing other ministries mention a similar number of offices but fail to articulate the salary ranks in such detail. In these other entries, we read only of the ranks of subordinate officials calculated in equivalent terms. For instance, the description of the superintendent of ceremonial (*fengchang* or *taichang*) mentions dozens of subordinate officials but does not give the salary ranks for any of them, with one exception: the academicians (*boshi*), ranked at equivalent (*bi*) to 600 bushels.[37]

Neither the counselors nor the academicians had subordinate personnel underneath them, and the *Hanshu* "Table" shows that they and other offices with equivalent ranks expanded over the course of the Western Han. For instance, the "superintendent of the palace" entries describe the growth in gentlemen-at-arms (*lang*) positions, though the language of equivalencies was used to link the gentlemen both to other specific offices *and* to salary rank categories: "The attendants at the gates [*qimen*] were charged with providing armed escort to and from [the palaces]. They were first established in the third year of the Jianyuan period of Wudi [138 BCE). They were equivalent to the gentlemen-at-arms and had no personnel. The number installed in these positions could reach as many as one thousand people. They had a supervisor whose rank was set in equivalent terms at 1,000 bushels."[38] This passage provides some justification for the fact that thus far I have refrained from offering a set definition of what *equivalent* actually meant in the Western Han context. The simultaneous existence, seen in the description of the attendants at the gates, of equivalencies between different categories of offices, on the one hand (gentlemen and attendants at the gates), and office and salary categories, on the other (the "supervisor" set as equivalent to 1,000 bushels), suggests that, in fact, it is perhaps premature to assume that one systematic definition of equivalent ranks can even be offered. What is clear, however, is that the *Hanshu* "Table" was primarily concerned not with the ranks of officials serving in central government ministries but rather with articulating the equivalent ranks of palace security officials and other irregular offices without subordinates or a set number of incumbents.[39] In this sense, the *Hanshu* "Table" evinces a clear focus on describing a particular subset of offices and institutions within the palaces, as opposed to central government ministries or officialdom as a whole.

Even if we cannot organize the sources discussed here into a smooth narrative, based on current evidence it seems that the articulation of institutional categories and divisions within the imperial court was keyed to frameworks provided by the salary ranks and orders of honor, drawing most importantly upon the regulations over gift-giving and sumptuary practices reflected in the "Statutes on Bestowals." As the number of officials serving in the palaces grew and rulers continued to disburse gifts and sumptuary privileges to groups of all kinds, these divisions gradually attained harder institutional form, most clearly in the court ranks calculated in equivalent terms, used mostly to organize large groups of bodyguards under the superintendent of the palace, as well as the consort ranks. At least, that is the impression given by the *Hanshu* "Table," which went out of its way to describe as equivalent the ranks of officials closely associated with the palace and the emperor. When and precisely why these equivalent ranks were assigned to guards and officials is difficult to say with any certainty. What is clear, however, is that the organization of the imperial court was an accretive process of institutional comparison among different groups.

This final point merits emphasis, for all of the sources I have discussed thus far have drawn internal equivalencies. In other words, I have not discussed comparisons and equivalencies between the Han realm and other realms, the regional kingdoms being the most important during early Western Han. As we already saw in the punitive measures called for in Jingdi's edict, this does not mean that such comparisons were not made. Indeed, comparing and equating Han institutions with those located outside Han borders, with particular reference to sumptuary privileges, was both a central strategy and a conceptual problem for those seeking to assert the supremacy of the Han court and condemn insurgent royal rebellions. The power of this rhetoric of comparison would only have been strengthened by the fact that comparison and equivalency provided the institutional framework for those within the imperial court who wrote accounts of royal rivalry and insurgency. However, it cannot be coincidental that the eventual stabilization of institutional categories at court, detailed earlier, was paired with a radically changed explanation about the nature and root of royal insurrection.

YELLOW CHARIOTS AND REBELLION, LUXURY AND MORALITY: THE RHETORIC OF EQUIVALENCY AND THE STATUS OF THE IMPERIAL COURT

In the years after the rebellion of 154 BCE, Jingdi eliminated several kings, appointed his sons in their place, and instituted a series of reforms, all measures aimed at bolstering the power of the imperial household and diminishing the autonomy of the regional kingdoms. The most well-known of these reforms were administrative in nature: beginning in 145 BCE, the kingdoms were no longer allowed to appoint their senior officials, all such appointments thenceforth made by the central government. Additionally, the chancellors (*chengxiang*) of the kingdoms were renamed administrators (*xiang*), a simpler title that further underscored the lower status of the kingdoms vis-à-vis the Han.[40] These administrative changes have received greatest emphasis in scholarly accounts of the kingdoms.[41] They came, however, three years *after* a series of changes to the regulations governing appointments and funerals for royals and nobles.[42] These reforms, some of them sumptuary in nature, established a hierarchical arrangement that delineated the officials responsible for completing appointments, assigning posthumous names, composing funerary dirges, and directing funeral ceremonies. In the scheme, higher ranked officials managed these matters for the kings, while officials at lower ranks did so for the nobles.[43] The very establishment of this hierarchy is significant: since nothing of the sort previously existed, the creation of such a ceremonial hierarchy went a long way toward putting the regional kings in a lower position vis-à-vis the Han. Noteworthy, too, is that these changes received more detailed description in the *Hanshu* "Annals of Jingdi" (Jingdi ji) than did the administrative changes.[44]

Such facts speak volumes about the prominence of appointment and funeral ceremonies in Western Han political culture as well as the important role played by sumptuary regulations and ritual performances in asserting the preeminent status of the imperial court. The *Shiji* is replete with such stories, which regularly emphasize that acting the part was a necessary prerequisite for actually becoming the ruler.[45] Nonetheless, the *Shiji* also regularly allowed that such indices of status were often subverted and that sumptuary regulations had a complicated relationship to, and were sometimes outdone by, the familial bonds linking emperors and royal relatives. By contrast, the *Hanshu* definitively categorized sumptuary privileges as matters of law and regulation, highlighting the moral failings of those who did not fulfill them. Indeed, the *Hanshu* took pains to emphasize that only the morally perfect ruler could appropriately enjoy his incomparable luxuries and privileges.

The *Shiji* "Basic Annals of Gaozu" (Gaozu ben ji) can be read as an extended, at times puzzled meditation on the circumstances by which Liu Bang, a man of relatively low status, managed to rise to the imperial throne and become the first Han emperor. The "Basic Annals" offers no clear explanation: though it describes Liu Bang accumulating auspicious signs that portended his ultimate triumph, it also depicts him as almost comically inept, with only his immediate supporters, not the man himself, recognizing the significance of such omens.[46] One prominent theme is precisely the importance of these supporters, since the chapter emphasizes Liu Bang's genius in employing able men by affording them a material stake in Han's victory and allowing them to utilize their talents to Han's benefit.[47] Such bonds and reciprocal exchanges between the new emperor and his supporters perhaps explains a puzzling suggestion in the appraisal to the "Basic Annals": that Han's success was brought about by the "loyalty" (*zhong*) of Gaozu's supporters.[48] The appraisal, however, is hardly unambiguous on this point. In a jarring contrast with the chapter proper that one eminent scholar termed "bizarre," the appraisal does not summarize the preceding narrative but rather inserts the principle of loyalty into an elaborate system of cyclical change.[49] This passage, highly unique compared to other *Shiji* appraisals, thus begins by speaking not of the Han but of the ruling houses of high antiquity: "The governance of the Xia was loyalty. With the decline of loyalty lesser people acted in a wild manner, which the people of Yin took on by means of reverence. With the decline of reverence lesser people became occupied with the spirits, which the people of Zhou took on by means of refinement. With the decline of refinement lesser people acted in a shallow manner. Therefore, when it comes to saving people from shallowness, nothing can compare to loyalty. The way of the three kings is like a cycle that starts again after it has come to an end."[50] The appraisal respectively associates the ancient Xia, Yin, and Zhou periods with three distinct modes of action, which presumably characterized the rulers and their policies: loyalty (*zhong*), reverence (*jing*), and refinement (*wen*). Each of these states, however, eventually and inevitably degenerated into debased forms of their originals. These paired modes of action, one pure and the other corrupted, were linked in an endless cycle. The appraisal thus opens with the intriguing claim that loyalty, reverence, and refinement were the three driving forces behind the rise and fall of political regimes. Transformations from one to another drove historical change.

What were the implications for the Han? By the logic of the appraisal's tripartite system of cyclical change, the ruling house that replaced Zhou needed to resurrect the mode of loyalty. The author of the appraisal, however, recognized that the problematic place of Qin in this cycle required explanation:

> The period between Zhou and Qin can certainly be characterized as the degeneration of refinement. Qin's governance did not change but instead featured cruel punishments and laws. How could this not have been an error? Therefore Han arose, took on this degenerated state, and replaced it with its transformation, "ensuring that the people were not weary."[51] Han truly achieved a heavenly concordance![52]

Qin was unable to depart from a debased form of refinement (in the vocabulary of the appraisal, they were "shallow") and resorted to refinement's precise opposite: harsh punishments and laws. The appraisal thus argues that Qin failed to recognize the changes necessary to accord with the cycle of political transformation. Only with the establishment of Han did such a change occur. The appraisal does not explicitly say that Han returned to loyalty, but it leaves open the possibility that such a return had or at least should have occurred, for with the achievement of a "heavenly concordance" (*tian tong*) Han completed and restarted the cycle of political change that began in high antiquity. For readers familiar with early imperial intellectual history, talk of a "heavenly concordance" immediately conjures up other theories of cyclical change applied to transfers of dynastic power. Ideas similar to those expressed in the *Shiji* appraisal are found in other texts, while the appraisal to the *Hanshu* "Annals of Emperor Gaozu" (Gao di ji) is much less ambiguous in attributing the rise of Han to a more specific scheme of cyclical change.[53]

The end of the *Shiji* appraisal sharply shifts gears. Even though the invocation of a "heavenly concordance" provides a logical conclusion,[54] in fact the appraisal ends with a curious statement that seems almost entirely disconnected from the preceding discussion of cyclical modes of political action and dynastic change: "Gaozu held a New Year's court audience [*chao*] in the tenth month. According to the carriage and robe regulations he rode a chariot with a yellow canopy and pennant on the left side. He was buried at Changling."[55] We can only speculate as to whether or not this description of court audiences, sumptuary regulations, and Gaozu's mausoleum was written by somebody other than the author of the rest of the appraisal. Perhaps the writer was responding to an obvious objection that any Han loyalist could have lodged against the cycle of "heavenly concordance": by its logic, the Han too would decline and eventually be vanquished by a successor dynasty that "took on" the degenerate "wildness" of Han and replaced it with "reverence," the next mode of action in the cycle. Possibly the final line was meant to demonstrate that the rituals and practices established by Gaozu, from the annual New Year's court audience to the emperor's grand burial place, would be a bulwark against this sort of decline. On a more speculative note, the ritual practices mentioned in the line might even have been meant to evoke reverence and refinement, which would have paired with the loyalty Han had already demonstrated. By this reading, the appraisal advanced the claim that Han managed to embody the three modes of action simultaneously, thus bringing the cycle to a close and ensuring the continuation of the Han realm.[56]

The problem, however, is that holding court audiences, riding in yellow canopied chariots, and building mausoleums were not exclusive to Han. They were part of a shared symbolic language of rulership whose origins and history, if by no means clear, long predate the Han.[57] Since chapter 2 explores the court audience in greater detail, I will focus here only on the chariots and mausoleums. Early texts and the archaeological record alike both indicate that royal families began building mausoleums over their tombs (to say nothing of the tombs themselves, which had always been elaborate) long before unification under Qin in 221 BCE.[58] The yellow canopy is more problematic, not least because stories from early texts indicate that those with royal or imperial pretensions could easily adopt the canopy to bolster their status claims.[59] Gaozu himself was hardly innocent on this count, as seen in one *Shiji* story that describes an episode in the post-Qin civil war between Xiang Yu (d. 202 BCE) and Gaozu. The future Han emperor found himself in the city of Xingyang at an especially low ebb in his fortunes, besieged by Xiang Yu's troops. A general told Gaozu to sneak away from the city, advice that the future emperor readily heeded. In the meantime, the general rode out to Xiang Yu in a chariot with a yellow canopy, declaring from inside, "The grain in the city has been exhausted, so the King of Han surrenders." When Xiang Yu looked inside the chariot and saw only the general, he realized the deception and immediately had the man burned to death.[60]

The story illustrates the indexical significance of the yellow canopy and also the strange and quick about-face that the Han founder had to perform after seizing the throne: a symbolic vocabulary of royal and imperial power that Gaozu and his advisers cleverly drew upon for strategic advantage had to be transformed into a protected privilege enjoyed only by the ruler and forbidden to other specified groups. By assuming the title "emperor" (*huangdi*), Gaozu could hardly allow others to draw upon a language of imperial rulership that by rights now belonged to the Liu household alone. Long after the establishment of the empire, significant anxiety persisted regarding potential threats to the Western Han monopoly on imperial regalia, including the yellow canopy. Such concerns swirled around tales of conflict between the imperial court and the courts of the Liu household kingdoms and realms at the Han borders.

For instance, stories in the *Shiji* about the far southern realm of Nanyue, ruled by the lineage of a former Qin official that maintained independence from Han until 111 BCE, highlight a particularly complicated politics of ritual representation. Some Nanyue rulers, for instance, nominally proclaimed submission to Han suzerainty. At the same time, shielded by their location in the distant south, they adopted imperial titles and practices used by Qin and Han rulers while selectively drawing upon local customs to bolster their legitimacy.[61] Throughout the many incidents regarding Han-Nanyue relations described in the *Shiji*, Nanyue's use of titles such as *di* (emperor or lord) and luxury goods such as the yellow canopied chariot continued to stoke controversy and clearly indicated Nanyue's refusal to recognize a submissive political relationship to Han. Less commented upon are statements in the *Shiji* noting that Han efforts to reign in Nanyue equally focused on slotting the upstart southern empire into the same ritual category as the regional kings. For instance, according to the "Account of Shen Yiji and Lu Jia," Lu Jia being a key Han envoy who helped bring Nanyue into line, the kingdom was made to "eliminate yellow canopied chariots and the proclamation of imperial edicts." In doing so Nanyue thus became "equivalent to the regional kings" (*bi zhuhou*).[62] In other words, bringing Nanyue into submission was a process of rejecting certain imperial symbols *and* adopting practices that were equivalent to the status group to which Han rulers and advisers believed Nanyue rightfully belonged.

Other sections in the *Shiji*, however, highlight the fact that the precise meaning of acting in a manner equivalent to a regional king was not always clear, complicated as regional king status was by the deep, sometimes fraught kinship ties that bound the Han court to the courts of the kings. Quite simply, even if all kings were theoretically equal in status, the vicissitudes and complexities of imperial family life afforded some kings special privileges at court. A striking story in this regard is that of Liu Wu (d. ca. 144 BCE), king of Liang, one of Wendi's four sons, the half-brother of Jingdi, and a favored son of Jingdi's powerful mother, Empress Dowager Dou (d. 135 BCE). The *Shiji* chapter "Hereditary House of the Filial King of Liang" (Liang Xiao wang shijia) begins not by focusing on Liu Wu alone but by listing the four sons of Wendi: Liu Qi (the future Jingdi), Liu Wu, Liu Can, and Liu Yi.[63] Liu Wu had initially been appointed king of Dai and then Huaiyang but was ultimately installed as king of Liang only after the youngest of the brothers, Liu Yi, died while still on the Liang throne. According to the "Hereditary House" chapter, the love and favor that Liu Yi enjoyed was "distinct compared to the other brothers."[64] This favor might partially explain why Liu Yi, rather than his elder brothers, was assigned to the comparatively plum realm of Liang, far from his elder brothers' more dangerous border kingdoms of Dai and Taiyuan, which were subject to regular attacks from northern nomadic groups. Moreover, Wendi had to specially reestablish Liang as a kingdom for Liu Yi to rule, since prior to Wendi's reign it had been converted into a commandery.[65]

Liu Wu, however, also enjoyed a close relationship with the empress dowager. Moreover, the *Shiji* suggests that Jingdi showed favor to Liu

Wu in order to appease their mother, who appears positively obsessed by the fate of her younger son. Regardless, Liu Wu was allowed to visit Chang'an repeatedly to participate in the New Year's audience ceremony, in some cases making the trip in consecutive years. By carefully noting all of these trips, the "Hereditary House" chapter clearly indicated the favor that the king enjoyed. During one particular visit Jingdi casually intimated that he might be willing to install Liu Wu as the imperial heir, much to Liu Wu and the empress dowager's delight.[66] Meanwhile, the empress dowager showered Liu Wu with numerous gifts.[67] At his capital in Liang, Wu constructed elaborate palaces with elevated walkways, was given the privilege to fly pennants reserved for the emperor, and embarked on wide-ranging hunts, all in a manner that, according to the chapter, "imitated the Son of Heaven" (*ni yu Tianzi*).[68] The situation soured when Liu Wu assassinated a Han official who had successfully opposed a move to name Wu the imperial heir. After this incident, Jingdi began to distance himself from his brother. In the end, upon receiving an ominous gift of an ox with a leg sticking out of its back, Liu Wu died of a feverish illness.[69]

The appraisal to the "Hereditary House" chapter sums up Liu Wu's fate, emphasizing the convergence of factors that ultimately resulted in the king's undoing: "The Grand Archivist states: Though King Xiao of Liang ruled as king over a fertile land due to parental love, it was precisely at this time that the Han imperial family flourished and the many clans became prosperous. He was therefore able to increase his wealth, expand his palaces, and have chariots and robes that imitated the son of Heaven. In this manner, for his part, he certainly overstepped."[70] Though the appraisal, to be sure, does not laud Liu Wu's behavior, neither does it blame him for his ultimate fate. For instance, the mention of parental love here should be understood in terms of the favor Liu Wu received from the empress dowager and also in relation to her love for the deceased Liu Yi, the youngest of the brothers. Recall that at the beginning of the "Hereditary House" chapter, Liu Yi, the youngest and most loved of Wendi's four sons, was installed as king of a newly reincarnated Liang. In other words, the very establishment of Liang as a kingdom was due to love for Liu Yi, not Liu Wu, who thus came to "rule as king over fertile land" only because of the favor enjoyed by his youngest brother. Moreover, even though the chapter proper attributes Liu Wu's luxurious lifestyle to favors granted him by the empress dowager, the appraisal backs away from this explanation, pointing out instead that the king's growing wealth and splendor coincided with an ascendant imperial house and a populace that was growing wealthy. "Imitating the Son of Heaven," then, was hardly a matter of Liu Wu's premeditated rebellion, nor even of conscious favoritism on the part of the empress dowager. Rather, it was almost the natural outcome of circumstances that were not entirely in any one person's control. The concluding statement that the king had nonetheless "overstepped" thus raises questions: By what criteria and at what stage can "imitating" cross over to inappropriately and dangerously exceeding authority? Who (or what) is ultimately responsible for such overreach?

The appraisal in the *Hanshu* to "The Account of the Three Kings of Emperor Wen" (Wen san wang zhuan) provides one possible answer to these questions. The discussion of Liu Wu in this *Hanshu* chapter is almost identical to the narrative in the *Shiji* "Hereditary House of the Filial King of Liang." Even the appraisal is exactly the same, with the exception of the following concluding statement, tacked on to the very end: "He relied upon his family without any restraint, and the calamity of the ox announced his punishment. In the end he became troubled and died. How sad!"[71] Whereas the *Shiji* left open the question of how Liu Wu came to overstep his authority, the *Hanshu* appraisal shifts the focus back to the king, arguing that it was his own pleasure-seeking that ultimately led to his demise: he had indulged "without restraint" in his family's favor. The *Hanshu* thus transforms a much more complicated story of family relations and larger political and economic trends to a question of personal behavior and absence of limits, buttressed by an ill-advised reliance on family connections that could not prevent Liu Wu's destruction.

This contrast in treatment between the *Shiji* and the *Hanshu* of insurrectionist behavior on the part of the Liu kings is hardly limited to their respective assessments of Liu Wu. For instance, the *Shiji* "Hereditary House of the Five Imperial Lines" (Wu zong shi jia) and the *Hanshu* "Account of the Thirteen Kings of Jingdi" (Jing shisan wang zhuan) describe in quite different terms the fate of Jingdi's sons, all of whom were installed as regional kings. Both chapters detail the collapse of many of these royal lineages, some of which ended in shocking criminal and sexual scandals. The *Hanshu* "Account" is far more detailed, but some of the differences between the "Hereditary House" and the "Account" are clearly rooted in different emphases rather than mere level of detail. Probably the best example comes in the case of Liu Jian, Jingdi's grandson and king of Jiangdu, who has been justifiably described as a ruler whose "depravity and wickedness . . . stand with few parallels in the annals of Han history."[72] Be that as it may, the admittedly shorter discussion of Liu Jian in the *Shiji* "Hereditary House" reveals more ambiguity as well as an easier recognition of the family connections that bound Jian to the imperial household. By contrast, the *Hanshu* is quite willing to paint Jian as an unrepentant lawbreaker who deserved to be executed.

A few details are in order. Jian was the son of Liu Fei, the first king of Jiangdu, who had played a key role in suppressing the rebellion in 154 BCE. For his efforts, Fei was given pennants reserved for the Son of Heaven.[73] After Liu Fei died but before his burial, both the *Shiji* and *Hanshu* note, Liu Jian had already begun to show evidence of depravity and completely unrestrained concupiscence; for instance, he slept with several of his father Fei's former consorts while still residing in the mourning hut.[74] The *Hanshu* goes on to describe the various crimes of Liu Jian in much more detail, some of it painful to read: drowning consorts, starving people to death in his palace, forcing attendants to copulate with animals, and using a slave girl as a shaman to curse the emperor. When he heard about a rebellion brewing in the realms of Huainan and Hengshan, he made plans to join the insurrection: cutting imperial seals; constructing a yellow canopied chariot; disbursing seals, tallies, and ranks to his officials; and sending envoys with gifts to Nanyue in an effort to secure that southern kingdom's aid when the rebellion broke out.[75] Late in his reign, in a dramatic episode described in the *Hanshu*, a defiant Liu Jian, conscious of his crimes, declared that when he was finally called to account for his actions he would not idly accept execution. Instead, he stated elliptically that he would "desire to do that which people are unable to do." Jian then drove out in his chariot, flying the pennants of the Son of Heaven that his father had received years earlier.[76]

Liu Jian was certainly correct that the emperor would eventually discover his wrongdoing, but the *Hanshu* and *Shiji* describe the adjudication of the king's crimes in different terms. The *Hanshu*, for instance, offers a detailed account of the legal process by which the king was condemned. A subordinate of the Han chancellor was sent to Jiangdu to investigate, and he found the weapons, seals, ribbons, tallies, and other items indicating Jian's plans to rebel. An imperial edict then requested that nobles and court officials debate Liu Jian's sentence. They unanimously condemned Jian for behavior that exceeded even the lasciviousness of the legendarily wicked rulers Jie and Zhou, concluding with the statement "Heaven punishes those whom it does not pardon, so it would be proper to follow the laws against rebellion and execute [Liu Jian]." After the director of the imperial clan (*zongzheng*) and superintendent of trials (*tingwei*) served Jian with the order, he committed suicide, and all the members of his court were executed. Contrast this image of a dispassionate imperial court dispensing punishment according to the law with the following conclusion to the story of Liu Jian in the *Shiji*: "After these matters had been reported, the lords and ministers of Han requested the arrest and punishment of Jian. The Son of Heaven was unwilling to do so, but sent a senior vassal to immediately interrogate the king. The king confessed to his wrongdoing, and thereupon killed himself."[77] Unlike the *Hanshu*, the *Shiji* remains silent about any investigation yielding evidence of Liu Jian's crimes. We in fact read not of imperial edicts ordering the legal process to proceed but rather of the emperor's hesitation in formally investigating and charging Liu Jian with a crime. Moreover, and more important, the *Shiji* states that Liu Jian actually confessed to his crimes immediately after interrogation by the emperor's envoy, a detail omitted from the *Hanshu*. In sum, whereas the *Hanshu* paints Liu Jian as a morally depraved ruler who succumbs to the force of Han law, the *Shiji* evokes the continued relevance of the family ties that bound Jingdi to Liu Jian. Instead of the impassive application of law, the case of Jian in the *Shiji* seems more like a matter internal to and resolved by the Liu imperial household.

The *Shiji*, then, quite openly recognized the fact that ritual regulations were not always executed in a consistent manner and that other factors, especially familial and personal relationships, could circumvent them. At the same time, neither did it deny the long-term effect on the regional kings of tightened restrictions, as in the *Shiji*'s appraisal to the "Hereditary House of the Five Imperial Lines":

> The Grand Archivist states: During the period of Gaozu, the regional kings were all given their lands, and were allowed to make their own appointments of officials from the metropolitan superintendents [*neishi*] on down. The Han only installed the chancellor with a golden seal. The regional kings appointed the imperial counselor, director of trials [*tingwei zheng*], and academicians in imitation of the Son of Heaven. After the rebellion of Wu and Chu and the appointment of the generation of kings from the five imperial lines, the Han installed officials at 2,000 bushels and eliminated the title chancellor, replacing it with an administrator [*xiang*] who received a silver seal. The

> regional kings received land rent and taxes only to provide household income, which took away their political power. Later, there were impoverished regional kings, with some reduced to riding around in ox carts.[78]

The story told in the *Shiji* appraisal emphasizes the gradual, almost pitiful reduction of power and wealth endured by the Liu regional kings. Note the appearance here of the phrase "imitated the Son of Heaven" (*ni yu Tianzi*), also mentioned in the *Shiji* story about Liu Wu. Though the precise valence of the phrase (positive or negative?) is somewhat difficult to discern, the appraisal makes perfectly clear that such "imitation" was woven into the institutional fabric of the kingdoms themselves. As a result, imitating or being equivalent to the imperial household was not necessarily or wholly a matter of kings asserting illegitimate claims to authority. It could be a problem inherent in the system, which did not clearly differentiate between the Han imperial court and the courts of the kingdoms. When that system was reformed after the 154 BCE rebellion, the kings experienced a corresponding decline in status. The *Shiji* appraisal thus highlights the long-term power of these regulations, underscored by the pathos of the image of kings in oxcarts. At the same time, the chapter itself, not to mention other sections of the *Shiji*, openly recognize the fact that familial and personal relationships could supersede rules that were applied inconsistently or, at times, for strategic purposes.[79] For the *Shiji*, then, the most important question seems to be the ambiguous role of ritual order: even while it promised to establish political order, it could not be treated separately from other systems of regulation and value.[80]

The appraisal to the "Account of the Thirteen Kings of Jingdi" from the *Hanshu*, however, adopts an entirely different tone, not least because it fails to mention the 154 BCE rebellion, a surprising omission given the uprising's importance for the reigns of many of Jingdi's royal sons. Instead, the appraisal begins with a telling rereading of a *Xunzi* passage, before continuing on to lament the corrupting effects of luxury:

> In appraisal, we state: In the past, Lord Ai of Lu said, "I was born deep within palaces and raised at the hand of women. Not even once have I known worry or fear." How true were his words! Even if he desired to not be in peril, such wishes could not be achieved. This is why the ancients believed the comforts of a palace banquet to be like

> a poison. Wealth and status without virtuous power: this is called misfortune.
>
> From the establishment of the Han to the reign of the filial emperor Ping, the number of regional kings can be counted in the hundreds. Most of them were arrogant, licentious, and departed from the Way. What was the reason for this? Mired in unchecked indulgence, their positions made them act this way. Since even common people can still be caught up in vulgar practices, how much more must be the case for a ruler like Lord Ai? As for the most refined sort of behavior whose preeminence cannot belong to the ordinary crowd, King Xian of Hejian came quite close.[81]

In the *Xunzi*, after the statement from Lord Ai quoted in this appraisal, Kongzi (Confucius) reminds the lord that he is nonetheless not immune from worry or fear; he will feel these emotions as he goes about his ritual and political duties, since the slightest indication of things or people amiss in his ceremonies or court audiences will make the lord reflect on the implications such signs hold for his realm's safety and stability.[82] The *Hanshu*, however, completely ignores this statement and focuses only on the corrupting effects of luxury. Instead of claiming that a virtuous king feels worry despite his material comforts, the *Hanshu* emphasizes that such comforts necessarily endangers all rulers; indeed, the extreme amount of luxury enjoyed by rulers put them in particular risk. This reinterpretation of the *Xunzi* passage sets up the appraisal's claim that the Han regional kingdoms fell because of their rulers' indulgence in the luxuries of their positions. Only King Xian of Hejian, lauded elsewhere in the *Hanshu* for his devotion to classical principles and collection of ancient texts, came "close" to exhibiting the sort of reverence and virtue necessary to avoid the pitfalls and temptations of his throne.

For the *Hanshu*, then, the story of the kings of Jingdi and their descendants had nothing to do with the effectiveness of sumptuary regulations. In fact, as the story of Liu Jian confirms, the *Hanshu* repeatedly emphasizes the failure of such regulations to prevent the most egregious abuses of power. Instead, it casts the downfall of the kings as a process of moral degeneration. Rather than lowering the kingdoms to a status much humbler than the imperial court, the only true solution was to promote morally charismatic rulers. Given that a long-established and codified sumptuary regime had nonetheless repeatedly failed to prevent reprehensible behavior by Liu household royals, such a conclusion is understandable. According to the narratives in the *Hanshu*, even if the categories had been established, far more important were the kind of people who filled them.

As many of the statements from early texts analyzed in this chapter underscore, sumptuary rules were by definition designed to bolster the imperial court's power and status. A study of their actual effectiveness in this regard, however, would require scouring the material record, especially evidence from excavated tombs, for concrete evidence that the rules were actually enforced. Given the spotty nature of archaeological preservation and excavation, however, as well as myriad local variations in funerary practices, such an enterprise would yield only provisional conclusions, at best.[83] It is exceedingly difficult to prove whether or not any given regulation was actually effective or consistently enforced. How, then, can we evaluate the extensive, almost obsessive discussions of sumptuary regulations and rank in early texts? In order to answer this question, I have analyzed rank-based regulations not as clearly defined tools for asserting power but as a collection of processes that ultimately raised conceptual problems about the nature of ritual categories.

As a process, sumptuary regulations required Han officials at all levels to draw comparisons or equivalencies (*bi*), to use the administrative language of the time, between different ranks. The excavated legal statutes from Zhangjiashan, dating to 186 BCE, illustrated the mechanics of such equivalencies, stipulating equivalent amounts of cash and material items to be given to officials with salary ranks (*zhi*) or to those holding an order of honor (*jue*). Equivalencies, however, did not only link together the two different rank systems. The Zhangjiashan statutes also show that specific groups of people, especially those associated with the imperial court (e.g., "those who served the emperor," imperial princesses), were cast as equivalent to the salary ranks. Moreover, such equivalencies were used to divide up the imperial court as an institution, with consorts and court attendants categorized as equivalent to different offices or categories of offices. Though modern scholarship has tended to depict these "equivalent ranks," especially as they are articulated in the *Hanshu* "Table of Offices and Ministerial Posts," as a set hierarchy, in fact we have precious little evidence that this harder, institutionalized form of the "equivalent ranks" emerged before late Western Han at the earliest. We see instead the gradual emergence of different rank and institutional classifications, especially at court, through the implementation of sumptuary regulations. It is in this sense that sumptuary regulations should be understood as a process, even if it was a process still intimately related to the consolidation of imperial power. My emphasis here, however, is less on the effectiveness of such regulations in asserting power and more on the subtler institutional ramifications of sumptuary law. In short, sumptuary regulations were significant not just or even primarily because they helped maintain authority but because they established social and institutional categories that provided structure for the imperial court and the empire as a whole.

It is this question of the larger empire that raised important conceptual problems. As we saw in Jingdi's 154 BCE edict, issued in response to a devastating royal rebellion, equivalencies were drawn between groups within the Han realm as well as beyond its borders, especially between and among the regional kingdoms. We thus read regularly of privileges and powers that were "equivalent to the Han court" (*bi Han chao*) or "equivalent to the regional kings" (*bi zhuhou*). In the case of the regional kingdoms, the Han imperial court took particular exception to those kings who "imitated the Son of Heaven" by adopting the symbols and trappings of imperial power (e.g., yellow chariots). At least according to some stories, however, after the civil war that followed Qin's collapse, such symbols were appropriated by many different contenders for power; they could even be used as acts of deception or diversion. By what means would the newly established Han be able to assume a monopoly over the symbolic language of imperial rule as well as the sumptuary privileges theoretically reserved for the emperor?

Certainly, convincing performances and displays were key to the success of the Han ritual program, a point made in many stories found in the *Shiji*. At the same time, the *Shiji* quite openly allowed that sumptuary regulations and the larger ritual order of which they were a part were by no means consistently applied or impossible to subvert. Moreover, the failure of or exceptions to ritual categories were hardly rare and could not always be easily dismissed or explained away. The story of Liu Wu, king of Liang, is an important case in point, for his biography explained the special privileges he enjoyed as simultaneously the result of being favored by his mother and larger political and economic trends that no single person fully controlled. Thus, even if the *Shiji* acknowledged that sumptuary privileges were central to the Han's successful assertion of imperial authority, it also equivocated on their very stability. The ritual categories were established, but they were not always clearly defined and hardly remained impervious to external factors.

We see an entirely different picture of the sumptuary order in the *Hanshu*, which appears much less willing to admit that sumptuary regulations did not always operate in a consistent fashion. As demonstrated in the narrative of Liu Jian's prosecution, the *Hanshu* consistently depicted ritual and legal regulations operating quickly and dispassionately. At the same time, however, the *Hanshu* lamented the fact that the sumptuary system did not prevent such insurrections from arising in the first place. In other words, even while, in contrast to the *Shiji*, it assumed the stability of sumptuary categories, it also called attention to problems with the people who filled those categories. Rather than tweaking the system, it seemed to argue, the entire approach and strategy of asserting imperial power had to be redirected toward transforming the kings into morally proper rulers.

In making this argument, of course, the *Hanshu* revealed its fidelity to a rhetoric informed by classical principles (note its valorization of Liu De, the classicist king par excellence) that began gathering strength in the closing decades of Western Han. However, certain institutional changes had to occur in order for the argument to make sense. For instance, the *Hanshu* could not have depicted the quick punishment of sumptuary violations if the sumptuary system had not been established and operational for some time. The hardening of practices, categories, and boundaries at the imperial court provided the necessary conditions for claiming that such institutions were ultimately insufficient. The institutional definition of the court, a project far from finished even in mid–Western Han, eventually allowed other questions and problems to assert themselves. In turn, such questions informed the way the *Hanshu* depicted the imperial court as a whole. The next chapter turns to a more specific example in order to show how this process played out in relation to a particular ritual event.

CHAPTER 2

Who Gets to Praise the Emperor?

In the fall of 52 BCE, a leader of a group from the foreign Xiongnu traveled south toward Chang'an. The man, named Jihoushan, encamped with his entourage outside a mountain pass several hundred miles north of the city. Beset by conflicts with rival *shanyu*, the title held by Xiongnu leaders, Jihoushan asked for permission to attend the annual New Year's audience (*chao*) held at the Han imperial court. In making the request, the first ever from a *shanyu*, Jihoushan signaled a willingness to submit to Han power.[1] After a court debate, the emperor, Xuandi, granted permission for Jihoushan to participate in the audience, which he held at Ganquan Palace, a complex of imperial palaces and shrines north of the capital. Xuandi accorded the *shanyu* special ritual treatment during the ceremony, which was a truly spectacular performance, at least according to the following description from the *Hanshu* "Annals of Xuandi" (Xuandi ji):

> The *shanyu* of the Huhanye Xiongnu, Jihoushan, came for the court audience. When summoned forth he was termed a "protective vassal" but was not called by his given name. He was given a seal with ribbons, cap, robe, passenger chariot with a four-horse team, gold, silk brocade, and silk thread. Officials were ordered to take the *shanyu* ahead to his mansion in Chang'an, overnighting in Changping.[2]
>
> From Ganquan, the emperor spent the night at Chiyang Palace.[3] Then, he ascended the slope at Changping but ordered that the *shanyu* was not to be summoned. The *shanyu*'s group of left and right *danghu* all assembled to observe the emperor.[4] Leaders of foreign groups, kings, nobles, and those who came to greet the emperor numbered some several tens of thousands, lined along both sides of

> the road. The emperor ascended the Wei River Bridge and everybody called out "long live the emperor!" The *shanyu* then went to his mansion. The emperor offered wine at Jianzhang Palace. Entertainment was provided for the *shanyu*, with precious treasures put on display. In the second month, the *shanyu* left Chang'an and returned home.[5]

The audience at Ganquan, and the banquets and entertainment in Chang'an, provided the *shanyu* with a dramatic display of the material wealth and political might of the emperor and the imperial court. For Xuandi's officials and the thousands who caught a glimpse of the emperor as he crossed the Wei River, the dazzling spectacle demonstrated that the *shanyu* had officially submitted to Han suzerainty.

The "Annals of Xuandi" thus characterized the 51 BCE audience, the first ever to include a Xiongnu *shanyu*, as an event of monumental size, pageantry, and diplomatic significance. The surprisingly few secondary studies that mention the audience have largely adopted this interpretation, arguing almost exclusively that 51 BCE marked Western Han's triumph over a previously powerful Xiongnu confederation, one that had caused problems for the Han since the dynasty's inception.[6] Such an interpretation is by no means incorrect. Other chapters from the *Hanshu* lend support to understanding the 51 BCE audience as an event primarily significant for the history of Han foreign relations.[7] According to this narrative, 51 BCE provides an endpoint for a dramatic story told in all textbooks of Chinese and East Asian history: the large-scale expansion of the Han Empire, starting some seventy-five years earlier, during the reign of Wudi, into areas northwest and south of the Yellow and Yangzi river regions. From this perspective, 51 BCE marks a high point for an empire of unprecedented size and power.[8]

The 51 BCE audience, however, was more than a military and diplomatic milestone in a narrative of Han imperial expansion. The particular terms used and moves made within the ceremony must have held tremendous symbolic importance for participants, and this symbolism was far more specific than a generalized celebration of imperial power. For instance, the "Annals of Xuandi" mentions the *shanyu* was called a "protective vassal" (*fanchen*), without reference to his given name.[9] It also notes that the emperor, upon arriving at Changping, did not summon the Xiongnu leader and his entourage. Such points of ritual protocol distinguished the *shanyu* in distinct and significant ways from other participants in the 51 BCE audience. Given the unprecedented nature of the visit, such ceremonial details were by no means intuitive; they were determined after a vigorous court debate, portions of which are included in the *Hanshu*, regarding the consequences and significance of different protocols for the audience ritual.[10]

Descriptions of both the 51 BCE audience ceremony and the attendant debate thus open windows on to ongoing problems as much internal as external to the empire, allowing us to delve further into the issues of institutional change and ritual representation explored in chapter 1. While chapter 1 focused on sumptuary regulations and the larger ritual order that those regulations supported, this chapter zeroes in on one particular ceremony, the annual court audience (*chao*), as well as the body of "court ceremonial" (*chao yi*) to which it belonged. Even though most secondary studies have focused on the imperial sacrifices, court ceremonial and the court audience were arguably just as important in the court's ritual calendar.[11] Most of the particulars around both, however, remain murky. Nonetheless, compared to the imperial sacrifices, whose ceremonial details are virtually unknown, students of court ceremonial enjoy a wealth of sources that provide more specific information, particularly when it comes to the court audience. Historian Derk Bodde examined many of these sources in his seminal study of Han dynasty rituals and festivals, showing that kings, nobles, and officials were required to participate in the annual audience and proclaim their loyalty to the emperor. This political importance of the audience can hardly be underestimated, since failure to participate could be interpreted as an act of insubordination or even rebellion. As Bodde showed, however, there was more to the audience than politics alone, since the ceremony was just a single, if central event in a series of New Year's celebrations at court, including an annual presentation of administrative reports from the commanderies as well as various entertainments and amusements.[12]

Without denying the impressive picture Bodde painted of the court audience and its place in the New Year's festivities, this chapter emphasizes gaps between different descriptions of the audience as well as institutional shifts that changed the ceremony's organization and the demographic makeup of its participants. We begin with a famous description in the *Shiji* of the first court audience, designed by the ritual specialist Shusun Tong and performed by Gaozu, at the beginning of Western Han. The *Shiji* casts this particular court audience as an important moment in the establishment of Han authority, a critical performance and display that solidified the ruling household's political control. The next detailed records of a particular court audience, however, those of the 51 BCE ceremony, paint an entirely different picture. The *Hanshu* provides three different descriptions of the *shanyu*'s audience, as well as an attendant debate about ritual protocol, in three different chapters: the "Account of the Xiongnu" (Xiongnu zhuan), the "Account of Xiao Wangzhi" (Xiao Wangzhi zhuan), and the "Annals of Xuandi." Comparison of these three accounts shows the audience and debate to have been multifaceted events that raised questions about the nature of Han imperial power and the best way to represent it; culminated a long process of demographic and institutional change at the imperial court, one that established it as the undisputed center of imperial power while simultaneously raising new concerns about that power; and became retroactively recast as a clash between an autocratic emperor acting unilaterally against a corps of classically minded officials, all of whom were devoted to a conservative understanding of imperial power.

While the first two points receive emphasis in the "Account of Xiao Wangzhi" and the "Account of the Xiongnu," the third and final point emerges from a close reading of the "Annals," since it shows that Ban Gu clearly altered records in the former in order to produce a more classically inflected narrative in the latter. The final section argues that Ban so wrote the "Annals" in order to situate 51 BCE within his larger call to revamp the Han ritual program, including the precedents and practices of court ceremonial, so that it accorded with classical principles. Instead of a diplomatic denouement in the history of Han-Xiongnu relations, Ban refashioned the audience as a beginning: an early salvo in an increasingly strident struggle to reorganize court ceremonial in particular and the imperial court in general according to principles enshrined in classical texts. The court audience thus became just one piece that had to fit into the empire's larger ritual puzzle. Even if the court audience was consistently practiced over the course of the Han, its significance changed greatly: from a transparent affirmation of Han power, the audience became a highly articulated ceremonial form, justified in classical terms, that provided a ritual position for a larger and more diverse imperial population.

DEBATING THE AUDIENCE: RITUAL PRINCIPLES AND PRACTICE

The first court audience ceremony performed by a Han ruler also received the most detailed description in early sources. The "Account of Liu Jing and Shusun Tong" (Liu Jing Shusun Tong liezhuan) in the *Shiji* relates the circumstances under which Shusun, a former Qin official and ritual expert who became one of Gaozu's top advisers, designed and performed this first audience. According to the *Shiji*, in the seventh year of Gaozu's reign the newly enthroned emperor grudgingly allowed Shusun to devise a new "court ceremonial" (*chao yi*), though only after he expressed concern about the difficulty of such rituals and urged Shusun to make them "easy to understand," something he "would be able to do." Brushing aside the concerns of specialists who protested that such rituals could be established only after the accumulation of virtuous power, Shusun convened thirty experts to devise an audience ceremony, which he then performed in a newly constructed Chang'an palace:

> The ceremony commenced before dawn. Messengers governed the ceremony, leading people in by rank as they entered the gates of the hall. Within the center of the courtyard were arrayed chariots, cavalry, soldiers, and guards. They set up their weapons and set high the flags and emblems. An order was passed on: "Forward." At the foot of the hall the gentlemen of the palace assembled to the sides of the stairs, and the stairs themselves held several hundred people. Organized by rank on the west, and facing east, were the meritorious ministers, nobles, generals, and military officers. Organized on the east, and facing west, were the civil officials from the chancellor [*chengxiang*] on down. The *taixing* set them into nine ranks, while heralds transmitted orders to them.[13] Thereupon, the emperor emerged from his chambers in a litter and the many officers grasped their halberds and passed on orders with urgent precision. By order of rank, the regional kings on down to the officials at the salary level of 600 bushels were brought forth to offer their praise. From the regional kings on down, nobody failed to tremble in terror and shrink back in deference.
>
> When the ritual was complete, they returned to their positions as the regulation wine was set out. Everybody in the hall bent over, with heads pressed down. From highest to lowest, each raised his head and wished the emperor a long life. They drank from their goblets nine times, and then the messengers said: "Set aside the wine." Imperial counselors commanded the rules of the proceedings and immediately led out anybody who did not conform to the ceremonial protocol. Throughout the court audience and presentation of wine, nobody

> dared to cry out or falter in maintaining ritual decorum. Thereupon, the emperor said: "Only now do I understand the nobility of being the emperor." He appointed Shusun Tong to be superintendent of ceremonial and gave him five hundred catties of gold.[14]

The *Shiji*'s description pays particular attention to the arrangement of ranks within the ceremonial space. It repeatedly notes that rank governed all of the movements of ceremony participants, from their entry into the courtyard, to their position on the stairs, to being seated in the hall itself. As they toasted the emperor, Gaozu's men simultaneously displayed both their fealty to the ruler and their position within the hierarchy. Small wonder that the ceremony caused participants to "shrink in deference" and Gaozu to marvel at the power of ritual to make him realize his own supreme status and authority. As the *Shiji* noted elsewhere, these court ceremonies, devised by Shusun Tong on the basis of Qin practices and precedents, proved immensely effective in "venerating the ruler and restraining the vassal" (*zun jun yi chen*).[15]

This statement should be taken seriously, for many other stories in the *Shiji* highlight the central roles played by court audiences and ceremonial in imperial efforts to maintain authority and show favor to particular people. Recall, for instance, that Liu Wu, the king of Liang, was repeatedly allowed to visit the capital to participate in the New Year's court audience. In one instance, he actually stayed in Chang'an for the entire year, a clear reflection of the favor he enjoyed.[16] Other stories show emperors keen to see kings fulfill their court audience duties, with some harboring an almost paranoid fear of the significance of a missed court ceremony, since in theory absences required special permission.[17] Moreover, one of the *Shiji* tables, the "Annual Table of the Regional Kings from the Rise of the Han" (Han xing yi la zhuhou wang nian biao), recorded not just the years that the kings assumed the throne and died but also the years in which kings were either deposed or came for the court audience. Even if we cannot assume that the table is complete, by annually noting which kings attended court and which rebelled or committed a crime, the table distinguished between kings who fulfilled their duties and remained loyal to the imperial court and kings who turned against it. Qing commentators writing in the early eighteenth century were probably correct, then, when they claimed that the table recorded court audience attendance in order to indicate whether or not the kings were acting in a properly deferential manner.[18] The regulations over the court audience and court ceremonial that Shusun Tong established and, all evidence indicates, wrote down, thus held enormous significance for court ritual life long after the ritual expert's death.[19]

When Jihoushan asked to participate in the 51 BCE New Year's audience, the general purpose of the court audience was hardly in question. Nonetheless, the *shanyu*'s impending visit still caused a vigorous debate. According to the *Hanshu* "Account of Xiao Wangzhi," after Jihoushan made his request Xuandi ordered officials to "discuss the ceremonial protocol [of the audience]."[20] Perhaps many weighed in, but the "Account" records only a joint proposal from Huang Ba (d. 51 BCE) and Yu Dingguo (d. after 43 BCE), as well as a response to Huang and Yu from Xiao Wangzhi (ca. 107–47 BCE). At the time, Huang served as chancellor (*chengxiang*), the highest office in the government bureaucracy, and Yu was imperial counselor (*yushi dafu*), while Xiao held the post of senior tutor to the heir apparent (*taizi taifu*). As their respective statements make clear, a key point of debate was the ceremonial position of the *shanyu* vis-à-vis the Liu regional kings, all of whom formally ranked just below the emperor. When the audience took place, would the *shanyu* be positioned above or below the kings? Huang and Yu argued forcefully that the lower position was preferable, citing classical texts and precedents:

> The institutions of the sage kings spread virtuous power and enacted ritual. They esteemed the capital before the kingdoms and the kingdoms before foreigners. The *Odes* say:
>
> > Following the rites without overstepping,
> > Throughout he examined and fully enacted them.
> > Xiang-tu was very glorious,
> > And beyond the seas he ruled.[21]
>
> The sagely virtue of Your Majesty fills Heaven and Earth and your bright rays pervade the four corners of the world. The *shanyu* of the Xiongnu has leaned toward your example and desires a moral transformation, offering up precious items and giving his praise at court. Since ancient times, this has never occurred. Ritual protocol for him should properly be set as analogous to the regional kings, and his court position should be below theirs.[22]

Huang and Yu cited a hoary past in which the royal capital sat above the kings, who themselves ranked above foreign groups. They thus situated the emperor and his court at the center of a series of nested zones extending out toward increasingly wild and uncivilized lands. Even if Huang and Yu offered no explicit citations of classical texts, the model of imperial space expressed in their proposal is similar to that articulated in the "Tribute of Yu" (Yu gong) chapter of the *Documents* (Shangshu). The final section of the "Yu gong" located the capital at the center of "five realms" (*wu fu*), each of which entailed hierarchical tribute obligations and ritual status that increased with proximity to the imperial center. We need not prove that Huang and Yu explicitly cited the "Tribute of Yu" in order to recognize that they plainly invoked the "tributary orders," derived from classical texts and principles, that articulated a centralized and hierarchical imperial space.[23]

By contrast, when Xiao expressed his opposition to Huang and Yu, he provided no guiding model for how the court should rank vis-à-vis foreigners but rather rooted his argument in Western Han patterns and politics alone: "The *shanyu* is not subject to our calendar, so his is called an adversarial kingdom. It is proper both to receive him with a ritual that does not treat him as a submitted vassal and to fix his position above that of the kings. A foreigner has bowed his head and proclaimed his desire to submit. If the central states demur and do not treat him as a vassal, such an action would manifest the propriety of holding the reins loose [*ji mi*] and the 'good fortune of modesty being prevalent.'"[24] As Xiao allowed, participation in the New Year's audience necessarily implied acceptance of Han suzerainty. Since the *shanyu* led an "adversarial kingdom" not subject to Han laws and practices, Xiao argued that it would be ill-advised to suddenly treat him like a regular participant in the audience ceremony. If the emperor used rites other than those reserved for vassal lords, then he could avoid the complicated obligations that treating the *shanyu* as a vassal would entail. As Xiao continued, this strategy was particularly appropriate due to the unreliability of foreigners, who were always "disordered and inconstant."[25] Correspondingly, the descendants of the *shanyu* could not be depended upon to maintain their obligatory court audience visits and tribute offerings. By not treating the *shanyu* as a vassal and rather installing him in a position higher than the kings, the emperor signaled the *shanyu*'s status as distinct, one that would allow the Han court to sidestep complicated political and military entanglements.[26] This is what Xiao meant when he urged the emperor to "hold the reins loose," for when the *shanyu*'s descendants inevitably faltered in fulfilling their court audience obligations he could ignore them and "not treat them as rebellious vassals."

Why did Xiao adopt a position so different from that of Huang and Yu? I cannot offer a definitive answer nor entirely discount political motives. The "Account" in fact hints that Xiao might have had reason to bear a grudge against his debate opponents.[27] At the same time, the "Account" does not depict the opinions as mere political posturing or attempts to jockey for power, since it emphasizes Xiao's reputation as a major expert in ritual. For instance, he got his early start as an assistant in an office subordinate to the superintendent of state visits (*da honglu*), a ministerial-level office that by the first century BCE managed both the distribution of noble titles and relations with foreign groups. Moreover, the "Account" reproduces a lengthy debate between Xiao and another official, who had recommended that convicted criminals be required to make expiatory payments in support of efforts to quell uprisings by foreign groups in the west. Xiao opposed the idea, arguing that it would lead to increased crime.[28] His opinion eventually won out, earning him promotion to the post of superintendent of state visits.[29] In that capacity, he argued on two occasions that marital relations between the imperial court and the Wusun peoples should not be maintained, for the Wusun were too far away and the marital policy had no effect in stabilizing the border regions.[30] Xuandi ultimately agreed with Xiao's suggestions, resulting in his promotion to imperial counselor. From that post, Xiao further argued, contra others at court, that the Han should not send troops to intervene in the internecine struggles afflicting Xiongnu leaders, including Jihoushan. He instead advocated sending envoys to render assistance to people negatively impacted by the Xiongnu wars, a recommendation that the "Account" implies seems to have signaled the coming submission of Jihoushan at the 51 BCE court audience. As Xiao put it, when foreign groups heard about this aid, they would "all esteem the humanity and propriety of the central states" and "necessarily proclaim their status as vassals and render their submission."[31]

From these policy proposals we cannot definitively ascribe to Xiao a consistent approach to ceremonial protocol and foreign relations, even while his "Account" emphasizes his deep experience and knowledge in both subjects. Prior to its discussion of the debate, with just two exceptions every single statement from Xiao quoted in the "Account" somehow relates to relations with foreign groups. The topic remained controversial throughout Xiao's lifetime: the dangers of an assertive policy could hardly be overestimated, even while the Han found itself in an advantageous position that afforded opportunities to flex the empire's military and political might. Xiao and Huang and Yu presented their proposals in this context, advancing two contrasting models. Huang and Yu argued that the hierarchy of state power, crowned by the Han emperor and his court, did not allow for exceptions. The *shanyu* therefore had to be incorporated into the court audience in a manner that recognized his more distant ritual relationship with the emperor, as compared to the Liu household kings. Xiao, meanwhile, argued that the court audience was sufficiently flexible to allow for the recognition of particular political situations and relationships that did not necessarily fit into the standardized hierarchy advocated by Huang and Yu. Idealistic principles of Han supremacy thus clashed with more concrete realities of ritual practice and foreign relations, even if both proposals cited classical texts for support (the *Odes* for Huang and Yu; the *Changes* for Xiao).

Nothing in the statements by Xiao and Huang and Yu disagrees with the spirit of Shusun Tong's first audience ceremony as an effort to "esteem the ruler and restrain ministers." That the emperor was to be praised in the audience ceremony was beyond dispute. The debate, however, evinced concern with a rather different set of questions: How, exactly, was the emperor to be praised? Toward what end, and guided by what purpose or principle? As the disagreement between Xiao and Huang and Yu demonstrates, there was no consensus answer. Moreover, that these questions were even raised highlights deeper changes occurring in the century prior to 51 BCE that promoted new perspectives on court ceremonial.

THE COURT AUDIENCE: CHANGING DEMOGRAPHICS AND INSTITUTIONAL CONSOLIDATION

Since the "Account of Xiao Wangzhi" opposes the ritual expertise and realpolitik of Xiao Wangzhi with Huang Ba and Yu Dingguo's more rarified, aspirational notion of imperial power, it behooves us to gain a better understanding of the precise duties executed by court ritual officials such as the superintendent of state visits, as well as changes to those duties over time. "The Account of the Xiongnu," our second source for the 51 BCE audience, highlights the importance of such changes, since by the reign of Xuandi they had become integral to Han-Xiongnu relations and even the internecine struggles of Xiongnu leaders. As the "Account of the Xiongnu" makes clear, by the time of Xuandi the Xiongnu had fractured into a bewilderingly complicated welter of warring groups, fighting to control the "court of the *shanyu*" (*shanyu ting*).[32] Jihoushan, son of a former *shanyu*, fled when his uncle became *shanyu*. The uncle was in conflict with a powerful rival, who after fleeing to the Han imperial court was installed as a noble with the title "The Noble of Surrendering to Virtue" (Gui de hou).[33] As the "Account of the Xiongnu" details, after his uncle committed suicide Jihoushan became *shanyu*, but several other rival claimants immediately emerged. When Jihoushan defeated one such rival, two of the latter's supporters quickly surrendered to the Han. Such a strategy, however, was hardly limited to Jihoushan's opponents. The "Account" relates that two of Jihoushan's top officers, judging conditions among the Xiongnu to be in total chaos, also decided to surrender to the imperial court, which duly gave both of them noble titles.[34]

Regardless of the intricacies of Xiongnu political struggles, the key point is this: prior to the 51 BCE audience, surrendering to the Western Han imperial court, receiving court rank, and participating in court ceremonies were all accepted political strategies among Xiongnu groups. These were not sudden, one-off shifts in Xiongnu-Han relations during Xuandi's reign. Rather, they were the result of longer-term changes in Han foreign policy as well as concomitant adjustments in institutional organization. As is well known, the reign of Wudi saw the initiation of a more aggressive foreign military strategy, with the emperor launching numerous campaigns that forced the Xiongnu confederation into a defensive position and expanded Han military forces deep into Central Asia. The success of these efforts meant that by the beginning of the first century BCE the Xiongnu had become "unable to assert authority" against the Han.[35] The internecine fights detailed earlier only compounded Xiongnu impotence and, as the "Account of the Xiongnu" made clear, rendered alliance with the Han court a viable and attractive course of action in the context of an extremely unstable political situation.

One strategy, pioneered by Wudi and clearly reflected in the "Account of the Xiongnu," was the practice of ennobling Xiongnu leaders who surrendered to the Han. This development, however, was just one in a much longer series of demographic and institutional changes to the nobilities. Gaozu's top military supporters received the first nobilities, which, as the highest and only fully heritable of the twenty orders of honor (*jue*), gave title holders the privilege of collecting tax money from a specified number of households. Several of the first nobles appointed by Gaozu filled the highest official posts in the government during the opening decades of Western Han. As table I.1 showed, however, after Gaozu's reign nobilities given for military "merit" became comparatively less common, while nobilities given to the sons of kings and for reasons of "favoritism" were more frequent.

The biggest increase in disbursed nobilities came during the reign of Wudi, a hardly surprising fact, since during his long fifty-four years on the throne he would have had comparatively more opportunities to bestow noble titles. More important is the fact that Wudi's reign witnessed a complete transformation in the type of nobilities conferred. For instance, most of Wudi's nobles were sons of regional kings. In addition, many of the men who received nobilities for merit had distinguished themselves in military campaigns that expanded the borders of the empire to the west and south. Particularly germane for our understanding of the "Account of the Xiongnu" and the 51 BCE audience is the fact that fully forty of Wudi's seventy-five nobles appointed for merit were members of foreign groups, including many Xiongnu, who had surrendered to Han suzerainty.[36] In other words, the reign of Wudi saw a complete transformation in the nobilities: whereas at the beginning of the Western Han they were held almost entirely by people who had rendered military service to the Han imperial court or their descendants, by mid–Western Han they were mostly held by members of royal families or foreigners.

We cannot understand these demographic changes, however, without understanding a series of institutional transformations that, based on current evidence, folded management of noble titles into the realm of court ceremonial. The *Shiji* on several occasions records that when Gaozu ennobled his military supporters, he gave the new title holder a tally while pledging that the nobility would be passed on to descendants "generation after generation without end."[37] After Gaozu's death, this pledge seems to have been reaffirmed during Empress Lü's reign in a more systematic fashion. A 186 BCE edict issued in her name and recorded in the *Hanshu* ordered the ranking of all nobles by merit into "court positions" (*chao wei*[a]), an obscure term that probably refers to the positions nobles assumed in court ceremonies as well as their place in the noble hierarchy. Regardless, the edict ordered that this record of noble rank be stored, again for "generation after generation without end," in the ancestral shrines dedicated to Gaozu, with the stated aim of guaranteeing that nobles' descendants would inherit the noble titles.[38]

The pledge, however, was not as immutable as these descendants might have hoped. Later, according to one source, beginning in

Wendi's reign, the imperial court levied a tax on nobles to pay for the brewing of a special sacrificial wine. Significant questions about this tax and the wine remain unanswered, not least because we know about them only from fragmentary statements by Eastern Han writers or even later commentators.[39] According to these sources, the wine was brewed yearly and, in the eighth month, given as an offering in the shrines dedicated to deceased emperors. Nobles were required to pay the tax in gold, which they presented in an annual ceremony presided over by the emperor, presumably in Chang'an, though sources are not clear on this point. It is clear, however, that the tax was collected regularly by the time of Wudi, whose reign saw a dramatic purging of nobles in 112 BCE on charges that they submitted insufficient or low-quality gold.[40] Even if Gaozu's first nobles received promises that their titles would be held in perpetuity, the reigns of later emperors saw the establishment of various regulations that determined whether or not a nobility would be maintained. Adherence to these regulations and ritual obligations, rather than "meritorious" acts (martial or otherwise), was far more important to hereditary holders of noble titles who wished to maintain their status.[41]

A series of institutional reforms accompanied this change in the nature and expectations of the nobles. These reforms culminated late in the reign of Wudi, a period that saw the consolidation of both court ceremonial and management of many aspects of court rank under a single office: the superintendent of state visits (see table 2.1). Some ranks, of course, remained outside the superintendent's purview; overseeing and maintaining records related to the Liu household regional kings, for instance, remained the province of the director of the imperial clan (*zongzheng*).[42] As table 2.1 shows, however, the responsibilities of the superintendent of state visits also extended to the kings, for by 104 BCE the superintendent coordinated the dispensation of posthumous names and funerary dirges of kings and nobles as well as the orders of appointment for all nobles and royal tutors. To these tasks was added management of the villas that visiting guests used while staying in Chang'an. (Recall that Jihoushan stayed in such a villa in 51 BCE.) The fact that the superintendent of state visits had long been responsible for welcoming visiting dignitaries perhaps helps explains why eventually, in 28 BCE, he was put in charge of the dependent states located at the peripheries of the empire.

Table 2.1 Timeline of Institutional Reforms of Court Ceremonial

Early Western Han	Following Qin practice, the director of guests was in charge of relations with foreign groups. He might also have managed the disbursal and confiscation of some official seals and ribbons.[43]
148 BCE	Jingdi (r. 157–141 BCE) assigned the director of guests the responsibility of presenting a posthumous name and funerary dirge upon the death of an imperial household king. He was also made responsible for the official orders of appointment given to newly enfeoffed nobles. An official with the position of *taixing*, meanwhile, perhaps a subordinate of the director of guests, was made responsible for the posthumous names and dirges of nobles as well as the official orders of appointment for the tutors assigned to Liu kings.[44]
144 BCE	As part of a series of changes to official titles, Jingdi renamed the director of guests *taixing*. The old *taixing* was renamed *xingren*. The old *taixing* thus became a subordinate officer of the old director of guests (who from 144 to 104 BCE would confusingly be called *taixing*).[45]
104 BCE	The *taixing* (old director of guests) was renamed superintendent of state visits (da honglu), and to his duties were added all responsibility for the mansions used by visitors from the commanderies and kingdoms.[46] The superintendent of state visits also assumed responsibility for the nobles, which had previously been managed by the *zhujue duwei*. Finally, the *xingren* again became *taixing*.[47]
28 BCE	The office of director of dependent states (*dian shuguo*) was eliminated, with all duties combined under the superintendent of state visits.[48]

By 104 BCE and for the remainder of the Western Han, the bureau of the superintendent of state visits directed an institutionalized framework for organizing kings, nobles, officials, and other figures into various court ceremonies, including the audience, and ensuring that they adhered to ceremonial regulations. Whereas in the early Western Han noble rank, court ceremonial, and diplomatic visits were managed by

different officials, by the mid- and late Western Han all were consolidated under the superintendent of state visits and his subordinate officials. Elite rank and court ceremonial thus simultaneously expanded to include a larger number of people, even while in institutional terms it narrowed into a body of technical knowledge and bureaucratic practice managed by the single office of the superintendent of state visits. We must imagine him supervising all of the new appointments, keeping track of who held what title, and incorporating all royal and noble titleholders into ceremonial performances at the imperial palaces. This pattern had been established for over fifty years by the time Jihoushan asked to participate in the 51 BCE New Year's audience.

While this shuffling of rank and ceremonial duties seems to have temporarily settled questions about the organization of elite society and the imperial court after a period of rapid imperialist expansion, it also allowed new questions to be raised. How was the power of a newly dominant Han court to be represented? Could its ritual protocol be adjusted in order to accommodate shifting political and diplomatic circumstances? Or did it comprise a fixed set of practices, rooted in purportedly ancient principles, that brooked no adjustment, regardless of the vicissitudes of contemporary affairs? These questions animated the debate between Xiao Wangzhi and his opponents. Huang Ba and Yu Dingguo advocated for a court audience that reflected an assertive understanding of Han imperial power, one rooted in classical ideals of the peerless and universal status of the imperial capital. Xiao, though, advocated for the more flexible understanding of court ceremonial.

It is impossible to determine if there was a link between Xiao's opinion and his previous service as a superintendent of state visits. Surely the knowledge of court ceremonial that he gained in the office informed his proposal for the audience, but we cannot know the precise connection. At the very least, however, as the previous section showed, the narrative in the "Account of Xiao Wangzhi" seems to suggest such a connection. After all, the detailed understanding of ritual protocol reflected in Xiao's opinion pairs more naturally with the duties of the superintendent of state visits. As a result, in the context of the debate, the isolation of court ceremonial knowledge and practice within the office of the superintendent was reflected in the divide between Huang and Yu's aspirational ritual theory and the more concrete realities of ceremonial practice in Xiao's statement. This divide, however, had implications not just for the debate and planning for the *shanyu*'s visit but also for the representation of that visit in later historical writing.

REGULATIONS VERSUS RITUAL: REWRITING THE 51 BCE AUDIENCE

The "Annals of Xuandi," as we have seen, painted a dramatic picture of the *shanyu*'s audience with the emperor. The "Account of the Xiongnu" includes an almost identical passage that describes the audience, but with a starkly different description of Jihoushan's gifts: "[The *shanyu*] was given hats, sashes, outer robes, and inner skirts; a golden seal with green ribbons; a sword with a jade handle; a waist dagger; one bow; four arrows; ten halberds draped in cloth; one passenger chariot; one saddle and bridle set; fifteen horses; twenty catties of gold; twenty-thousand cash; seventy-seven quilted robes; eight thousand bolts of sundry silk fabric, including brocade and patterned gauze; and six to seven thousand catties of silk thread."[49] The superintendent of state visits would have been responsible for assembling these gifts, documenting them, and presenting them to the *shanyu* and his entourage. That such documentation, or copies thereof, served as sources for the *Hanshu* is suggested by comparing the gift list in the "Account of the Xiongnu" with its counterpart in the "Annals of Xuandi." Strikingly, the list in the "Annals" is much less detailed: it gives no amounts but rather provides only general categories: robes, ribbons, chariot, money, and so on. By contrast, specific figures are in the list from the "Account" (e.g., *one* saddle and bride set, *fifteen* horses, *seventy-seven* robes). Whether or not the precise figures given in the "Account of the Xiongnu" accurately reflect the gifts exchanged in the 51 BCE ceremony is unknowable. The greater level of detail in the "Account," however, illustrates that the officials working under the superintendent who organized the ceremony and directed its performance must have originally produced a list of gifts. Surely, the list in the "Account" more closely reproduces the original list than the general description in the "Annals." In other words, the "Annals" went through more significant editing and, compared to the "Account," was one further step away from the activities of the superintendent of state visits and the realities of court ceremonial practice.

The "Annals" went rather far in this editorial work, since it completely eliminated any hint of gifts of weapons. We read instead only of seals, ribbons, sashes, robes, chariots, and other gifts commonly given to kings, nobles, and officials, who almost never received weapons from the imperial court, at least according to the imperial annals of the *Hanshu*.[50] In other words, even if the "Annals" acknowledged the special status given to the *shanyu* during the audience, its list seems to have deliberately downplayed the distinctiveness of his treatment. The "Annals of Xuandi" thus simultaneously reveals the special nature of Jihoushan's 51 BCE audience as well as an impulse to slot him into more standard ritual categories. As a result, the tension between the actual execution of the audience and a more aspirational idea of how the audience *should* have transpired only underscores the distance between the work of the superintendent of state visits and the normative depiction of that work in the "Annals." It also suggests that the central problematic between Xiao and Huang and Yu continued to color the depiction of 51 BCE long after it occurred.

Further comparison shows that the "Annals" went so far as to entirely change the record of the debate and reverse Xiao's opinion. First, the "Annals" omits the different opinions from the officials, stating only that "all" (*xian*) who participated in the debate were unified and offered the same proposal.[51] Second, in the "Annals" that proposal combines language found in the two opinions of Huang and Yu and Xiao. The "Annals" version of the proposal begins with an almost verbatim quote of Huang and Yu's opinion, but then introduces an intriguing variation of Xiao's proposal. In the interest of clarity, and at the risk of repeating myself, the entire debate given in the "Annals" is reproduced here. Standard roman font indicates portions identical to statements by Huang and Yu in the "Account of Xiao Wangzhi," while italics indicates statements attributed to Xiao in the "Account." Bold text is found only in the "Annals of Xuandi."

> **All stated:** The institutions of the sage kings spread virtuous power and practiced ritual. They esteemed the capital ahead of the kingdoms and esteemed the kingdoms ahead of foreigners. The *Odes* say:
>
> > Following the rites without transgression,
> > Everywhere observing their enactment.
> > Men of service were majestic,
> > And beyond the seas all was ordered.
>
> The sagely virtue of Your Majesty fills Heaven and Earth and your bright rays pervade the four corners of the world. The shanyu of the Xiongnu has bent towards your moral force, **and his entire realm is of one mind**, offering up precious items and giving his praise at court. Since ancient times, this has never occurred.

> *Because the shanyu is not one who receives our first-month calendar,* **he is treated as a guest of the ruler.**[52] Ritual protocol for him should properly be set as analogous to the Liu household kings. **He shall state that he is a vassal, attending on pain of death, and repeatedly bow.** His court position should be below the kings.[53]

As the contrasts between different styles attempts to make clear, most of the opinion included in the *Hanshu* "Annals" reproduces the statement of Huang and Yu, and the ultimate policy position that it advocates is the same: the *shanyu* should be ranked below the kings in the audience ceremony. Xiao's points, however, are not neglected, but this time they support rather than oppose the opinion of Huang and Yu. Recall that in his "Account" Xiao concluded that the *shanyu* should be placed above the regional kings since he did not use the Han calendar and was from an adversarial realm. The opinion in the "Annals," however, uses the same statement about the calendar to conclude that the *shanyu* should be treated the same as the Liu kings and situated below them during the ceremony.

The opinion is very confusing, not least because its reasoning seems to contradict an edict, issued in Xuandi's name, which comes immediately after the debate in the "Annals." The edict called for using a "guest ritual" (*ke li*) to receive the *shanyu* even while it said the *shanyu* would be put in a position *above* the kings: "During the reign of the Five Lords and Three Kings, wherever ritual order did not apply was not reached by government policies. Now, the *shanyu* of the Xiongnu has called himself a northern protective vassal and he desires to attend the first-month court audience. This was not something that We caused nor can it be broadly encompassed under Our virtuous power. Guest ritual will be used to receive the *shanyu* and his position will be placed above that of the kings."[54] In other words, the notion of the *shanyu* as a "guest" supports two entirely different conclusions. Xuandi's edict argued that guest ritual could be used while situating Jihoushan above the kings. The opinion of "all" officials in the "Annals," however, held that as a guest the *shanyu* should be in a position subordinate to the regional kings. Recall that the "Account of Xiao Wangzhi" showed a divide: Xiao's detailed understanding of court ceremonial and realpolitik approach to the audience ceremony clashed with Huang and Yu's muscular assertion of the imperial court's peerless status, based on the classical tribute hierarchy. The "Annals," however, combined the two perspectives, suggesting that there was no disagreement, contradiction, or room for interpretation when it came to court ceremonial. Rather, all ritual regulations, including guest ritual, upheld a classically informed vision of the imperial court as a peerless center that attracted tribute and declarations of loyalty from subordinate groups. In making this claim, the "Annals" further depicted Xuandi as a more autocratic ruler, since he unilaterally contradicted the unanimous opinion of his advisers, all of whom supported this understanding of the court.[55] As the "Account of Xiao Wangzhi" demonstrated, however, in 51 BCE no such unanimity existed, and court ceremonial regulations were hardly free of contradictions.

In addition to rewriting the history of the debate and audience, then, Ban Gu's description in the "Annals" of both events was also an argument about how court ceremonial *should* look: instead of a grab bag of sundry rites that could be adjusted according to circumstance, the ideal court ceremonial would be a linked system of practices, all rooted in classical principles, that put the Han at the heart of a centralized tribute order in which all participants had a clearly defined position. Such a purpose for and understanding of court ceremonial represented a dramatic departure from the early Western Han and Shusun Tong's first court audience ceremony. Shusun and his work were never entirely rejected, perhaps not least because early sources recognized him as the Han's "founding classicist" (*ru zong*). His legacy and his success in "esteeming the ruler while restraining ministers" continued to receive qualified praise as late as the closing years of late Western Han, as demonstrated by several memorials by important Western Han ritual experts that Ban quoted in his "Treatise on Ritual and Music" (Li yue zhi).

The interesting change, however, is that these ritual reformers characterized Shusun's work not as a successful reformulation of Qin court ceremonial but as an unfinished project that needed to be reestablished on completely different terms.[56] As Ban argued in his own concluding statement in the "Treatise," even in early Eastern Han the precedents and practices of Shusun's court ceremonial had collapsed into a confusion of contradictory regulations:

> However, the reason that moral transformation has not yet spread to all corners and the rites and music are incomplete is because the masses below have no place to recite and explain [the classics], since the Xiangxu ritual schools are not yet established.[57] Kongzi said: "It is like the building of a mound: if you stop before the last basket of earth, it remains forever unfinished."[58]
>
> Today, Shusun Tong's rituals and ceremonies are recorded together with the Han statutes and ordinances and stored with legal officials. Moreover, specialists in the law have not transmitted them further.

> With the Han ritual canons unused and no further writings on them, among the people and ministers nobody ever talks about the subject. Additionally, after Shusun Tong died, King Xian of Hejian chose ancient precedents related to the rites and music. Gradually these [manuscripts] increased and were edited, totaling more than 500 fascicles.
>
> Learned men of today are unable to clearly understand them. They only push rites meant for men of service to be applied to the Son of Heaven. Their explanations are disordered and different. As a result, the Way of associating between ruler and minister, elder and younger, is mired, without any proper form.[59]

Ban Gu's emphasis here is on establishing ritual schools, which would theoretically provide the instruction necessary for the entire realm to follow the proper "Way of associating" between different status groups. In so doing, he categorized the rites of Shusun as legal writings recorded with statutes and ordinances. Though we might expect Ban to favor the classical rites of King Xian of Hejian, this passage does not single out Xian's ritual texts for particular praise. Instead it describes all of the ritual writings as so voluminous and jumbled together, hardly different from mere legal regulations, that it would be virtually impossible to separate the wheat from the chaff.[60] The key for Ban was the reanimation of classical ritual institutions. In order to achieve this goal, the proper rituals had to be separated out from a confused mass of regulations and then unified into a coherent set of models that would provide a lasting and appropriate form for moral conduct throughout the empire. Ban thus distinguished between a jumble of inconsistent ceremonial regulations and a unified set of rituals supported by classical education. He did something rather similar in his depiction of the 51 BCE debate about the *shanyu*'s court audience.

At the beginning of Western Han, one of the top objectives of rulers and their advisers at the imperial court was to craft a body of court ceremonial that "esteemed the emperor and restrained vassals." The ritual expert Shusun Tong was probably the most important figure in this process. Many sources cite the central role he played in retooling, though not fundamentally altering, the practices and precedents of court ceremonial employed by the Qin. The dramatic court audience designed for Gaozu, which allowed the new ruler to "understand the nobility of being emperor," was merely the most important example of Shusun's success. This understanding of court ceremonial never disappeared. When Jihoushan asked to participate in the 51 BCE

New Year's audience, 150 years after Gaozu's very first ceremony, participants in the resulting debate about ritual protocol hardly disagreed on the point of the audience: for participants to declare their loyalty to the emperor and their recognition of Han suzerainty. Indeed, this fundamental purpose of the New Year's court audience was precisely what motivated the *shanyu*'s request in the first place, for by participating in the ceremony and thus allying himself with the Han he hoped to gain leverage over rivals in a violent civil war that had erupted between Xiongnu groups. In this sense, the 51 BCE court audience was a significant milestone in the history of Han-Xiongnu relations.

The debate over ceremonial protocol for the *shanyu*'s visit, however, demonstrates that quite a bit more was at stake than diplomatic relations and that the factors that allowed the debate to happen in the first place were more complicated than political instability among the Xiongnu. The opinions offered by Xiao Wangzhi on the one hand and Huang Ba and Yu Dingguo on the other presented starkly different visions of the imperial court and the empire as a whole. Xiao's opinion cast the imperial court as a relatively flexible body, one whose protocols and self-presentation could be adjusted in order to accommodate political exigencies. By contrast, the opinion of Huang and Yu asserted a vision of the court as a more rigid, conservative institution that would not brook exceptions to a ritual hierarchy extending concentrically from the imperial center out into distant lands. While both parties in the debate agreed that the *shanyu* had to praise the emperor in the audience, they sharply disagreed on the nature and presentation of that praise and the proper relationship between the *shanyu* and other participants in the audience ceremony, especially the regional kings.

These other participants had experienced fundamental demographic changes since the beginning of Western Han, changes that were accompanied by institutional shifts in court ceremonial that provided important background to the 51 BCE debate. One of the starkest changes occurred among the Han nobles, who by the time of Jihoushan's visit had transformed from a group dominated by Gaozu's military supporters into a much more heterogeneous category filled by members of different groups: sons of kings, exemplary officials, favored advisers, and indeed foreigners whose lands had now been incorporated into or at least abutted an expanded Han Empire. A transformation in the institutional organization of court ceremonial accompanied these changes.

Though the evidence is far from complete, sources indicate that by the end of Wudi's reign regulations over court ceremonial and the maintenance of noble titles, previously spread among different offices, had been consolidated into just one bureau, that of the superintendent of state visits. By late Western Han, control over foreign "dependent states" also came under the control of the superintendent. Even if we cannot identify a direct connection between the 51 BCE debate and the emergence of the superintendent of state visits as the bureau in charge of court ceremonial knowledge and practice, surely Xiao's experience as both a subordinate official in that bureau and even as the superintendent would have informed his opinion in the debate. Indeed, the isolation of court ceremonial and management of noble rank in the office of the superintendent reflected the disagreement between Xiao and Huang and Yu. Xiao's knowledge of and experience with court ceremonial paired naturally with his realpolitik approach to the *shanyu*'s visit, grounded as his opinion was in the concrete realities of ritual protocol, while the opinion of Huang and Yu showed little familiarity with or concern for such details.

When Ban Gu compiled the *Hanshu* and especially the "Annals of Xuandi," however, he presented a narrative that evinced rather different concerns. Most important, Ban combined the opinions of Xiao and Huang and Yu into a unanimous policy proposal, calling on Xuandi to place the *shanyu* below the regional kings as a guest. Ban thus effaced the disagreement between the two parties and presented a vision of court ceremonial in which the details of protocol (in this case, the protocol for guest ritual) conformed to a conservative, classically informed understanding of the imperial court. This editorial move correspondingly depicted Xuandi as contradicting that same understanding, for in his edict the emperor ordered the *shanyu* to be treated according to guest ritual and placed *above* the kings. By framing the debate about the court audience in this manner, Ban depicted it as a flashpoint in a larger disagreement between the emperor and classically minded officials who advocated a unified vision of court ceremonial, in which all protocols and precedents conformed to principles enshrined in classical texts. Ban called for precisely this kind of reform in his "Treatise on Ritual and Music," which recast Shusun not as the official who successfully established the Han ritual program but as a man whose work was never finished and had to be entirely reformulated so that it accorded with the understanding of court ceremonial that Ban advocated.

Given the clear classical predilections evinced in Ban Gu's editorial work, it would be tempting, and not entirely wrong, to ascribe attempts to change and reform the rituals and protocols of court ceremonial to a growing vogue for classicist ideals in the late Western Han. In other words, some of the factors driving changes in imperial court ceremonial were certainly rooted in different interpretations of classical texts.[61] At the same time, this chapter and the previous chapter have emphasized that changes in the understanding of the imperial court were not rooted in "ideological" changes or interpretive shifts alone. Changes in the office of the superintendent of state visits were driven by a total demographic transformation in holders of noble titles, as well as a process of imperial expansion that began during the reign of Wudi, expanding the scope of court ceremonial and including ever more groups and people in its purview. The isolation of court ceremonial and practice into the office of the superintendent of state visits was in part a response to these changes, since it was probably easier for one office to manage a much larger and more complicated body of practices and precedents.

This change, however, might have had unanticipated consequences. Experts such as Xiao Wangzhi, having experience in and familiarity with the office of the superintendent, could draw upon expertise in court ceremonial protocol. Others, however, including Huang Ba and Yu Dingguo, looked outside the purview of the superintendent for different principles and precedents that could guide their policy proposals. In other words, the division between Xiao and Huang and Yu was not just "ideological." It was also rooted in institutional patterns and changes stemming from imperial expansion and the consolidation of political power in the imperial court. When Ban Gu compiled the *Hanshu*, after classical ideals had gained more sway among highly educated advisers at the imperial court, he could cast the divide as a struggle between an autocratic emperor and a unified corps of classically minded officials. We should not be deceived, however, and forget the institutional and policy changes that raised important questions, not to mention the entirely unexpected and contingent request from the *shanyu*, all of which ultimately allowed Ban's narrative of the 51 BCE debate to make sense.

The evidence assembled thus far in this and the previous chapter has led us behind and beyond the assertions of imperial power that were necessarily part of imperial sumptuary regulations and court ceremonial. Even if court ceremonial was designed to "esteem the emperor and suppress the vassals," in fact the "suppressed vassals" appear to have had quite a bit of latitude in proposing formulations of court ritual that addressed different problems and served interests and concerns other than exalting the ruler. Even if the initial project of the imperial court was to establish the sumptuary and ritual categories, by mid- and late Western Han other questions were more important: Who should fill those categories, and how should they relate to each other? Such a dynamic was no less at play in the spatial understandings of the court discussed in the next chapter. Whether commenting on the court as a body of ceremonial practice or as a space, officials did not just assume the status of the imperial court as an unambiguous center but actively participated in crafting a center that better fit their particular ambitions and experiences, be they intellectual, political, or social.

PART 2

Spaces

CHAPTER 3

Parks, Palaces, and Prestige

In the autumn of 30 BCE, during a period of heavy rain, rumor spread that a dangerous flood threatened Chang'an. With capital residents in turmoil, a top official advised Chengdi (r. 33–7 BCE) that the populace should scale the city walls to avoid the rising waters.[1] On the advice of a dissenting official, the emperor ultimately decided not to issue such an order, and in the end no flood occurred. Nonetheless, many people clambered to the top of the walls anyway. The account of the incident in the *Hanshu* "Annals of Chengdi" (Chengdi ji), however, was not limited to the panicked reaction of city residents. It also described a parallel security breach in another set of walls, those that surrounded Weiyang Palace, where the emperor lived:

> In the autumn, a flood occurred within the passes. In the seventh month, a little girl from Sishang, Chen Who-Carried-the-Bow [Chen Chigong], heard that the floodwaters were coming.[2] She traveled through the Heng Gate of the Chang'an city walls and then without authorization entered the barred side gate of the Imperial Workshop, traveling all the way to the bureau of the Intendant of the Imperial Palaces and Parks within Weiyang Palace. Officials and commoners, in terror, had scaled the city walls.
>
> In the ninth month, the emperor issued an edict: "Recently, the commanderies and kingdoms have suffered from flooding. The number of people swept away and killed has risen into the thousands. Within the capital, baseless rumors claimed that floodwaters were coming. Officials and commoners were terrified, so they fled to climb the city walls. It appears that punitive and cruel officials have not let up, and there are many good people who have been wronged and

> strayed from their duties. I will send my Advisory Council, Lin, and others on a tour of inspection throughout all under heaven."[3]

The account leaves no doubt that the flood was of grave concern for the emperor, who in his edict blamed the chaotic incidents surrounding the deluge on the sorry behavior of government officials. The edict connected the chaotic scene of terrified Chang'an residents climbing city walls to the unrelenting cruelty of those officials, conduct that had caused good and honest people to "stray from their duties" (*shi zhi*). Chengdi stated that the resulting lack of good officials had allowed Chang'an residents to act in such a reckless manner. In other words, Chengdi concluded that he had a personnel problem.

The *Hanshu* "Annals" hinted at a different interpretation, however, when it paired the story of the girl Chen with Chengdi's edict, which made no mention of Chen's entry into Chang'an. For the "Annals," the 30 BCE flood saw a total breakdown in the concentric rings of security and control that protected the capital and the palaces.[4] The ominously named Chen Who-Carried-the-Bow, after all, surmounted or breached all defensive walls, from the city's perimeter ramparts to the barriers surrounding the innermost sanctum of the emperor.[5] Another version of the story, this one from the "Treatise on the *Wuxing*" (*Wuxing* zhi) included in the *Hanshu*, articulated this narrative more clearly: "Chen entered Weiyang Palace through a side gate of the imperial workshop. At the gates to the palace halls, none of the guards were to be seen. She made it all the way to the office of the intendant of the imperial palaces and parks within the forbidden zones of the palace before she was discovered and apprehended."[6] The "forbidden zones" (*jin zhong*) were quarters reserved for the emperor, his palace ladies, and those with special permission to enter. The "Treatise on the *Wuxing*" invoked the symbolic value of these inner areas of the palace in its interpretation of the girl Chen's entry: "This incident of a young girl entering into the inner areas of the palace halls was a sign that low people intended to take advantage of a woman's favor and set up residence within palace chambers."[7] Even without considering the specific identity of the "low people" mentioned here, this interpretation of Chen's entry into the palace's forbidden zones alerts us to the fact that the spaces alluded to in these passages were not incidental details in a story about a chaotic flood. They constituted highly politicized criticism of undesirables who used access provided by a palace woman to establish themselves in the emperor's inner sanctum.[8] The story of Chen Who-Carried-the-Bow served as a vivid metaphor of a coterie of people who, having invaded the most privileged areas of the palace, threatened the security of the throne.[9]

Even if the Chen Who-Carried-the-Bow story drew especially tight connections between particular areas of the imperial palace and groups of people, it was hardly unprecedented to use important spaces as metaphors or symbols for powerful people. However, symbolic understandings of palace and court space became significantly more complicated over the course of Western Han. While palaces were always understood as representations of imperial power, by the end of the period their metaphorical value was more nuanced: far beyond the emperor alone, the palaces of Chang'an in general and the imperial residence of Weiyang Palace in particular came to represent a much larger and more complicated court society. The reign of Wudi was a turning point in this regard, not least because he embarked on an ambitious program of building palaces and expanding Shanglin Park, the imperial preserve located to the west of Chang'an. The series of debates and policy shifts that occurred after Wudi's death included a reassessment of this construction program. The final century of Western Han thus saw the emergence of a complicated rhetorical landscape in which officials and advisers wrestled with the benefits and problems of parks and palaces. Broadly speaking, Shanglin Park and palaces outside of Weiyang came under increasing attack as illegitimate spaces that should be entered only occasionally, while Weiyang emerged as the only true and legitimate center of imperial power. This change was driven not just by a classicist turn toward frugality but also by a complicated collection of ritual practices, legal regulations, and social patterns. Behind all of this talk of palaces and parks was an increasingly wealthy elite court society that by the late Western Han had come to imagine Chang'an in general and Weiyang Palace in particular as the privileged if morally suspect center of its social and cultural world.

EXPANDING THE PALACES AND PARKS: POLICIES, CRITIQUES, AND REPRESENTATION

From their Qin predecessors, Western Han rulers inherited the sprawling capital Xianyang, which straddled the Wei River in a broad basin located in what is now southern Shaanxi Province. Based on current archaeological evidence, the older portion of Xianyang, located north of the river, was not surrounded by an external perimeter wall.

Neither was such a wall constructed when the First Emperor began to expand the capital by erecting palaces and temples south of the Wei River. According to the *Shiji*, the First Emperor constructed those buildings within the "imperial parks and forests" (*shang lin yuan*).[10] The area was ill-defined, and it seems likely that it comprised many different parks, not one of which was known as "Shanglin Park," a name that came into use only during Western Han.[11] Many of the buildings in these "imperial parks and forests" were probably destroyed in the fires that consumed Xianyang after the fall of Qin.[12] Nonetheless, perhaps in a natural effort to avoid labor and material costs, Gaozu built palaces on the foundations and ruins of old Qin structures after establishing the Han capital of Chang'an south of the Wei River.[13] When Gaozu's successor Huidi built a perimeter wall around Chang'an, the city and its palaces were demarcated from the surrounding space for the first time. Huidi was thus the first emperor to move into Weiyang Palace, but since his mother ruled from Changle Palace after his death, Weiyang did not truly emerge as the imperial residence until the reign of Wendi.[14]

Wudi embarked on a series of construction projects that brought huge changes to this pattern, erecting structures in and around Chang'an as well as in the distant reaches of the empire. Many of these construction efforts were related to Wudi's vigorous program of sacrifices, which saw the emperor embarking on several long journeys outside of the capital. His predecessors, of course, visited temples in the capital region and the Wei River valley, especially those at Yong.[15] Wudi went much farther afield, however, traveling long distances from Chang'an, including to points along the eastern coastline and as far south as the Yangzi River.[16] In doing so, he partially followed the model of imperial progress completed by the First Emperor of Qin and also asserted imperial suzerainty over areas that had formally been controlled by the regional kingdoms.[17] Wudi did not just pause briefly at these distant sites. In addition to constructing temples at Taishan, in modern-day Shandong Province, and at Ganquan, an old Qin site located about 100 miles north of Chang'an, at both of these sites Wudi also ordered the construction of mansions for the regional kings, on several occasions performed the New Year's court audience, and received accounts from the commanderies.[18] In doing so, Wudi established a multicapital system of governance, with Taishan, Ganquan, and Chang'an serving as political and religious centers.[19] Thus, even if some Han texts claimed that Weiyang Palace was "where the emperor resided,"[20] by the end of Wudi's reign this statement was not true in practical terms.

Closer to Chang'an, Wudi also completely transformed the old imperial parks around the capital. He erected a perimeter wall, effectively establishing Shanglin Park as a clearly delineated area. Even if Shanglin is primarily understood as a pleasure park for emperors, sprinkled with temples and palaces, during Wudi's reign it also began to assume an increasingly important role in the political and economic life of the imperial court and the empire as a whole. Most tellingly, by the middle of his reign Shanglin had begun to house important manufacturing centers, including the imperial mint.[21] Such facilities produced cash and goods that emperors could distribute to foreign dignitaries, family members, favorite associates, and officials. After 115 BCE, Wudi established a new office, the superintendent of waterways and parks (*shuiheng duwei*), to administer Shanglin Park, including its imperial mint and factories.[22] If in the opening years of Western Han the capital and surrounding park were not highly developed or delineated spaces, by the end of Wudi's reign precisely the opposite was true: capital and park were sprawling areas demarcated from the surrounding area by a long series of walls, which protected important and immensely valuable production facilities.

In the decades after Wudi's death, officials and advisers debated whether the myriad costs associated with this kind of extravagant construction were worthwhile, just one of the many moves toward retrenchment and away from the activist policies of Wudi that occurred in late Western Han.[23] Significantly, the development of this critique brought about a shift in the metaphorical significance of palaces and capital space, as demonstrated by a comparison of two stories from the *Shiji* and *Hanshu*. Even if both illustrate that political space and political rhetoric were closely interrelated, differences between the accounts suggest that the rhetorical value of such spaces had shifted by late Western Han. I will begin, however, with a story from the *Shiji*'s "Basic Annals of Gaozu" (Gaozu ben ji), which describes Xiao He's (d. 193) justification for building Weiyang Palace.

As the story goes, in 200 BCE Gaozu return to Chang'an after several difficult military expeditions—one nearly cost him his life—aimed at suppressing challenges to his newly established rule. Such conflicts were troubling reminders that the new emperor, who had assumed the throne only four years earlier, had only a tenuous hold on power. Gaozu thus expressed dismay to find Xiao He, his chancellor (*chengxiang*) and most trusted adviser, in the midst of constructing Weiyang Palace mere months after he had already completed Changle immediately to the east. The emperor angrily chastised the chancellor, pointing out that with control of the empire still unresolved, it was unwise and presumptuous to build grand structures. Xiao offered a brilliant and famous response: "Precisely because All Under Heaven has not yet been settled, it is right to seize the opportunity to build palaces and chambers. Furthermore, the Son of Heaven takes the four seas as his household. Unless you impose grandeur you will have no means to consolidate your authority, nor will you afford later generations the ability to augment it." Gaozu, the passage concludes, was "delighted."[24] The story thus articulates an underlying motivation for Xiao He's building program as well as an ideological basis for palace architecture: palaces were spectacular in order to command the majesty befitting the emperor, preserve his legacy and the legacy of the Liu ruling house, and allow for later generations to build (literally and figuratively) upon his work.

A much less famous but still important passage, this one from the *Hanshu*, highlights Wudi as a palace builder to rival Gaozu. It comes in a memorial written by an adviser named Yi Feng (fl. 40s BCE) during the reign of Yuandi (r. 48–33 BCE). Yi Feng extolled the supposedly economical practices of Wendi in order to criticize Wudi's building program: "I have heard that the efflorescence of Han's virtuous power rested in Filial Emperor Wen's personal enactment of measured and frugal policies, which reduced the use of conscripted labor outside of the capital. During Wendi's reign there was no Ganquan Palace and Jianzhang Palace, nor were there the traveling palaces and buildings of Shanglin Park. Moreover, Weiyang Palace did not yet have the halls of Towering Gate, Martial Pavilion, Qilin, Phoenix, White Tiger, Jade Chamber, or Golden Blossom. It had only the Front Hall, Curved Pavilion, Jian Pavilion, Announcing Chamber, Heated Chamber, and Hall of Receiving Brilliance."[25] Without explicitly naming Wudi, Yi Feng's memorial clearly attacked him, since he was the emperor responsible for expanding Ganquan Palace and constructing Jianzhang Palace.[26] Even though archaeologists have used Yi's statement to reconstruct the architectural history of Chang'an, the memorial is perhaps best read in contrast to the story about Xiao He's construction of Weiyang Palace. Whereas Xiao emphasized the "authority" (*wei*) that palaces provided to the newly established Han, Yi argued that a restrained building program would demonstrate the

Han's "virtuous power" (*de*). For Xiao, construction was the best way to show imperial power, whereas for Yi, imperial power was demonstrated by precisely the opposite approach: *not* building palaces. The two theories reflected the larger debate in late Western Han about the true purpose of palaces, their benefits, and their significant costs: while Xiao He's statement presented a blanket claim about the symbolic power and authority of palaces, Yi Feng described a hierarchy of palaces and a related assumption that certain structures were necessary while others were superfluous and wasteful. To cast Yi's statement in Xiao's terms, Yi effectively claimed that certain palaces embodied legitimate power, whereas others symbolized an overly extravagant, even illegitimate authority.

The significance of this criticism runs deeper, however. By claiming that Weiyang Palace (and even then only certain buildings within that palace) was the only legitimate structure, Yi Feng implicitly advanced a tight connection between the emperor and Weiyang Palace. To stray from Weiyang and spend significant time in other palaces would be to deviate from proper forms of imperial authority. Of course, as described earlier, Wudi completed precisely this kind of travel when he journeyed around the empire to perform sacrifices at Taishan, Ganquan, and elsewhere. It is no coincidence that other portions of Yi's memorial addressed the imperial sacrifices, lamenting that the rituals employed at ancestral temples of the Han imperial household "mostly [did] not accord with ancient practice."[27] Noting that it would be extremely difficult to change these rites in Chang'an, Yi proposed a radical solution: move the capital hundreds of miles east to the old Eastern Zhou capital of Chengzhou! Yuandi, needless to say, did not heed this advice. Nonetheless, Yi's memorial provides an example of the many calls to "restore antiquity" (*fu gu*), often in conscious contrast to Wudi's imperial progresses and sacrifices, that became more strident during the reigns of Yuandi and Chengdi. The culmination of this classicist movement came in 5 CE, when Wang Mang eliminated altars outside of the immediate Chang'an area and relocated all sacrificial rites to altars near the capital.[28]

Scholars have thoroughly examined these changes to the imperial sacrifices, but they have generally paid less attention to the first issue addressed in Yi Feng's memorial: the reconceptualization of imperial space as centered in Chang'an and Weiyang Palace.[29] Criticism of the peripatetic journeys of Wudi to different cult sites and the elevation of Chang'an as the rightful center of the empire were necessarily related.

Moreover, they did not just occur at the level of policy proposals or critiques but also emerged in the style by which Han emperors and their travels were represented, especially in annalistic accounts of the emperors. The *Shiji* represents imperial movement and journeys in ways subtly but importantly different from the *Hanshu* imperial annals. For instance, the "Basic Annals" of Wendi in the *Shiji* records one trip by that emperor to Yong, noting that Wendi in the fifteenth year of his reign "for the first time visited Yong and performed sacrifices to the Five Lords."[30] The *Hanshu* "Annals of Wendi" adjusts the wording, writing that Wendi "visited Yong and for the first time performed sacrifices to the Five Lords."[31] The change is slight, seemingly inconsequential, but the difference in emphasis is nonetheless undeniable: for the *Shiji* the visit and the performance of the sacrifices were one and the same event, whereas the *Hanshu* separated the description of travel to Yong from the fact that Wendi "for the first time" performed sacrifices there.

The pattern appears clearer when we compare the *Hanshu* "Annals of Wudi" with descriptions corresponding to the same trips in the *Shiji* "Treatise on the *Feng* and *Shan* Sacrifices."[32] From the "Treatise on the *Feng* and *Shan* Sacrifices":

> During the winter of the next year, the Son of Heaven offered sacrifices at Yong . . . then the Son of Heaven traveled east and for the first time erected the shrine to Houtu atop a hill south of the Fen River. . . . When the ritual was completed, the Son of Heaven then went to Xingyang before returning. When he passed by Luoyang, he issued an edict that said . . .[33]

From the "Annals of Wudi":

> In the tenth month during the winter of the fourth year, the emperor went on progress to Yong and made offerings at the altar to the Five Lords. . . . His progress continued from Xiayang and went east to visit Fenyin. On the day Jiazi in the eleventh month, he set up the shrine at Houtu atop a hill to the south of the Fen River. When the ritual was complete, he went on progress to Xingyang. Returning, he arrived at Luoyang and issued an edict that said . . .[34]

Significantly, the *Shiji* does not use the binomial term "went on progress" (*xing xing*). The *Hanshu*, however, frequently uses the term, describing with much more precision all of Wudi's movements. The result is a destination-by-destination pairing of imperial movement with ritual action: the emperor goes somewhere, conducts a sacrifice or offering, and then goes elsewhere. According to the *Hanshu* imperial annals, then, travel outside of Chang'an was limited and enjoined only for discrete purposes, especially religious purposes.

At the same time as it represented imperial travel in this manner, the *Hanshu* imperial annals appear to have occasionally downplayed or omitted other types of travel and thus occasionally reinforced the idea that Wudi's travels were anomalous. For instance, while the "Annals of Wudi" notes that Wudi convened people in Shanglin to observe the so-called *juedi* games, the "Annals of Xuandi" do not mention the fact that Xuandi also performed the *juedi* in Shanglin, for the benefit of a group of foreign dignitaries.[35] Also revealing is the 51 BCE court audience at Ganquan analyzed in the previous chapter. The occasion was a spectacular event featuring a Xiongnu ruler and allies, as well as the regional kings and nobles. The *Hanshu* "Annals of Xuandi," however, records only that the emperor "went on progress to Ganquan and offered sacrifices [at] the altar to Taiyi," before listing the gifts to the Xiongnu ruler.[36] Contrast this description with the *Hanshu* "Annals of Wudi," which specifically records when Wudi "held court" (*chao*) at Ganquan and Taishan and received accounts at both places. Xuandi did the exact same thing in 51 BCE, and we might logically suppose that Yuandi and Chengdi did as well when they traveled to Ganquan in the first month to offer sacrifices to Taiyi. The *Hanshu* annals of these later emperors, however, make no note of such political activities at Ganquan, thus implying that in contrast to Wudi, later emperors went to Ganquan rarely and only to conduct imperial sacrifices.

In sum, using a specific vocabulary, representational style, and omissions from the record, the *Hanshu* annals advanced the claim that Chang'an and Weiyang Palace were the rightful place of the Han emperors. As a result, Wudi's construction projects and his travels implicitly emerged as unwelcome and disruptive aberrations rejected by later emperors. The *Hanshu* annals thus supported Yi Feng's claim that straying from Weiyang and spending significant time in other palaces would be a deviation from proper forms of imperial authority. The story of Chen Who-Carried-the-Bow, however, reminds us that there were yet other formulations of imperial space that extended to groups of people beyond the emperor. These broader sociospatial metaphors developed in concert with changing critiques of imperial parks and along with the development of legal regulations that governed the imperial palaces themselves.

PARK, PALACE, AND COURTIER: EXCEEDING LIMITS AND DRAWING BOUNDARIES

With the physical development and expansion of Chang'an and Shanglin Park, marked most prominently by the construction of perimeter walls, later Western Han figures began to wonder: Who belonged on which side of the barriers? Why? Such questions were especially prominent in discussions of Shanglin Park, whose extravagant size and wealth prompted pressing and uncomfortable questions. Where did all of this wealth come from? Who should benefit from park resources? Such questions were not entirely new, since several pre-imperial texts debated the purpose of royal parks and preserves. Most focused on their appropriate use by rulers in self-cultivation programs, while a minority view advocated sharing park resources with imperial subjects. Even if the latter perspective enjoyed increasing prominence in later Western Han writings, the implications extended beyond victory for a classically informed "ethics of thrift."[37] In calling attention to the danger posed by imperial parks and palaces that "exceeded proper limits," to quote a memorial I discuss in more detail below, late Western Han officials and advisers took care to place themselves on the "proper" side of the wall: outside of the parks and within the space of the capital. Implicit in this critique of imperial excess, which extended from historical narratives to poems and pieces of political persuasion, was the creation of a spatial identity confined to the capital, applicable to the ruler's morally and ritually proper officials as much as to the emperor himself.

Discussion of royal parks and palaces in pre-imperial texts turned on whether they were primarily for the ruler or for the benefit of his realm's populace. The former idea seems to have been more common. Several different texts describe the role played by parks and palaces in elaborate self-cultivation programs, which seem to have gained some level of popularity among the Zhanguo and early imperial elite.[38] A passage from the *Annals of Lü Buwei* (Lüshi chunqiu), for instance, included parks and gardens among the tools available to rulers seeking to "nurture their lives" (*yang xing*). The pleasures offered by parks and gardens, among other luxuries, allowed rulers to practice "tempering their dispositions" (*jie hu xing*), so that they pursued only the amount of pleasure needed to preserve their lives in an optimum manner and, ultimately, ensure the longevity of their lineage and ruling household.[39] The *Xunzi*, meanwhile, emphasized the importance of state regulations of pleasures such as parks and preserves, which everybody naturally desires, in order to maintain political order.[40] Even if the means of controlling indulgence were perhaps debated, passages such as these evince a common understanding of parks and palaces as part of the material pleasures and privileges rightly enjoyed by rulers and fundamental to enhancing their power and ensuring the stability of their realms.

Other texts, however, emphasized the material riches contained within royal parks and, by extension, the capacity of such parks to deprive subjects of their livelihoods, or even their lives. The *Mengzi*'s condemnation of King Xuan of Qi's tightly regulated preserve is by far the most famous in this regard. According to the *Mengzi* story, the king protested to Mencius that his preserve was not nearly as large as the park maintained by the storied founder of the Zhou, King Wen. Nonetheless, the people of Qi still complained that King Xuan's park was too large. In reply, Mencius stated that the king's subjects expressed an entirely logical concern. After all, by enlarging and barring entry to his park, King Xuan risked impoverishing the people of Qi or, worse, causing them to be criminally prosecuted and perhaps even executed. Small wonder, then, that King Xuan's people saw the park as a huge "trap within the realm."[41]

Western Han discussions of Shanglin Park highlight both the role of parks and preserves in the cultivation of the emperor's moral dispositions and the danger they posed to imperial subjects. Any study of imperial parks during this period, however, is necessarily haunted by their starkly different treatment in the *Shiji* and *Hanshu*: whereas they hardly receive mention in the former, the latter includes several memorials and descriptions that directly address the parks. The few discussions in the *Shiji* focus almost exclusively on the moral hazards the park posed for the emperor, especially for Wudi, who dangerously indulged in park pleasures. See, for instance, the following discussion of Wudi's expansion of the park in the *Shiji* "Treatise on Balanced Standards" (Ping zhun shu):

> At first, the grand secretary of agriculture managed the salt and iron offices and coinage. The planned additional establishment of the superintendent of waterways and parks was done out of a desire to control salt and iron revenues.[42] After Yang Ke's accusations over [undeclared] strings of cash, however, the money and property of Shanglin increased tremendously. At that point, by imperial order the superintendent of waterways and parks came to direct Shanglin.

> Since Shanglin was already full to bursting, it was further broadened in size.
>
> During this period, the Yue people were planning to fight the Han and drive them out by using boats. Thereupon, Kunming Lake was greatly expanded with an array of towers surrounding it, while towered boats several tens of *zhang* tall topped by flags and streamers were built. They were incredibly majestic. The Son of Heaven was moved by the sight and so constructed the Boliang Terrace, some several tens of *zhang* tall. Construction of palaces and chambers became ever more grand from then on.[43]

Even if military preparedness against the Yue people was the apparent reason for enlarging Kunming Lake, the narrative itself neglects all details about the conflict, not even discussing, for instance, the weapons and armor that were installed on the "towered boats." Rather, it highlights the impressive flags that fluttered atop their masts and spars. The sight of boats and flags so "moved" Wudi that he constructed their terrestrial analogue, Boliang Terrace, which equaled the height of the magnificent boats. Construction of palaces thereupon progressed with abandon.[44] This description of Shanglin Park, Kunming Lake, and Wudi in the "Treatise on the Balanced Standards" thus corresponds with strands of the Zhanguo "cultivating life" discussions that linked parks and preserves to desire, pleasure, and self-cultivation. According to the "Treatise," Wudi abandoned all pretense of fulfilling his desires in a properly limited and cultivated manner. To borrow the language of the *Lüshi chunqiu* passage, the emperor exceeded the minimum level of consumption necessary to "temper his disposition," embarking instead on a reckless pursuit of opulence.

Such barely concealed criticism of Wudi is not to deny that other stories in the *Shiji* support the idea that expanding parks threatened the general welfare of imperial subjects. Most prominent in this vein is an account of a conflict over imperial parks between Gaozu and Xiao He. In the event, Xiao He suggested opening up empty portions of the imperial parks for cultivation by farmers. Gaozu rejected the suggestion, angry that the chancellor made a request that infringed upon his "personal park."[45] In the context of the *Shiji* account, this story was primarily important for the light it shed on the occasionally rocky relationship between Xiao He and Gaozu rather than for answering the question of who rightfully controlled the park and its resources.[46] Nevertheless, Xiao's question and Gaozu's anger hinted at the controversy that dogged the imperial parks as they expanded: To what extent were parklands meant to benefit the larger populace?

This question received significantly more attention in the *Hanshu*, a fact highlighted by its depiction of Dongfang Shuo, an adviser at Wudi's court. The only statements we have about Dongfang in the *Shiji* come in a short addition, composed not by Sima Qian but by Chu Shaoshun (104?–30? BCE), to the "Accounts of the Sarcastic Jesters" (Gu ji lie zhuan). The *Hanshu* includes an entire separate biography of Dongfang. The disparate treatments in these two sources make it almost impossible to differentiate fact from fiction, and Ban Gu very well might have inserted into the *Hanshu* stories about Dongfang in order to criticize Wudi.[47] This possibility actually makes the figure of Dongfang more valuable for our inquiries, since Ban included a long memorial supposedly written by Dongfang that criticized Wudi's plans to expand the imperial park. That memorial drew upon ideas from the *Mengzi* critique of King Xuan of Qi, suggesting that the different descriptions of Dongfang were part of a larger trend toward criticizing the park that started in late Western Han.

Chu Shaosun's discussion is undeniably brief, though compared to the *Hanshu* account Chu's comments provide a more complex, contradictory, even human picture of Dongfang Shuo. According to Chu, Dongfang was from Qi, and his love for ancient writings and "classical techniques" (*jing shu*) drove him to accumulate a wide range of knowledge. When he first went to Chang'an, he submitted a huge body of writings to the prefect at the palace gates. Wudi spent a full two months reading all of the texts, after which he appointed Dongfang gentleman-at-arms (*lang*). Delighted with his new retainer, the emperor often rewarded Dongfang with silk, which he promptly used to secure brides from among the finer women of Chang'an. Dongfang, however, was never promoted beyond gentleman-at-arms, and his unorthodox behavior earned him a reputation at court as a "wild man." According to Chu's narrative, when Wudi heard of this appellation he expressed his own willingness to indulge Dongfang's eccentricities. Moreover, when another gentleman-at-arms told Dongfang that everybody thought he was mad, Dongfang replied, "A person such as myself is somebody who 'retreats from the world [by going] within the court.' The ancients, by contrast, retreated from the world [by going] deep within the mountains."[48] In other words, by his own wit and ability to please the emperor, Dongfang had ingeniously carved out a comfortable and secure life for himself at court, untroubled by court politics or the concerns of gaining promotion or enhanced status. Under Chu's brush, far from being a moral paragon, Dongfang appeared as a clever courtier who gained the emperor's favor, thus ensuring his own security and that of his family.

By contrast, the *Hanshu* account of Dongfang Shuo takes him out of the inner world of the court, telling us nothing about his collection of texts or his close relationship with Wudi highlighted in Chu's comments. Indeed, Dongfang received a lowly post after submitting a rather arrogant memorial to the emperor, but he was never able to gain an audience with the emperor in his private quarters, to which only close advisers gained admittance. Dongfang managed to gain the emperor's confidence and a higher position as "gentleman in constant attendance" (*chang shi lang*) only after presenting a series of riddles that confounded everybody else. Ban Gu's account then takes a sharp turn, detailing Wudi's secret trips through the capital region and his plans to expand the imperial park. Dongfang submitted a memorial in protest, noting first that Heaven disapproved of overly large imperial parks and preserves: "Now your Majesty has accumulated corridors and pavilions, but fears they are not high enough; locations for shooting and hunting, but worries they are not broad enough. If Heaven did not produce anomalous warnings, then the entirety of the capital region could be converted into a park. Why would you need to limit it to Zhouzhi, E, and Du? With opulence and extravagance that exceed proper limits, however, Heaven will produce anomalous warnings. Even if Shanglin were small I would still find it large."[49] Echoing the *Mengzi*, Dongfang's memorial claimed that a park's size did not necessarily have anything to do with whether or not it is impressive. Rather, such a determination is rooted in the ruler's activities within the park and the ambitions that drove park expansion. The emperor, Dongfang argued, created the park only to fulfill his extravagant desires. As a result, he had "exceeded proper limits" (*yue zhi*), behavior that would bring about signs of Heaven's disapproval.

The concluding line about Shanglin being large is a clear reference to the *Mengzi* story discussed earlier. Indeed, the wording is almost exactly the same.[50] The memorial's warning is thus clear: Wudi's park plans, rooted in his lust for pleasure, risked impoverishing and destabilizing the realm. Dongfang concluded his memorial with three reasons why the park should not be fenced off and transformed into the emperor's personal domain. While the third and final criticism emphasized the dangers the park posed to the emperor's person, the first two called attention to the importance of the park for the larger populace. Specifically, Dongfang's memorial stated that park expansion would take farmland out of production and damage gravesites and homes.[51] We thus see in this transformation of Dongfang a rhetorical shift in criticism of the park: from a dangerously opulent temptation for the emperor, the park also became an oppressive institution that damaged the body politic and also the health of the imperial subjects who constituted its foundation.

The fact that the *Hanshu* kept some distance between Dongfang and the emperor, implying that the adviser never fully entered into the ruler's inner sanctum but remained on its periphery, also suggests the ways by which the spatial symbolism of parks and palaces could bolster the identity of the morally righteous, remonstrating official. After all, the very idea of "exceeding proper limits," to quote Dongfang Shuo's memorial, implied a set of normative boundaries within which parks, palaces, *and* moral rulers and subjects were to remain. In that vein, another statement in the *Hanshu* account has Dongfang accusing Dong Yan, a favorite of Wudi, of three different capital crimes, one of them being Dong's reckless indulgence in luxury. In response, Wudi said he would address the problem during the drinking parties he regularly held with Dong Yan in the Announcing Chamber (Xuan Shi), assuring Dongfang that Dong would change his ways. Dongfang protested, noting that the Announcing Chamber, located in Weiyang Palace, was a "proper location" (*zheng chu*) established by former emperors to be used solely for state matters. Chastened, Wudi moved the drinking parties to the Northern Palace (Bei gong). He also started admitting Dong Yan from a gate located on the eastern side of the palace, which was renamed "Eastern Meeting Gate" (Dong Jiao Men) instead of "Eastern Marshal Gate" (Dong Sima Men). The exchange thus has Dongfang enforcing a spatial order that kept unofficial business and people who did not follow ritual and governing precedents out of Weiyang Palace.[52] By extension, the ritually proper and morally righteous remonstrant was spatially associated with Weiyang.[53]

This transformation of Dongfang Shuo in the *Hanshu* becomes clearer when read in light of rhapsodies (*fu*) on the imperial park. Scholars have emphasized that even if the rhapsody was far from a tightly defined genre, it nonetheless became the dominant form of poetic performance at the Western Han imperial court.[54] Some of the most influential rhapsodies directly addressed imperial parks and palaces, including the "Rhapsody on the Excursion Hunt by the Son of Heaven" by Sima Xiangru and the later "Rhapsody on the Plume Hunt" by Yang Xiong (53 BCE–18 CE). As several scholars have discussed in different ways, descriptions of parks and palaces in these and other rhapsodies were inevitably connected to celebrations (or critiques) of imperial power.[55] However, the moral conundrums of imperial power explored in the rhapsodies came to have implications for people beyond the emperor, as demonstrated by a comparison of the Sima Xiangru and Yang Xiong rhapsodies and their depiction of the emperor's moral "turn."

The turn was central to the narrative and persuasive message of both the "Rhapsody on the Excursion Hunt" and the "Rhapsody on the Plume Hunt."[56] Both poems describe hunts in Shanglin Park, with the emperor mounting his chariot and summoning horsemen and hunters to gallop through the park, flushing out a veritable fantasia of exotic fowl and game and shooting or trapping an ever greater number of animals. Then, at the climax of killing, the emperor retires to a hunting lodge to enjoy a great feast. In Sima Xiangru's "Rhapsody on the Excursion Hunt," however, this feast is prefaced by a cosmic journey in which the emperor journeys into the heavens and shoots spectacular creatures, such as the "roving simian" and the "flying chimera."[57] He and his guests then enjoy the feast and entertainment. The emperor's mood, however, completely changes when he realizes the waste and folly of his exuberant hunt. He thereupon executes a series of morally proper actions, including opening up the park to his subjects and hearing policy proposals and criticisms from his officials.[58] This moral transformation is the key moment in Sima Xiangru's poem, for it is just as much a celebration of the emperor's power as is the description of his cosmic journey. Sima allowed Wudi to have it all: hunt, banquet, and "virtuous renunciation." As a result, "the imperial prestige [could] only be enhanced by the magnitude of his unselfish gesture."[59] By allowing Wudi to experience the twin climaxes of sensual pleasure and moral perfection, Sima created a balanced celebration of the emperor's martial and political power on the one hand and his moral authority on the other.

The moral turn in Yang Xiong's "Rhapsody on the Plume Hunt" is more complicated, but Yang clearly did not depict the emperor's turn away from park pleasures as a moment of solitary, moral apotheosis. Even though Sima Xiangru described the emperor listening to policy proposals from his officials, in his rhapsody these officials do not play a role in convincing the emperor to change his ways. By contrast, at the end of his poem Yang Xiong surrounded the emperor (at the time of composition, Chengdi) with envoys and officials who play an important role in effecting the emperor's "virtuous renunciation." Specifically, after the imperial hunt has ended, rather than a cosmic journey, Yang Xiong described the emperor retiring to a hunting lodge. The space is not without its fantastic elements, however:

> Thereupon, the game exhausted, shot to extinction, they gathered at a lodge of peaceful seclusion:
> Overlooking a precious pool,
> Watered from Mt. Qi and Mt. Liang,
> Overflowing to the Yangtze and Yellow Rivers.
> Looking eastward as far as the eye sees,
> Extending westward through a boundless expanse.
> With Sui pearls and He jades,
> Shining and sparkling upon their banks.
> Jade rocks peaked and pointed,
> Dazzle and sparkle in blue brilliance.
> The Han River nymphs in watery depths,
> Strange creatures in dark shadows,
> They cannot be fully described.[60]

Yang Xiong's description of the pool and its connections to the vast Yangzi and Yellow rivers opens up the vistas of the imperial hunt to an empire-wide scale, while the precious, sparkling treasures lining their banks hint at the fantastic and magical. So too do the Han River nymphs and "strange creatures." As the poem states, however, from the hunting lodge by the pool the form of the water beings cannot be fully discerned. This land-based perspective of the emperor and his hunting party receives further emphasis in the lines that follow, which describe the movements of various birds as they soar by, call out, and play in the waters of the pond.

Yang Xiong does not deny the emperor a cosmic journey of sorts, but it is only by proxy envoys with a mission of moral transformation:

> Then, he sent off tattooed men to demonstrate their skill, and in the water wrestle scaly reptiles.
> They cross solid ice,
> Breach the inaccessible pool,
> Exploring rocky shores and twisting banks,
> Deftly searching for dragons and crocodiles.
> They step over otters and muskrats,
> Grab turtles and lizards,
> Seize the magic tortoises.
> They enter the grotto;

Come out at Cangwu.
They mount huge sea monsters,
Ride giant whales,
Float over Lake Pengli,
See You Yu.
They beat the beryl gem that glows:
Cut open the pearl embryo of the bright moon.
They flog Consort Fu of the Luo River,
Offer food to Qu Yuan, Peng, and Xu.[61]

Recall that in Sima Xiangru's "Rhapsody on the Excursion Hunt," it was the emperor who shot the "roving simian" and "flying chimera," while his cosmic journey concludes with elaborate entertainment from singers, "dwarves" (*zhu ru*), and exotic foreigners.[62] By contrast, Yang Xiong describes a group of tattooed envoys, perhaps a reference to men from the southern lands of Yue, who are not entertainers.[63] They journey on the emperor's behalf, meeting ever more fantastical creatures in the waters, which the emperor and his hunting party cannot see from their position in the lodge. The envoys finally end their magical swim by flogging Consort Fu and feeding Qu Yuan, Peng Xian, and Wu Zixu. By the Western Han all three of these long-dead, quasi-legendary officials from pre-imperial times had become famous as "martyrs . . . who died in an attempt to save their rulers from perdition."[64]

The tattooed envoys are thus ultimately devoted to finding proper officials and advisers. The point receives further emphasis in the immediately following passage, which matches the glow of the beryl gem and pearl embryo with the magical radiance of a group of learned men:

Thereupon, great teachers and grand scholars,
In high carriages and hats,
Colored jackets and skirts,
Men who study the Canon of Tang,
Rectify with the *Odes* and *Hymns*,
Bow ceremoniously at front.
Their lustrous shine shimmers and sparkles,
Swift and sudden as if divine.
Humane repute tame[s] the Northern Di,
Martial justice moves the Southern Lin.[65]

The feeding of the officials by the tattooed envoys marks the hierarchical reordering of the emperor's social surrounding, with his learned officials, the "great teachers and grand scholars," assuming their rightful place above the emperor's frivolous entertainers. The glow emanating from the scholars recalls the pearls discovered by the swimming envoys and describes their powers of moral transformation: "their lustrous shine shimmers and sparkles, swift and sudden as if divine." The poem continues with a description of foreign envoys coming to the emperor to submit tribute, while a group of nobles praises the emperor's virtue, comparing him to the sage rulers of high antiquity.

This height of praise and ecstasy, brought about by moral perfection (as opposed to the sensory indulgence in Sima Xiangru's poem), provides the emperor with his own opportunity for "virtuous renunciation." In the poem's final section the emperor "modestly declines and does not assent [to the praise]." After opening up the park to his subjects, the emperor rejects the park's pleasures entirely, turning away from an extravagant Qin palace and back toward the capital:

> He has no time for the beauty of his parks and preserves,
> Or the frivolity of tours and hunts.
> Thus, he turns his carriage, reverses the yoke.
> He turns his back on Epang Palace,
> And returns to Weiyang Palace.[66]

The role of the shining officials in the "Rhapsody on the Plume Hunt" is thus somewhat ambiguous: they appear but momentarily and do not seem to follow the emperor in turning toward Chang'an and away from Epang and the extravagant pleasures of the imperial park that the Qin palace symbolized. On the other hand, their moral power, spread as "humane repute" and "martial justice" to foreign lands, caused all to praise the emperor and thus prompted him to leave the park. Yang Xiong's rhapsody drew upon spatial hierarchies that associated court officials with a turn away from Shanglin Park, especially the moral problems that the park represented, and toward the imperial capital and Weiyang Palace, where the emperor should reside.

Such spatial hierarchies received much clearer articulation in an essay that had little impact when it was written in early Western Han but enjoyed a rise in stature toward the end of the dynasty. The essay, entitled "Sublime Sayings" (Zhi yan), was purportedly written by Jia Shan, an early Western Han cavalry commander who served at the court of Wendi. Jia does not appear to have had a major influence on policy during his lifetime; the *Shiji* does not even mention him.[67] Starting in late Western Han, however, he gained posthumous repute, and the *Hanshu* included an account of his life, primarily consisting of his essay.[68] The reasons behind Jia Shan's heightened profile are unclear, but many of the themes in "Sublime Sayings" correspond with trends in late Western Han learning, including a widespread reassessment of the Qin and its legacy.[69] More important for our purposes is the fact that Jia's critique of Qin rulers and their parks and palaces resonated with the social and spatial symbolism found in Yang Xiong's rhapsody.

"Sublime Sayings" begins by reflecting on Qin's downfall, noting that the First Emperor recklessly indulged in every conceivable pleasure, building up palaces and grounds of such spectacular opulence that his successors could not possibly build or improve upon them, an argument that should be read as a counterpoint to Xiao He's emphasis on the symbolic power of majestic palaces.[70] Even more dangerous was that the First Emperor's pleasure-seeking behavior, including his obsessive enjoyment of the imperial hunt, exhausted the resources of the empire and established the conditions that ultimately led to the anti-Qin uprising:

> The First Emperor used all the people of the myriad kingdoms to provide for himself. Their strength was used up, but they were still unable to satisfy his conscription requirements. Their finances became exhausted, but they were still unable to meet his demands. He was just one person, but All Under Heaven could not provide the riding and hunting amusements by which he cultivated himself. Exhausted laborers received no rest. The hungry and cold received neither clothing nor food. Innocent people who had been condemned to death had no recourse. People began to hate him and households felt enmity toward him. As a result, All Under Heaven was spoiled. Even when the First Emperor was alive All Under Heaven was already spoiled, but he did not know it.[71]

The First Emperor's complete lack of restraint, Jia Shan argued, sowed the seeds of his regime's destruction. Moreover, the reason the First Emperor did not understand that he was undermining his empire was that "within All Under Heaven nobody dared tell him." The First Emperor's destructively indulgent imperial hunts should have been subject to criticism from officials. In other words, for Jia the problem with the Qin imperial hunt was twofold: it went unchecked by the emperor himself and uncriticized by the emperor's officials. The echo chamber that was the First Emperor's court, Jia implied, was powerless to prevent the excesses of the imperial hunt from sending the realm onto a destructive path.

When Jia turned to Wendi, he noted with approbation that the emperor had filled his court (*chaoting*) with the worthiest of officials (not least Jia himself!) but that he had still fallen short of effective rule because of his obsession with hunting. Most disturbing was the fact that the emperor took his worthy attending officials along with him on his hunts, a practice that Jia argued would cause discipline at court to slacken and result in officials neglecting their duties. Even if, Jia allowed, Wendi's behavior was upright and he had performed various good deeds, this indulgence in hunts threatened to destroy his legacy and completely went against the example of legendary rulers:

> Now, your heroic ministers and upright men of service go out hunting and shooting with you every day. You shoot hares and chase foxes, harming the grand enterprise and cutting off the hopes of All Under Heaven. I view this with great sadness. . . .
>
> In ancient times, the grand ministers did not act indecently, so the superior man rarely revealed his stern countenance and his expression. The grand ministers did not accompany the ruler on his tours and his upright and cultivated men of service did not follow along on hunting trips. This allowed all to devote themselves to their jurisdictions and to improve their comportment. In this manner, among the multitude of ministers none dared slacken in righting and cultivating his behavior. They expended full effort in order to conform with ritual propriety.[72]

Not surprisingly, Jia claimed that the end result of this rule by properly cultivated ministers, undistracted by imperial tours and hunts, was a reverent and respectful mode of rulership that spread throughout the empire. He concluded with a recommendation to Wendi, writing that the emperor should only take his "minor vassals" (*zhong chen*) on his pleasure outings and tours, while "grand vassals" (*da chen*) were to remain within the court to discuss and debate affairs of state. As Jia put it, "Your tours will not lose their pleasurableness, your court will not lose its ritual propriety, and debates will not lose their precision." In other words, the gravity of imperial affairs required an equally rarified group of officials located in a space, the court, that befitted their importance. For Jia Shan, the social and spatial boundaries of the imperial court ended where the hunts and tours of the emperor began. In making this argument, he cast hunts and tours in the imperial parks as personal ventures of the emperor, activities unrelated to the state.[73]

Statements by Dongfang Shuo and Jia Shan thus drew upon a spatial rhetoric that equated Chang'an in general and Weiyang Palace in particular with the morally proper remonstrating official. The *Hanshu* by no means equated Dongfang and Jia, since it expressed some ambivalence about the former and his unpredictable and inconsistent actions, not to mention his flowery language.[74] Nonetheless, the *Hanshu* accounts of both men situated them away from the pleasure parks of Shanglin and within the walls of Chang'an, a moral "turn" toward ritually proper behavior that seems to have applied as much to officials as to the emperor himself. It would be a mistake, however, to understand the turn toward the capital as only a triumph of classicizing rhetoric. Legal regulations also shaped late Western Han understandings of court space, especially the "forbidden zones" (*jin zhong*) reserved for the emperor and his closest associates, areas that became the subject of anxious meditations on access and social status.

FORBIDDEN ZONES: THE LEGAL AND SOCIAL ARTICULATION OF A PRIVILEGED SPACE

As noted, the *Hanshu* states that though Dongfang Shuo received a salary and post at court after submitting his memorial in response to a call from Wudi, he was not actually admitted into the emperor's private quarters. Specifically, the account states that Dongfang "was not yet afforded an inspection and audience."[75] Later, the account states that Wudi abruptly arose and entered the "inspection area" (*xing zhong*) after Dongfang toasted and praised the emperor at an inappropriate moment: the emperor, to his sorrow, had just determined that laws and precedents left him no choice but to execute a relative.[76] Wudi eventually invited Dongfang into his private quarters, where he angrily upbraided the adviser and demanded an explanation for the off-key praise. Dongfang managed to explain himself, saying that the toast was merely meant to snap the emperor out of his sorrow, since it was entirely proper to follow precedents established by previous emperors. Apparently satisfied with the explanation, Wudi commuted a punishment previously given to Dongfang after an inappropriate act in a palace hall and installed him as a gentleman of the palace (*zhonglang*).

The exchange is interesting for many reasons, not least being the underlying distinction in the story between official business (here, a criminal judgment) carried out in the palace and a more intimate one-on-one conversation in the emperor's "inspection zone" (*xing zhong*). While Western and Eastern Han writings contain many references to this "inspection zone" and the related "forbidden zone" (*jin zhong*), the terms are entirely absent from pre-imperial texts. The physical expansion of Han palaces seems to have been accompanied by the development of corresponding vocabulary indicating less restricted and more restricted zones within the palace. The most restricted "forbidden zone," sometimes described as the area within the Yellow Gates (Huang men), was reserved for the emperor and his consorts.[77] Only people with special permission or a specially endowed supernumerary title could gain entry into the forbidden zone, which was guarded by an officer corps reporting to the director of the Lesser Treasury (Shaofu).[78] Given these discussions in early texts of the specific spaces and personnel, it is hardly surprising that most scholarship has focused on identifying the precise buildings and locations that constituted the forbidden zone. One scholar, for instance, has combed all textual references that identify specific buildings within the forbidden zone and, on that basis, charted its spatial parameters.[79] A second went one step further, using this analysis to produce a map, based on archaeological excavations, that displays the location of the forbidden zone within Weiyang Palace.[80]

Even while interesting, such descriptions understand the "forbidden" areas as strictly defined in spatial terms, ignoring the fact that sources mention other forbidden zones outside of Weiyang Palace.[81] Certainly all palaces (even, perhaps, all buildings) contain areas of privileged and limited access, and scholars of other parts of the ancient world have emphasized that such spaces are perhaps best imagined as social groups of the highest status, not just discrete physical areas.[82] The same was true during Western Han, though a shared understanding and vocabulary linking high social status to privileged spatial access emerged only over time. On this point, it is important to note that the two terms for the emperor's private spaces, forbidden zone (*jin zhong*) and inspection zone (*xing zhong*), are not distributed equally across early imperial texts. In particular, "inspection zone" is entirely absent from the *Shiji*. The *Hanshu* uses both terms, though "inspection zone" is more common. Some commentators have explained that "inspection zone" emerged after *jin* became taboo in late Western Han.[83]

Whether or not a taboo existed, other factors seem to have been in play, since by late Western Han the term "inspection zone" began to have legal significance. Of the sixteen instances of the term in the *Hanshu*, seven come in the longer phrase "leaking talk from the inspection zone" (*xie xing zhong yu*). It is not possible to determine precisely when this phrase, particularly as a legal infraction, first came into use. Based on current evidence it does not appear to have been in operation prior to the reign of Wudi.[84] Leaks of privileged information, of course, had occurred long before late Western Han. For instance, the "Basic Annals of the First Emperor" (Qin Shihuang ben ji) in the *Shiji* described the First Emperor becoming enraged after attendants "leaked [his] statements" (*xie wu yu*). As the *Shiji* story noted, these leaks revealed the location of the First Emperor and allowed officials to track his movements, thus undermining an elaborate network of buildings and covered walkways that were designed to keep the ruler hidden, alone, and calm so he could commune with otherwise elusive spirits.[85] The contrast between the First Emperor's personal fury at the divulgence of his words and location and the more formalized late Western Han regulations about leaking illustrate that the idea of secrecy and privilege eventually spread to the court as a whole. As stories in the *Hanshu* make clear, the crime of "leaking talk from the inspection zone" often resulted in severe punishment. The following example from the account of Chen Xian (d. ca. 10 CE), who served as assistant to the imperial counselor (*yushi zhongcheng*) during the reign of Yuandi, shows that officials with access to sensitive information had to be particularly careful of such charges:

> During this period Zhu Yun, the magistrate of Huaili, cruelly murdered an innocent person. Officials had reported the incident in a memorial, but a decision had not yet been issued. Chen Xian held Zhu Yun in high regard. Zhu Yun made quiet inquiries through Chen regarding his case and was told to submit a statement accepting personal responsibility for the incident. At this point, Shi Xian was able to figure out what was going on through his spies, and he reported in a memorial that Chen Xian had leaked talk from the inspection zone. Chen was imprisoned and beaten. His punishment was commuted from death, but he was tattooed, sent to pound earth on the city walls, and stripped of his position.[86]

Stories in the *Hanshu* describe Shi Xian as a famously vindictive adviser to Yuandi, so it is hard to judge whether or not Chen Xian suffered a "standard" punishment for leaking information to Zhu Yun.[87] Even if Shi Xian used the charge as a pretext in a political battle, the story nonetheless suggests that officials were supposed to keep sensitive legal information confidential.

Other *Hanshu* stories, however, indicate that leaks were not limited to divulging information about legal cases or official affairs. An accusation against Zhao Ang (fl. ca. 60 BCE), son of the famous and influential general Zhao Chongguo (ca. 137–51 BCE), is a case in point:

> Some time prior, Xin Wuxian, the General Who Destroys the Qiang, and Zhao Ang, General of the Palace Gentlemen, had engaged in a casual conversation. Ang said: "Once, Zhang Anshi, the general of cavalry, displeased the emperor and the emperor wanted to execute him. The general from my household [i.e., Zhao Chongguo, Zhao Ang's father] believed that Anshi, having served Wudi for many years with his writing bag and brush at the ready, should be seen as loyal and circumspect and meriting the fullest consideration. Zhang Anshi as a result of this opinion managed to avoid punishment."
>
> When Zhao Chongguo returned to the capital to advise on military affairs, Xin Wuxian was dismissed and sent back to his old office [as commandery governor]. He was thus filled with a deep hatred. Xin Wuxian submitted a letter to the throne accusing Zhao Ang of leaking talk from the inspection zone. Zhao Ang was brought up on charges of entering into the inner areas of one of Chongguo's bureaus,[88] wreaking havoc among the garrisoned troops. The matter was sent down to officers for investigation. Ang committed suicide.[89]

As the story shows, the crime for which Ang was ultimately investigated differed from Xin Wuxian's accusation of leaking information. Nonetheless, the incident at least suggests that such a charge could be made against not only those who divulged information about formal legal proceedings but also those who spread stories about the palace. We hardly need mention that Zhang Anshi and Zhao Chongguo were two of the most influential military men and palace insiders during the reign of Xuandi. So far as we know, however, neither man held one of the supernumerary titles required to gain access to areas of the palace in which the emperor resided or in which sensitive and confidential business was carried out. The fates of Chen Xian and Zhao Ang together indicate that "talk from the *xing zhong*" covered a broad spectrum of information, everything from legal affairs to rumors about palace denizens. Here "inspection zone" referred not just to a specific space but also to a loosely defined category encompassing some of the highest status people in the empire.

This interaction between privileged space and social status expressed in the term "inspection zone" proved a tantalizing mix for late Western Han Chang'an residents who were hungry for news of palace doings. At least, such a conclusion can be drawn from a story about the famously circumspect Kong Guang (d. 5 CE). During the reign of Chengdi, Kong served in various capacities within the palace: he held one of the supernumerary titles that afforded him entry into the emperor's inner quarters and simultaneously served as superintendent of the palace (*guangluxun*) and director of the secretariat (*shangshu*).[90] In these positions, Kong was responsible for handling imperial edicts and official documents, many of them secret:

> On his leave days Kong Guang would return home to rest. When engaging in casual banter with his brothers, wife, and children, he would never stray into topics related to the affairs of court, inspection zones, or government. One of them once asked: "What sort of trees are growing within the Heated Chamber of the inspection zone?"
>
> Kong Guang kept quiet and did not respond, and then replied by talking about something else. In this way he did not leak information [*bu xie*].[91]

The story surely tells us more about the sensibilities of the Chang'an elite during late Western Han than it relates a "true" story of Kong Guang's respect for confidentiality. By this time, the inspection zone had come to symbolize the most privileged people and information as much as the most restricted space; note that the story claims Kong did not leak about "court [*chao*], inspection zone [*xing*], or government [*zheng*]." Regulations had sprouted up to regulate all of them, with stories about the inspection zone circulating among a larger populace eager to understand the activities of powerful people at court.

When Xiao He claimed that impressive palaces were necessary if Gaozu wished to achieve authority and legitimacy as emperor, he expressed an enduring understanding of the symbolic value of palaces that echoed even into the twentieth century.[92] There is no question that palaces and other buildings were important expressions of imperial power throughout the Han period. The many walls and buildings constructed in the first century of Western Han, especially during the reign of Wudi, were no doubt understood in this fashion, not least because many were topped with distinctive tiles that identified a building's function or marked it as a government structure.[93] Yi Feng's criticism of palace construction, by contrast, provided an alternative understanding of the relationship between imperial buildings and imperial power: rather than building palaces, *not* building would allow a ruler to accumulate moral power and authority.

As this chapter has attempted to demonstrate, even if Yi Feng's memorial contributed to increased criticism and reassessment of the legacy of Wudi's building program, it also participated in a much more complicated rhetoric of spatial authority that was beginning to accommodate a wider circle beyond the figure of the emperor. This development cannot be separated from the increasingly strident debates about the imperial sacrifices that erupted at the late Western Han court, particularly during the reigns of Yuandi and Chengdi. The ultimate relocation of all imperial cult sites to the immediate Chang'an environs changed the spatial logic of the capital: from a "mere collection of palaces," Chang'an became organized along a central axis, with Weiyang Palace as a starting point.[94] This spatial reorganization, however, was not limited to architecture. It also proceeded along rhetorical and representational lines, as we saw in the comparison of discussions in the *Shiji* and *Hanshu* of imperial travel to perform sacrifices. Compared to the former, the imperial annals in the latter text used a different vocabulary and syntax in order to more clearly differentiate between travel and sacrificial activity, suggesting in the process that emperors (especially post-Wudi emperors) left the capital only in order to perform discrete ritual acts.

All observers at the imperial court would have understood this claim to be aspirational at best, not least because everybody was well aware that emperors traveled regularly to Shanglin Park, located to the immediate west of the capital. This enormous preserve had expanded greatly over the course of Western Han, particularly during the reign of Wudi, who reportedly erected a perimeter wall around much of the park and built structures there, including the massive Jianzhang Palace. As Shanglin Park assumed a greater political and economic role in the life of the capital and, indeed, the entire empire (recall the imperial mint located in Shanglin), criticisms of the park became ever more strident. However, the nature of these critiques changed rather significantly. Instead of calling attention to the emperor's moral abandonment in the park's pleasures, by late Western Han ever clearer calls emerged within different literary forms (historical narrative, the rhapsodies, and political persuasion) to esteem the palaces of the capital over the pleasures of Shanglin Park. Most important, such statements were meditations on status that was as much social as spatial since they inevitably situated the morally righteous remonstrator and court official within the palaces and clearly separated him out from the park.

On the one hand, these critiques and the connection between palace and morally superior court officials were the result of classically informed rhetoric and forms of rulership, supposedly based on the example of ancient sage kings, that were gaining prominence at the imperial court. It would be too simple, however, to chalk up the recurrent motif of the morally superior, palace-based official as just another example of a late Western Han victory for classical discourse and more restrained forms of governance. As we saw in the discussion of "forbidden zones" and "inspection zones," for instance, legal regulations were also shaping new ideas of spatial and social authority at the capital. The development of regulations regarding the inspection zones of Weiyang Palace reflected a legal concern about limiting access to and knowledge of specific areas of the palace. It also provided a vocabulary for discussing the palace, especially the gossip and rumors that swirled around its halls and chambers, as the epicenter of a highly elite social world. Without question, the forbidden zones protected the emperor and limited access to him. The privileges and status that such zones provided to a much wider circle of elite insiders, however, were arguably just as important on a symbolic level. If Yi Feng's memorial presented a more specific and differentiated hierarchy of whole palaces in order to advance a moral critique of the emperor, the development of regulations over the forbidden zones at the same time provided a more articulated understanding of internal palace spaces, which in turn gave voice to social and political concerns, anxieties, and ambitions.

This possibility brings us back to the story of the 30 BCE flood. When Chen Who-Carried-the-Bow breached the walls of Chang'an, Weiyang Palace, and finally the forbidden zones, she infiltrated not just the physical space of the emperor but also his social surroundings. Physical as well as social access to high-status areas of the palace were inextricably interlinked. Indeed, they had become so interchangeable that most people probably did not reflect on the connections they drew between the inner sanctum of the emperor and the inner circle that surrounded him. Recall, for instance, that in his edict after the flood Chengdi lamented that the incident of Chen-Who-Carried-the-Bow indicated his officials had "strayed from their duties" (*shi zhi*). In other words, the "court" (*chao*) as a physical space had morphed into the "court" as a privileged social group, the end result being that the authority of imperial palaces and their interior spaces accrued to a much larger collection of people, not just the emperor alone. Palaces thus represented not only imperial power but also the privileges enjoyed by powerful groups of people, a symbolic value that late

Western Han writers (and gossipers) drew upon in crafting their own political critiques. Moreover, they point us toward a growing concern with membership and proper action within the imperial court: Who could belong? How should they be organized? How should they behave? Such questions drove political conflict and institutional reforms, which were supported by, and existed in complicated interaction with, new forms of writing and literary representation.

PART 3

Roles

CHAPTER 4

Politics, Rank, and Duty in Institutional Change

The short but critical reigns of the First Emperor of Qin (r. 220–210 BCE) and Wang Mang (r. 9–23 BCE), founder of the interregnum Xin dynasty, provide temporal bookends to the Western Han. Even if our sources depict two men with different temperaments who justified their rule in vastly different terms, both famously engaged in a shared activity: changing the titles of government offices. Indeed, for both the First Emperor and Wang Mang, reforms of titles were among their most famous, signature acts, since the changes were self-consciously designed to demonstrate their political ambitions and sensibilities. As the First Emperor purportedly put it after his rivals were defeated and the empire finally unified, "Names and titles have yet been changed, so there is no way to mark my accomplishments."[1] His ministers duly responded by proposing a set of new titles, emperor (*huang di*) being merely the most famous.[2] Wang Mang, meanwhile, is said to have explicitly changed official titles according to schemes found in texts outlining classical political institutions and organization.[3] He also highlighted the importance of name changes, though for reasons that differed from those of the First Emperor. For example, in an order discussing the different and sometimes contradictory geographic terms and schemas found in classical texts, Wang stated that all ancient rulers named and organized territorial regions "in order to improve local customs," so that even if "their standards were distinct, their project was certainly the same."[4] The contrast is telling: while the First Emperor sought changes in titles in order to commemorate his status as the imperial founder, Wang characterized his changes as an act whose aims were continuous with the policies of past sage rulers. Rather than reforming titles to celebrate an unprecedented achievement, Wang cast his title changes as fully bound by precedent and within the standard repertoire of a self-consciously classical model of rulership.[5]

Even if undeniably important and famous, however, contrasting these two sets of official title changes alone gives short shrift to the entire intervening history of administrative reform during the Western Han, adopting a perspective that solely privileges the power and agency of rulers. Of course, the importance of the First Emperor and Wang Mang in early imperial political history is undeniable. Both were founders of new dynasties, and both executed a series of changes designed to demonstrate their political legitimacy and authority. Their reforms of official titles were just one part of this larger project, which also included the adoption of dynastic colors and the institution of ritual and sacrificial programs. Something rather similar happened in 104 BCE, when Wudi promulgated a revised calendar that, among other things, established a new first month of the year. Wudi combined that effort with a comprehensive reform of court office titles; according to the descriptions of individual offices provided in the *Hanshu* "Table of the Many Offices and Ministerial Posts" (Bai guan gong qing biao), nineteen different offices experienced a change in title or were first established in 104 BCE. Moreover, this pairing of office title changes with reforms of other court institutions and practices echoes discussions of "reform" (*gai*) in other Han sources. We read, for instance, of Jia Yi (201–169 BCE) drawing up a plan for Wendi to "reform the calendar, change robes and colors, regulate institutions and measures, fix the titles of offices, and invigorate the rites and music." More than 150 years later, Wang Shun (d. 11 CE) and Liu Xin (46 BCE–23 CE) used remarkably similar language to praise the achievements of Wudi.[6]

Nonetheless, the history of reforming offices in Western Han is quite a bit more complicated, and not nearly as ruler-centered, as a First Emperor to Wudi to Wang Mang narrative would imply. Even if the "Table of the Many Offices and Ministerial Posts" shows that Wudi changed and established offices upon reforming the calendar, his 104 BCE adjustments to the offices make up less than 20 percent of all of the changes mentioned in the "Table." At least according to that source, over the course of Western Han changes to office titles as well as the establishment or elimination of offices occurred almost one hundred different times. Moreover, every single emperor, with the exception of Zhaodi, saw changes occur during their reign.[7] This fact alone suggests that changes to office titles happened for a host of reasons, and not always as part of a ruler's comprehensive program to transform imperial institutions. Some of them were probably more reactive in nature. For instance, we saw in chapter 1 that Jingdi, in the wake of suppressing the royal rebellion of 154 BCE, changed office titles and duties regarding appointments and state funerals in order to solidify a status hierarchy and sumptuary system that clearly differentiated emperor, kings, and nobles. Other title changes, however, are rather mystifying; why, for example, in the first year of the reign of Pingdi (r. 1 BCE–5 CE) were the Gentlemen Attendant at the Gates (Qimen Lang), part of the emperor's guard corps, renamed the Gentlemen Rapid as Tigers (Hufen Lang)?[8]

Given such puzzles, it is neither possible nor desirable to craft a unified narrative linking all changes and reforms of the high offices that collectively constituted an important part of the imperial court. This statement is true despite the fact that secondary works continue to call attention to the emergence of an "inner court" over the course of Western Han. According to this theory, starting particularly from the reign of Wudi, client-officials with direct patronage ties to the emperor came to dominate an "inner court," while the high court officials in charge of ministries and bureaus were relegated to powerless positions in the "outer court."[9] The following passage from the *Hanshu*, describing a group of officials serving under Wudi, has often been used to support this understanding of the imperial court:

> The emperor appointed Yan Zhu to be palace adviser (*zhong dafu*). Later, he appointed Zhu Maichen, Wuqiu Shouwang, Sima Xiangru, Zhufu Yan, Xu Le, Yan An, Dongfang Shuo, Mei Gao, Jiao Cang, Zhong Jun, and Yan Congqi. They were all installed at the side of the emperor. During this period, the emperor sent reprisal attacks against foreign groups, established commanderies in border regions, frequently dispatched military expeditions, and in the interior changed administrative measures. The court administered an increasing number of responsibilities and there were frequent recommendations of candidate who were "able and virtuous" or "cultivated in learning."
>
> Gongsun Hong had risen up from commoner status. After several years he reached the position of chancellor, whereupon he established a chamber to the east [of his bureau] and welcomed in worthy men with whom he made plans and debated. When he was at court audiences and submitted memorials on official business, he would use the opportunity to speak of what was expedient and proper for

> the imperial household. The emperor ordered Yan Zhu and others to debate with the great ministers. "Inner" and "outer" responded to each other with proper and well-reasoned writings, but the greater ministers often lost out.[10]

The passage depicts a power struggle between the chancellor Gongsun Hong and the emperor. Disputes between the two played out in court debates, with the emperor's position, as expressed by his clients, usually prevailing. The impression that the passage imparts is one of partisan (if not bitter) conflict at court, conflict that the emperor engaged in by proxy through personal advisers whom he installed as officials. The mention of "inner" (*zhong*) and "outer" (*wai*) has led many scholars to conclude that Wudi established an "inner court" in order to bypass regular bureaucratic channels and thus assert more direct control over the government.

Several scholars have convincingly rejected the "inner court" versus "outer court" model as misleading and simplified.[11] In this particular story about Gongsun Hong, it is not at all clear that "inner" and "outer" in the final line refer to set institutional arrangements at court; they could plausibly refer to inside and outside of Wudi's private chambers or even the palace itself, if in fact the Chancellery was located outside of the palace. In any case, "inner" and "outer" is not even the point of the story, which emphasizes the strategies that the emperor and Gongsun Hong employed to gather followers. For instance, the chancellor "set up a chamber on the eastern side" of his bureau, which one commentator explained as a strategy for Gongsun to provide entry to his own advisers, separate from the regular officials of the Chancellery, who entered through the main gate of the courtyard.[12] The "Account" of Gongsun in the *Hanshu* also suggests that he tried to amass his own coterie of supporters by building a "guest lodge" (*ke guan*).[13] It seems that Wudi and Gongsun alike took steps to consolidate a personal network, as the story emphasizes the importance of patron-client relations at the imperial court. In fact, membership in an inner or outer group of officials was just as much a function of relationships and alliances with powerful people as it was a specific orientation to the imperial court or even the emperor himself.

At the same time, in rejecting the dichotomy of "inner" versus "outer" and searching for an alternative understanding of early imperial court politics and changes to offices in the central government, we cannot simply conclude that a free-for-all of alliances based on "factions" (*dang*) dominated the early imperial court. It is true, of course, that several families came to prominence over the course of Western Han, monopolizing some offices and commanding sufficient prestige to wield power and disburse privileges to potential clients. The Huo family after Wudi's death and during the reign of Zhaodi, the Shi and Xu families during the reign of Xuandi, and most famously of all the Wang family during the reign of Chengdi each managed to achieve considerable institutional power at court, which they used to their advantage.[14] The dynamics governing the rise and fall of these different families were not the same, however, and the strategies they employed were not necessarily comparable.[15]

Moreover, overreliance on this family-factional model of late Western Han politics tends to ignore the institutional context at the imperial court, the critical role of rank, and the importance of normative concepts about official duties and how an ideal court "should" be organized and managed. An important series of reforms of high offices in 8 BCE shows that, by the late Western Han, one idea that gained institutional traction was an understanding of the court as a rigorously articulated and hierarchical body, whose offices were defined by clearly delineated official responsibilities or "discrete duties" (*fen zhi*). Neither the idea nor the term were new, since many pre-imperial texts, from many different perspectives, extolled the importance of "discrete duties" in government organization and official action.[16] However, by the late Western Han "discrete duties" seems to have garnered greater attention given the political conditions at court.[17] In particular, struggles to define duty, rank, and alliance drove courtly politics and institutional change during the reign of Chengdi, in the context of growing tensions among Chengdi, the consort families, particularly the Wang family, and some high officials. Shifts in ranks and duties during Western Han had increased the complexity of the bureaucratic structure, divorcing official ranks to some degree from actual powers, particularly at the capital. The emperor sought to consolidate and uphold his power with the new policies of 8 BCE, which aimed to reorganize ranks to reflect the powers that his highest officials were supposed to command. By doing so, he sought to establish the position of capital officials as the most senior in the administrative hierarchy, and above all assert his status as the presiding executive atop the entire bureaucratic structure.

Why did the emperor, in correlating rank with duties, follow this particular arrangement when trying to consolidate power? By

8 BCE the emperor and key advisers believed the Wang family to be their main obstacle to resetting the balance of power. Together the Wang nobles constituted one of the most formidable families in Chang'an, and control of certain court offices by senior men in their clan endowed the family with a strong institutional position that allowed it to forge an advantageous network of patronage-based alliances. Proponents of the policy changes, not coincidentally, were relative outsiders to the capital who had no familial connections to the emperor. Their reforms insisted upon correlating rank strictly with official responsibilities, implicitly downgrading the role of court patronage. This position undoubtedly attracted the emperor, eager as he was to diminish the Wang family's supremacy.

Reform proponents sought to stigmatize all alliances formed outside of the clear rank-and-duty hierarchy they intended to establish, particularly alliances with the Wang family. It is in this sense that the 8 BCE reforms not only reformed the central government bureaucracy but sought to tear down norms, even those based on kin relationships, that might have separated the court from officialdom writ large. This idea did not occur in a rhetorical vacuum but found purchase across many different types of texts in late Western Han, a point explored in chapter 5. Here, however, I will emphasize that defining a proper social and institutional configuration for the court was a messy and complicated process, driven simultaneously by shifting political considerations and normative ideas.

COURT REFORM, DUTY, AND RANK DURING CHENGDI'S REIGN

The three reforms that Chengdi approved in 8 BCE specified a new hierarchy for the highest officials in the empire, mostly by adjusting their salary ranks.[18]

The Three Lords of the Executive Council: Chengdi established an Executive Council (San Gong) composed of three offices at the equal rank of 10,000 bushels each: chancellor, imperial counselor (*da sikong*), and marshal of state (*da sima*).[19] Prior to this reform, the chancellor had been the head of administration and the highest-ranking officer in the bureaucracy, followed by his assistant, the imperial counselor (called *yushi dafu*).[20] Also, before 8 BCE, the marshal of state had an ambiguous position in the regular bureaucracy, since his was only an adjunct title that did not provide the usual ribbons and seals of office, even if the office was typically held by the most powerful generals or officials at court, who often controlled important administrative and consultative functions.

The Inspectorate: Chengdi approved a proposal to replace regional inspectors (*cishi*) at 600 bushels with provincial shepherds (*zhoumu*) at fully (*zhong*) 2,000 bushels, the same rank as the Nine Ministers (*Jiu qing*) who directed the government ministries.[21] Wudi had established the Inspectorate in 106 BCE.[22] Inspectors monitored and reported on the top regional officers, the commandery governors (*taishou*) and kingdom administrators (*xiang*). They were also to identify promising candidates for office.[23]

Administration of the Commanderies and Kingdoms: Chengdi reset the salary grade of all governors at 2,000 bushels,[24] and then approved a proposal to set the rank of the kingdom ministers at that same grade. Going beyond the reformers' suggestions in their proposal, he eliminated the metropolitan commissioners (*neishi*) appointed by the court to the kingdoms, and replaced them with the commissioners from the capital (*zhongwei*), who were made equal in salary-rank to their counterparts in the commanderies, the commandants (*duwei*), at a rank "equivalent to" (*bi*) 2,000 bushels.[25]

The foregoing reforms of 8 BCE, including Chengdi's decision to establish the three offices of the Executive Council at the new and equal rank of 10,000 bushels, were not Chengdi's first efforts to adjust the rank scale: in 23 BCE he had eliminated the grades of 800 and 500 bushels.[26] Nor was Chengdi the first emperor to alter the system of salary ranks. As we saw in chapter 1, among the legal documents excavated from the tomb at Zhangjiashan (sealed in 186 BCE) was a set of statutes entitled "Statutes on Salary Ranks" (Zhi lü). That statute's list of positions by salary ranks across much of Western Han officialdom allows comparison of the early Han ranks to the late Western and Eastern Han ranks outlined in several received texts. Table 4.1 lists three salary-rank scales in operation during 186 BCE (based on the Zhangjiashan statutes), 23 BCE (after which Chengdi abolished the two grades of 800 and 500 bushels), and 8 BCE, after implementation of the reforms considered in this chapter.[27]

Two points bear emphasis. First, as table 4.1 makes clear, before 23 BCE different salary grades emerged at the very highest salary rank of 2,000 bushels: officials ranked at "fully" 2,000 bushels ranked higher than those at 2,000 bushels alone. Most lists of Western Han salary ranks would include reference to the "equivalent" ranks, but as we saw in chapter 1 the evidence for these salary ranks is rather spotty for most

TABLE 4.1 SALARY RANKS IN WESTERN HAN

186 bce	*23 bce*	*8 bce*
—	—	10,000 *shi*
2,000 *shi*	Fully 2,000 *shi*	Fully 2,000 *shi*
	2,000 *shi*	2,000 *shi*
1,000 *shi*	1,000 *shi*	1,000 *shi*
800 *shi*	800 *shi*	—
600 *shi*	600 *shi*	600 *shi*
500 *shi*	500 *shi*	—
400 *shi*	400 *shi*	400 *shi*
300 *shi*	300 *shi*	300 *shi*
250 *shi*	—	—
200 *shi*	200 *shi*	200 *shi*
		Equivalent to 200 *shi*
160 *shi*	—	—
120 *shi*	—	—
	100 *shi*	100 *shi*

Note: The salaries (paid in kind and in cash) of Western Han officials were linked to a ranked scale, which also provided a framework for the rank hierarchy of the entire bureaucracy. As the table shows, the scale changed significantly over the course of the dynasty.

of Western Han, since they receive clear description only in the *Hanshu* "Table of the Many Offices and Ministerial Posts," an Eastern Han source. "Fully" 2,000 bushels is another matter, however. The highest ministers in the capital held this rank, while commandery governors and a few other capital officials ranked at the comparatively lower level 2,000 bushels. More important, "fully" 2,000 bushels appears in several imperial edicts and orders, included in the *Shiji* and *Hanshu*, issued from as early as the reign of Jingdi.[28] Compared to the later and scarcer evidence for the equivalent ranks, we can state with much more confidence that "fully" 2,000 bushels was a rank assigned and utilized from a relatively early period. At the same time, Jingdi's reign began some thirty years after the Zhangjiashan documents were interred. Over the course of Western Han, then, grades emerged within salary ranks, particularly among the highest offices.[29] However, such gradations by no means prevented conflict over status and authority among late Western Han officials, particularly when such conflict was coupled with questions about jurisdictional duties.

Second, the reforms in both 23 BCE and in 8 BCE created wider gaps in the salary scale, gaps that better reflected the disbursal of privileges and benefits to the officials concerned, as well as their differences in status. One key gap divided lower positions from those at 600 bushels or 1,000 bushels; officials at this higher level included county magistrates, as well as officials in the capital such as assistants (*cheng*) or senior officials in the ministries, and some of the senior gentlemen-at-arms (*lang*) who supervised and guarded the imperial palaces.[30] A second key jump in rank led to the most senior posts in the empire at 2,000 bushels, which included ministerial positions and governorships. In addition to increased status, these 2,000-bushel positions brought larger imperial gifts of cash and goods, regular bestowals of orders of honor (*jue*), and special legal and tax treatment.[31] Chengdi's reforms in 23 BCE created an entirely new divide between officials ranked at 400 and 600 bushels, thus highlighting the higher status accorded officials ranked at 600 and 1,000 bushels.[32] Meanwhile, the decision to establish the 10,000-bushel rank for the three members of the Executive Council asserted unequivocally that these three officers outranked all other officials at 2,000 bushels in status and in privilege.

The reforms of 8 BCE allowed Chengdi to regularize the rank hierarchy, reduce potential conflicts among his officers, and above all concentrate his power, since the reforms asserted his own status as titular head of the government. Figure 4.1 contrasts this new 8 BCE structure with the prior hierarchy.[33]

Implicitly, the 8 BCE reforms asserted several principles. First, all of the highest officials in the capital, inspectorate, commanderies, and kingdoms were to enjoy the same rank of 2,000 bushels, not to mention the privileges and status commensurate with this rank. Second, both the Nine Ministers based in the capital and the provincial shepherds, who reported regularly to the capital, were to enjoy a grade of "fully" 2,000 bushels that put them at a rank slightly higher than that of the governors of the commanderies and the kingdom ministers, who were all henceforth to have the same grades.[34] In doing so, the reforms

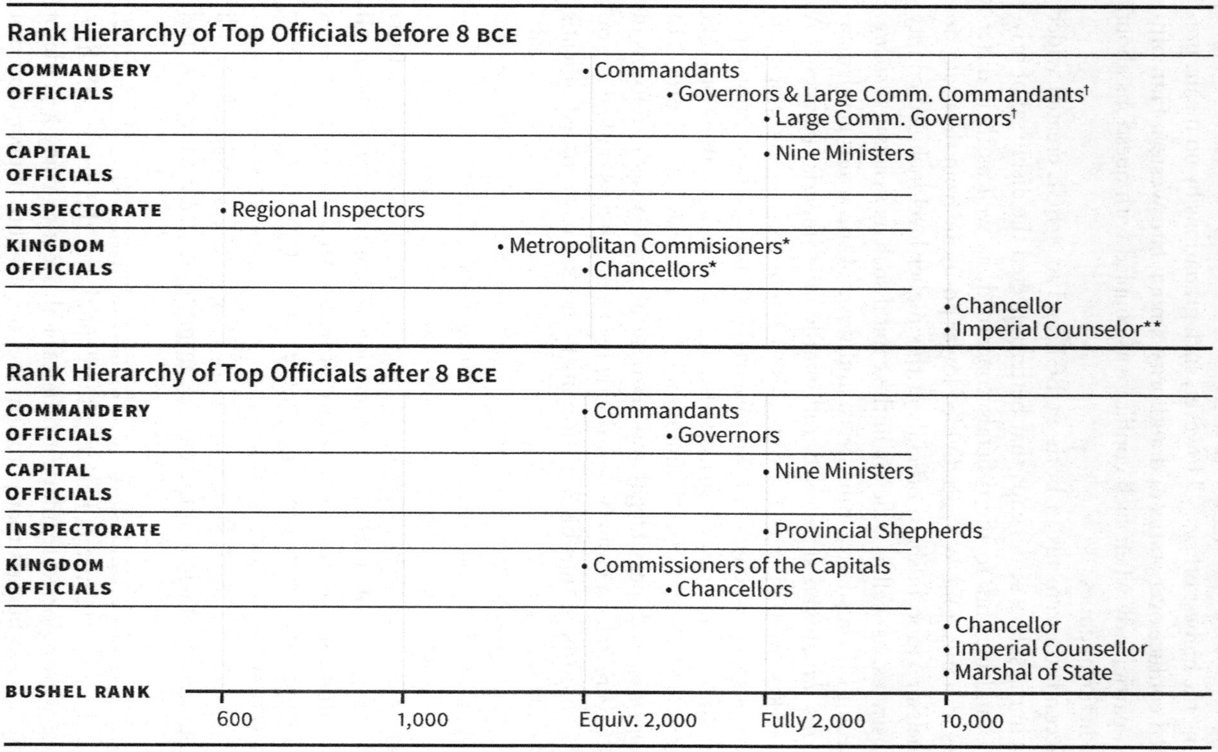

Rank Hierarchy of Top Officials before 8 BCE

COMMANDERY OFFICIALS
- Commandants
- Governors & Large Comm. Commandants†
- Large Comm. Governors†

CAPITAL OFFICIALS
- Nine Ministers

INSPECTORATE
- Regional Inspectors

KINGDOM OFFICIALS
- Metropolitan Commisioners*
- Chancellors*

- Chancellor
- Imperial Counselor**

Rank Hierarchy of Top Officials after 8 BCE

COMMANDERY OFFICIALS
- Commandants
- Governors

CAPITAL OFFICIALS
- Nine Ministers

INSPECTORATE
- Provincial Shepherds

KINGDOM OFFICIALS
- Commissioners of the Capitals
- Chancellors

- Chancellor
- Imperial Counsellor
- Marshal of State

BUSHEL RANK: 600 | 1,000 | Equiv. 2,000 | Fully 2,000 | 10,000

Figure 4.1. Rank hierarchy before and after the 8 BCE reforms.

effectively declared that the kingdoms were entirely equal in status to the commanderies, an important change in regional administrative policy. Chengdi thus reversed a policy going back to Jingdi that had steadily reduced the power and status of the kingdoms vis-à-vis both the central government and the commanderies. Finally, the three members of the Executive Council saw their ranks rise to 10,000 bushels, which better reflected the status of the Council as the highest administrative body in the government. Having styled himself the chief executive of the Executive Council, the emperor became the highest power in the hierarchy. Through these reforms, Chengdi asserted that he alone ultimately presided over a regular hierarchical system which rose at stepped intervals from regional government to the capital and inspectorate offices, then to the highest administrators in the realm, and ultimately to the emperor himself. Within a year of Chengdi's death, his successor was persuaded to rescind the Executive Council and Inspectorate reforms, but within the space of four years, in 2 BCE, the same emperor reinstituted Chengdi's basic model. That model remained in place through Eastern Han.[35]

THE REFORMS AND POLITICAL ALLIANCES

Why would Chengdi, in order to concentrate his power, have redefined the correlations between ranks and duties and reformulated the bureaucratic hierarchy in this particular manner? Even if his position as emperor theoretically endowed him with unmatched status, in reality the Wang family related to Chengdi's mother, especially her senior male relatives, oversaw many, if not most, of the day-to-day aspects of the administration. Chengdi naturally sought ways to curb their power.[36] In their proposals, reform proponents argued that the 8 BCE reforms would create a unified bureaucratic hierarchy, implicitly arguing that it would thereby be protected from complications caused by officials wielding powers that reformers deemed informal and illegitimate. The two friends and colleagues who jointly proposed the 8 BCE reforms, Chancellor Zhai Fangjin (d. 7 BCE) and He Wu (d. 3 CE), the newly appointed imperial counselor, emphasized the importance of clearly defined official responsibilities and powers within a bureaucratic hierarchy that allowed for no informal influence.[37] By carefully delineating the "discrete duties" (*fen zhi*) of the highest officers of the land, their reforms were designed to obviate situations where "authority would be severed from official position."[38] Such statements implied that nobody, not even members of the Wang consort family, should be able to encroach upon the emperor's rightful position at the apex of Han officialdom.

1. A PROPOSAL (*JIAN*) BY HE WU TO CREATE THE EXECUTIVE COUNCIL, (CA. 10–8 BCE)

In ancient times the people were plain and governing duties were simple. The advisers in the kingdoms were necessarily worthies and sages. They still, however, followed the model of the three luminaries of Heaven (sun, moon, and stars) and filled the three offices of the Executive Council, each having discrete duties.

In this declining age, customs and patterns have degenerated, and the duties of governing have proliferated. The talent of administrators is inferior to the talent of the ancients, but the chancellor on his own initiative has arrogated duties rightly belonging to an Executive Council. This is why over the long term they have been abandoned, not properly administered. It is right to establish the offices of the Executive Council, define the charges of the ministers and counselors, and divide up their responsibilities and dispense their governing duties. In this way we can evaluate effectiveness. (*Hanshu* 83.3404–5)

2. A MEMORIAL (*ZOU*) BY HE WU AND ZHAI FANGJIN, TO ESTABLISH PROVINCIAL SHEPHERDS, 8 BCE

The ancient rulers selected worthies from among the nobles and made them provincial lords. The *Documents* says: "He consulted with the twelve shepherds," and thus broadened his perception, lighting a candle on the darkness and hidden recesses. Now the regional inspectors occupy the position of the shepherds and lords, and they control the governance of one whole province. They select and rank the senior officials. Those they recommend to a position can reach as high as the Nine Ministers. Those they deem to be poor are immediately withdrawn. Their charge is heavy and their responsibilities great.

The meaning [*yi*] of the *Annals* is to employ the noble to govern the lower-ranked and to not have those at the bottom oversee those at the top. The inspector's grade is that of a low-ranking counselor [*dafu*], but he oversees those at 2,000 bushels. The weight of rank is out of balance; there has been a loss of the order properly due to official position. Your servants request that you eliminate the inspectors, and replace them with the provincial shepherds so as to accord with the ancient system. (*Hanshu* 83.3406)

3. A MEMORIAL SUBMITTED BY HE WU AND ZHAI FANGJIN TO EQUALIZE KINGDOM AND COMMANDERY OFFICIALS, 8 BCE

In the past the vassal kings decided trials and were in charge of governing. Their commissioners were in charge of judicial duties, their ministers coordinated administration and advised the kings, and their commissioners of the capitals had full command over [the control of] violence and wrongdoing. Now the kings do not make judicial decisions or parcel out governing duties. The commissioner of the capital's office is abandoned, its responsibilities folded under the metropolitan commissioner's office [in the kingdoms].

> Appointment of commandery governors and kingdom ministers is the means to unify and systematize, making the people trustful and secure. Now the metropolitan commissioner's position is low but his power is great, so authority and rank of position are at odds with each other. Since high-ranked officers are not strung together into one system, governing is difficult. Your humble servants request that the ministers be made equal to the governors, and the metropolitan commissioners be made equal to the commandants. In this way we will accord with the order of high and low, and level out the powers due to salary grade weights. (*Hanshu* 86.8485–86)

The Wang family's hand in recommendations and appointments to offices must have made these principles of clearly defined duty and rank attractive to the emperor. The senior members of the Wang family were extremely powerful in Chang'an. Close kinship ties to the empress dowager had given them high rank and position. They could thus recommend a great many candidates for higher office, which, in turn, strengthened their network of alliances.[39] This was particularly true for Chengdi's maternal male relatives, four of whom were designated marshal of state (*da sima*) while Chengdi was on the throne; together these four relatives asserted their authority for most of the emperor's reign. In the *Hanshu*, for example, Wang Feng (d. 22 BCE), Chengdi's oldest uncle and the first Wang marshal of state, duly sought out worthy officials to assist him.[40] As I suggested at the beginning of this chapter, the Wang family was not the first Western Han noble family to consolidate power by filling positions with kin and allies. However, Kamiya Masakazu has recently argued that the Wang men were distinct in that they commonly recommended and promoted officials into regional administrative posts, including as regional inspector, governor, and kingdom minister. Some of these officials eventually achieved posts at 2,000 bushels in Chang'an.[41] Such appointments provided the Wang family with a network of relationships that extended across the realm, serving to consolidate the stranglehold on power the family would soon exert.

On the other hand, the Wang family appears to have acquired such dominance that even some of the people they recommended and appointed expressed reservations about their power. In the most extreme case, an official recommended by Wang Feng urged Chengdi to sack his patron.[42] We also read of divisions within the Wang family itself over recommendations.[43] Such fissures are perhaps to be expected, but they also reflect a Wang family so confident in its hold on power that it did not need to maintain a constant, united front against potential rivals; after all, its members could close ranks and act as one whenever threatened.[44] The institutional positions held by the senior members of the Wang family necessarily gave them a particularly strong voice in decisions at court. Wang supremacy must have seemed a fait accompli to most in high office; the family's position had to be dealt with delicately and strategically.[45]

The challenge for the emperor and others who wanted to wrest power from the Wang family was to construct alternative alliances and power relationships. Zhai Fangjin and He Wu clearly fit the bill for Chengdi, or at least that is the picture provided in the *Hanshu.* It describes the two men as outsiders to Chang'an, with Zhai hailing from Runan commandery and He from Shu.[46] Both officials, after gaining recommendations, had advanced to the highest levels of the bureaucracy. Zhai and He were famous for their erudition in classical texts, consistent adherence to rules and regulations, and fair and honest governing practices.[47] He even won renown by refusing to protect a member of his own family from legal prosecution, while Zhai earned a reputation for acting against the powerful families in the Chang'an area who had engaged in profiteering.[48] In sum, the *Hanshu* paints He and Zhai as Chang'an outsiders and sticklers for the law—officials whose competence, honesty, and classical erudition won the admiration of many at court. The recommendations that spurred their advancement, and the privileges and power they had accumulated, we are led to believe, were entirely proper.

Even so, as Zhai and He rose up the bureaucratic ranks, they were hardly immune to charges of favoritism or cliquish behavior. Such accusations were commonly traded between different factions, even while everyone condemned factional politics. He took pleasure in raising up worthy candidates, even though he claimed to despise cliques, and took pains to double-check the advice of both government officials and classicists (*ru*) alike.[49] Zhai shared He's interest in identifying worthy candidates. Nonetheless, in a bitter memorial submitted after Zhai's death, Du Ye (d. 2 CE) accused Zhai of various improprieties, including promoting the careers of several unworthy officials who had "only to attach themselves to Zhai Fangjin, and thus receive exalted offices."[50] Not coincidentally, Du Ye was a native of Duling, one of the imperial mausoleum towns, scion of a powerful noble family that had maintained a prominent position in the capital for over a century, and nephew of Wang Feng's closest adviser. Since Zhai Fangjin had so zealously prosecuted Chang'an's noble families, Du's hatred for him is hardly surprising. These difficulties that He and Zhai experienced in negotiating the politics of alliances were hardly novel. Indeed, the Wang family itself was particularly vulnerable to charges of favoritism and cliquish behavior, though such charges tended to be swiftly punished on the rare occasions when they surfaced.[51]

Chengdi thus faced a number of obstacles when instituting the 8 BCE reforms. On the one hand, he had to craft a new bureaucratic structure that effectively sidelined the Wang family. But in order to do so, he had to ally himself with officials whose political connections were sufficiently robust to counter the Wang family's network of alliances yet untainted by accusations of favoritism and cliquishness (to the degree that this was possible). Tracing the proposal and enactment of the reforms allows us to see these considerations in action. At some point between 10 and 8 BCE, He Wu circulated the initial proposal (*jian*) for establishing the Executive Council.[52] The emperor implemented it after gaining the approval of his close confidante and former tutor Zhang Yu (d. 5 BCE), who had at best a tenuous relationship with the Wang family; for some time he had been in outright conflict with Wang Gen, then the marshal of state.[53] After approving the Executive Council reform, Chengdi kept He in the newly renamed position of imperial counselor, and Zhai Fangjin remained chancellor. Chengdi allowed Wang Gen to keep the title of marshal of state and thus become a member of the Council, but took away his position as general of Cavalry on the Alert (*piaoji jiangjun*). Moreover, for the first time Gen received the regular ribbons and seals of office; both items, in theory, marked his new status as a government functionary, which implicitly asserted his subordinate relationship to the emperor.[54] The reforms thus placed Gen at the same rank as Zhai and He in the Executive Council. Gen suddenly found himself and, by extension, the Wang family that he led, in a new institutional arrangement designed to underscore his inferior status toward the emperor.

The other reforms only further sidelined the Wang men. By late Western Han, many court officials had previous experience in regional posts; almost all of Chengdi's highest officials had served as regional inspectors, governors, or kingdom ministers. The Wang family certainly did not monopolize control over disbursal of these posts to the exclusion of others, but, as I noted, they had proven adept at moving officials through regional offices before bringing them to serve in 2,000-bushels posts in Chang'an. The 8 BC reforms disrupted that path.[55] As Zhu Bo later noted when he urged Aidi to rescind the 8 BCE reforms, Zhai Fangjin had ensured that the new provincial shepherds were ranked immediately below the Nine Ministers, virtually ensuring that those shepherds whose abilities were ranked at the highest level would be promoted to fill empty ministerial positions.[56] The Executive Council and Chengdi would have been able to oversee the assessment of the provincial shepherds, more closely monitoring who was placed in ministerial positions. Governors and kingdom ministers, now ranked lower than the shepherds, had been cut out of the promotional loop. Wang Gen could thus no longer utilize the promotional paths that his brothers had used to their advantage.[57] Not surprisingly, no record describes the emperor consulting Wang Gen as he implemented the reforms.[58] But Chengdi had to move discreetly since critics, some of whom might have been allied with Wang family members, argued that the reforms were little more than archaizing name changes that would have little practical effect.[59]

Why would He Wu and Zhai Fangjin, for their part, propose these reforms? What frustrations had these officials encountered in navigating through the world of the late Western Han imperial court, and how did the reforms propose to address them? As noted earlier, the emergence of different grades of the highest ranked offices at court, as well as the new office of provincial inspector established by Wudi, had tended to create confusion—potentially explosive confusion—in matters of protocol and jurisdiction by muddying the direct chain of command binding superior to subordinate.[60] One example of just such a dispute affected Zhai Fangjin's own career. It illustrates how officials tended to invoke claims of duty and rank when criticizing unofficial alliances forged outside the hierarchy of officialdom, which the "illegitimate" patron-client relations within the Wang family epitomized. Duty and rank thus became the terms by which "legitimate" versus "illegitimate" alliances were defined and policed.

To begin with a few background details: in the years leading up to 18 BCE, Zhai Fangjin served as deputy to the chancellor (*chengxiang sizhi*), ranking just below the chancellor in that head administrator's bureau.[61] On a trip outside the Chang'an city walls while accompanying the emperor to Ganquan Palace, Zhai's chariot had briefly traveled on the highway reserved for imperial use. The colonel of internal security (*sili xiaowei*) charged Zhai with a crime and duly confiscated his chariot. At a meeting held upon their arrival in Ganquan, the colonel and Zhai both submitted memorials. Zhai claimed that the colonel had divulged confidential matters while holding an earlier office. In the end, Zhai prevailed, and the colonel forfeited his post.[62]

The conflict was not merely a clash of personalities, since Zhai's and the colonel's jurisdictions overlapped to some degree. The deputy to the chancellor investigated the illegal activities of officials, while the colonel of internal security monitored officials of the capital region, in effect serving as an inspector for the capital.[63] To make matters worse, the colonel held a post ranked at 2,000 bushels, while the deputy's rank is slightly less clear: according to the "Table of the Many Offices and Ministerial Posts," that rank was set at "equivalent to" 2,000 bushels. The *Hanshu* states that according to Han "precedent" (*gushi*), the colonel of internal security ranked below the deputy to the chancellor.[64] But "precedent" hardly prevented conflict caused by overlapping authorities and jurisdictions. Zhai's immediate superior as chancellor once ordered members of his staff to help apprehend a murderous gang. The colonel of internal security, at that time one Juan Xun, protested that the chancellor was infringing on his responsibilities: "According to the *Annals*, those appointed by the king rank above the vassal lords in order to lend authority to the king's orders. I have been fortunate enough to receive imperial favor in being appointed as an imperial envoy [*shi*; i.e., inspector], with a duty to oversee and observe officials from the lords and ministers on down."[65] Juan Xun thus asserted the inspectorial nature of his office by citing its classical justification and casting it as a direct charge from the emperor himself, which gave him jurisdiction over all high ministers and officials at court. In doing so, Juan obliquely referred to a key difference between his office and that of the chancellor: the latter was ennobled only by virtue of his unassailably high position and did not enjoy a direct charge from the emperor himself that was rooted in principles articulated in the *Annals* (Chunqiu). In the event, officials agreed that the chancellor had overstepped his bounds, after which the gang's leader was duly apprehended and punished.

Zhai Fangjin did not let the matter drop. Perhaps he was offended, or perhaps he thought Juan Xun himself had previously offended against precedent by failing to visit the bureaus of the chancellor and imperial counselor, an omission whose rudeness seemed compounded by his show of arrogance when in the company of these officials. When Zhai launched a secret investigation against Juan, he discovered two things: that the colonel had met privately with the commissioner of the palace (*guangluxun*) and that he had once descended from his chariot to pay his respects to Wang Shang, yet another of the emperor's Wang family relatives.[66] Zhai's accusation is worth quoting in full for what it reveals about interministry conflicts:

> I have heard that when a ruling house is founded, it is to treat the honorable suitably and to revere the elderly, conferring rank and position according to courtesies reserved for high and low. In doing so, the kingly way is regulated. According to the *Annals*, we honor the highest lord by calling him "minister." Within all of the land bound by the seas, nothing falls outside his purview. When the chancellor has an audience with our sagely ruler, out of respect for the chancellor the ruler rises from the imperial throne or gets down from his chariot.[67] The ministers thus all receive and conform to sagely instruction, which is thereby put on display to the rest of the empire.
>
> Xun is an official ranked at 2,000 bushels, who was fortunate to be chosen to serve as an inspector. He does not respect ritual protocol, he belittles the chancellor, and he denigrates superior ministers. He moreover disdains decorum and fails to maintain probity. He is treacherous, sycophantic, and inconstant, "a coward who assumes fierce looks."[68] He damages the imperial structure, throwing the court ranks into disorder. He is not fit to occupy this position. I respectfully submit that the emperor should order the chancellor to remove Juan Xun from office.[69]

By failing to show proper respect to the chancellor, Zhai argued, the colonel had disrupted court protocols. Even worse, in dismounting from his chariot to show respect for Wang Shang, Juan displayed calculated deference to a member of the Wang family, hence Zhai's thinly veiled reference to Juan's "sycophancy." The implication was clear: Colonel Juan Xun put far more stock in the power of the consort family than he did in the emperor or the imperial bureaucracy under the emperor's supervision. The colonel, by insinuating himself into the powerful Wang patronage network for his own personal benefit, acted at the expense of his official duty.

Review of this memorial enables us better to understand the probable motivations that drove Zhai Fangjin and He Wu to offer their proposals to Chengdi. In theory, the Western Han bureaucracy administered the realm according to a strict hierarchy of duties and ranks at whose apex sat the emperor. In practice, however, differing interpretations of these duties and ranks, not to mention overlapping jurisdictions, easily gave rise to conflicts at the court, with the parties to these conflicts calling upon their allies for support. To revisit this example: had Colonel Juan Xun actually managed to attain the intervention of Wang Shang, for example, perhaps he could have looked to him for help against Zhai Fangjin. Zhai, however, called upon normative notions of rank and duty in order to cast Juan's attempt to curry favor with Wang Shang as illegitimate. The 8 BCE reforms attempted something similar: to clearly define the ranks and duties of high officers in order to firmly establish the emperor's position at the top of the hierarchy, and thus as every official's sole support, while in the process condemning all other alliances as illegitimate.

The Wang family represented a perceived threat to the body politic during the late Western Han. In order to suppress the Wang family and minimize its opportunities to build alliances, Chengdi and a circle of reform-minded officials put forth the 8 BCE reforms, which cast Chengdi as the leader of a new bureaucratic hierarchy where Wang power would be offset by that of two other officials named to the Executive Council. The 8 BCE reforms, in legitimizing some alliances at the expense of others that threatened to increase the power of the Wang family, reflected a fact of life at the Western Han court: the throne-Wang conflict drove court politics and institutional change. Still, factional politics alone are insufficient to explain the reforms. The reforms were not solely motivated by family or individual interests, nor even by any sort of public interest. Rather, supporters and critics of the Wang family alike had to heed norms and precedents relating to ranks, obligations, jurisdictions, and the bureaucratic procedures for recommendation and selection, knowing that all of these could be invoked in the course of political struggles and court debates on policy matters.

At no point throughout the 8 BCE debates did reforms mention or call upon notions of an "inner" or "outer" court, nor do we see clear dividing lines between inner and outer court factions. Indeed, an underlying thread of this chapter has traced the differing objectives and experiences of all the actors—among them Zhai Fangjin and He Wu, Chengdi himself, Zhang Yu, and a gaggle of Wang family members—their permanent or temporary alliances notwithstanding. Let us remember that Chengdi went beyond the proposal of Zhai and He, eliminating the metropolitan commissioners and introducing the commissioners of the capital; that Zhai invoked ranks and duties in order to prevail in a conflict he had with another official; that Chengdi and Zhang Yu, each in his own way, sought a precarious balance at court, whereby Wang family power would be at once acknowledged and limited by the institution of the tripartite Executive Council, which would enforce power sharing among Wang Gen, Zhai, and He; and that this new arrangement would have been personally enriching for both Zhai and He since it effectively awarded them a major salary raise and a big boost in status at court. All of these factors (and doubtless many more for which we have no records) contributed to a major institutional shift. Changing virtually congealed institutions after some two hundred years of Western Han rule was clearly no easy matter.[70] This convergence of interests is a more plausible explanation for the ultimate success of the 8 BCE reforms than a simplistic notion of conflict between an "inner" and "outer" court.

More important, the 8 BCE reforms provide a good view of the complicated interactions among political motivations, institutional reforms, and normative understandings of the imperial court. On this final factor, note that the driving principle cited by Zhai Fangjin and He Wu in their proposals was the importance of creating offices with "discrete duties." Moreover, by forcing even the Wang uncles into an institutional scheme supposedly characterized by discrete duties, Chengdi, Zhai, and He effectively pushed the concept into the innermost recesses of the court and every corner of the capital, from the emperor's family to the larger central government ministries. What did this phrase mean, precisely, for late Western Han audiences? The answer is not so simple, despite the fact that "discrete duties" had long received praise in a diverse range of texts. This talk of clearly defined official responsibilities was not merely an invocation of hoary classical principles, perhaps not least because classical texts provided different, even contrasting evidence for the duties of official posts. Note, for instance, the different conclusions offered by Juan Xun and Zhai Fangjin regarding information in the *Annals* about the relative status of the chancellor and the inspectors. Discussion of clear and clearly delineated duties appears to have been supported by thoroughgoing changes not just in the court's intellectual climate but also in the advancement of new types of literary production, a point explored in the final chapter. The court and its institutional organization, it seems, transformed just as much in response to changing modes of writing and representation as it did to the instantiation of an ideological program.

CHAPTER 5

The Literary Invention of Bureaucracy

A set of normative arguments about the proper organization of the court and central government, especially the importance of "discrete duties," provided support for the reforms of 8 BCE. Equally important, however, was a dizzying array of political considerations, driven by a complicated series of alliances, some of them tenuous, between and against Chengdi, members of the Wang family, and many different officials. A side story in the drama was the demotion of several associates of one Chunyu Zhang (d. 8 BCE). Chunyu was Chengdi's cousin and had at one time achieved a position of some importance at court after he successfully advocated abandoning the emperor's expensive tomb construction project at Changling. In 8 BCE, however, Chunyu was imprisoned after charges emerged that he had previously accepted bribes to speak in favor of Chengdi's former empress, who had been removed from her position so that the emperor could replace her with a favorite consort. While under suspicion for criminal activity, Chunyu Zhang purportedly feared that he might be expelled from the capital and so gave money to one of the emperor's uncles, Wang Li, who in return pled on Chunyu's behalf. Zhai Fangjin, who figured so prominently in the 8 BCE reforms, seized the opportunity to accuse Wang Li of conspiratorial behavior, successfully advocating for his dismissal along with the dismissal of several of his friends.[1]

These details are important, but so too is their representation in early sources. When we take a closer look at descriptions of the Chunyu Zhang and Wang Li story, it seems that the idea of discrete duties was not just a vaunted principle motivating the actions of reformers. It also became tightly and almost imperceptibly woven into the political narrative provided in the *Hanshu*. Take, for instance, the following passage, which describes the dismissals that occurred in the wake of Chunyu Zhang's and Wang Li's troubles: "That year (8 BCE), General of the Right Lian Bao and Rear General Zhu Bo were convicted in the matter of the Marquis of Dingling, Chunyu Zhang, and the Marquis of Hongyang, Wang Li. They were both reduced to commoner status. Kong Guang was made General of the Left and fulfilled the duties of the office [*guan zhi*] of General of the Right. The superintendent of the capital, Wang Xian, was made General of the Right and fulfilled the duties of the office of rear general."[2] At first reading, the language appears clear and straightforward: Kong Guang and Wang Xian were simultaneously executing the duties of several offices, a situation far from uncommon at all levels of Han officialdom.[3] Upon further reflection and comparison with other sources, however, the description of shuffled officials and new appointments seems curious. Why would Kong Guang fulfill the duties of the General of the Right even though Wang Xian was appointed to that same position? We cannot assume that Kong was substituting for an overworked Wang, since at this time Kong, like Wang, also held a third position that was not a general post.[4] The *Hanshu* "Table of the Many Offices and Ministerial Posts" (Bai guan gong qing biao) is also no help, since its description of these office changes notes only that Kong and Wang were appointed General of the Left and General of the Right, respectively, without mentioning additional responsibilities.[5] Indeed, the "Table" gives the impression that the rear general position was simply left unfilled.

Such a situation would hardly have been unprecedented, which raises the most important problem with the *Hanshu* passage: "general" posts were filled irregularly and often on an ad hoc basis, while more often than not those serving as generals had no specific military responsibilities.[6] Space limitations prevent a full investigation of Western Han military titles, but generals of various types existed from the early decades of the dynasty, and patterns are rather difficult to identify.[7] Even up until the late Western Han, however, it does not seem to be the case that only one person could hold any given military title. In fact, Lian Bao, one of the generals mentioned in the passage, served as General of the Right for two years while another man held the same title.[8] Moreover, appointments as General of the Rear were rare into late Western Han, so even if the position did have specific responsibilities they were hardly essential to government operations.[9] While appointment as a general surely "provided a higher measure of seniority and status," then, the evidence available in the *Shiji* and *Hanshu* does not support the idea that such posts were clearly delineated in terms of duties.[10] By mentioning "duties of the office" (*guan zhi*), however, the *Hanshu* seems to go out of its way to make precisely this claim. Why? As we saw in chapter 4, political conflicts at the imperial court would have made such rhetoric attractive. However, 8 BCE was hardly the only year to see intense political clashes in Chang'an, and persuasive texts going back to the pre-imperial period had emphasized the importance of clearly defined official responsibilities. Thus the rise of discrete duties in the late Western Han, and a near obsession with describing offices and the parameters of their work, was just as much a matter of changing and applying new conventions of representation as it was solely the result of political processes, let alone the adoption of a particular "ideology" or political program.

How did the idea of discrete duties develop and unfold at the imperial court? The concept emerged in a wide range of late Western Han sources, which pondered the nature of high court offices and the relationship between offices and incumbents: What were these offices, and where did they come from? Why were people appointed to certain posts? Why were they promoted or demoted? Three different sources will guide as through the answers provided to these questions during late Western Han. First, a series of biographies from the *Shiji* "Account of Chancellor Zhang [Cang]" (Zhang Chengxiang lie zhuan) profiles many of the people who became chancellor, the highest official in the empire. Importantly, roughly half of the "Account" was written long after Sima Qian's death, probably in the years after Yuandi's reign. A comparison of these two halves of the "Account of Chancellor Zhang" shows a shared concern with the fate of the offices and incumbents of chancellor and also imperial counselor (*yushi dafu*), which theoretically stood second to the chancellor in the hierarchy of officialdom. Indeed, rather than "Account of Chancellor," the chapter would perhaps more aptly be titled "Accounts of the Chancellors" or "Account of the Chancellery."

At the same time, the two appraisals in the "Account" show a different understanding of the link between offices and their incumbents, with the post-Yuandi era appraisal showing less interest in the individual characteristics, capacities, or histories that might have contributed to the promotion of a given official. Rather, in a move somewhat reminiscent of the board game that opened this book, the appraisal focused on the role of "fate" (*ming*) in determining whether or not an official made it to the highest posts. In doing so, however, and in contrast to the earlier appraisal in the "Account," the author implicitly accepted a connection between official posts and the qualifications of officeholders: fate determined whether or not "worthy men" (*xian*) gained appointment, but the connection between worthiness and holding a given office was simply ignored. Offices as entities linked to qualifications were the assumed field in which fate played its hand, since fate could prevent "worthy" men from gaining appointments that they otherwise were qualified for and deserved.

Our second, perhaps unlikely set of sources—two tables (*biao*), one in the *Shiji* and the other in the *Hanshu*—depict in chronological fashion the incumbents of the highest offices in the land. Even if the *Shiji* and *Hanshu* tables were composed on the basis of administrative records, however, they presented information about offices in starkly different fashion. Most striking is the fact that the *Shiji* table primarily represents high offices in relation to historical events and political conflicts at court. Only toward the end of the *Shiji* table can we detect a shift in representational style, since the final years outlined there mention only promotions and dismissals without reference to events. Instead of explaining the complexity of circumstances behind the appointment of any individual official, the table represents offices as more autonomous institutions whose incumbents gained promotion according to hidden (or, at least, unarticulated) factors. The *Hanshu* "Table of the Many Offices and Ministerial Posts" developed this pattern further; it depicted offices as historically constant posts disconnected from contingent events but also cast them as rule-bound entities held by people who were promoted or demoted according to clear rules and regulations.

Finally, a rather similar message is found in the *Admonitions of the Many Offices* (Bai guan zhen), a neglected and now highly fragmented collection of poems that began to be compiled in late Western Han and eventually established a whole new genre of "admonition" poetry. We might, of course, understand a late Western Han uptick in talk of offices, their histories, and their discrete duties as part of a general vogue for classical texts and rhetoric during this period. What would a classicizing vision of officialdom look like? The *Admonitions of the Many Offices* show that the matter is hardly simple. According to all accounts, the poems included in the *Admonitions* were initially based on an admired admonition verse attributed to an ancient Xia adviser and included in the *Zuozhuan*. The late Western Han admonitions, however, shifted the voice and structure of their *Zuozhuan* model in order to invoke normative and historically constant duties and performance standards pertaining to particular administrative posts. In other words, the admonitions were written in the voice of a depersonalized *office*, not an office's incumbent, and correspondingly were designed to criticize not only or even primarily the ruler but also officeholders who failed to live up to the standards of the posts described in the poems. As the *Hanshu* "Treatise on Arts and Letters" (Yi wen zhi) further illustrates, a classical vision of the imperial court thus rested in tension between supposedly ancient offices and the literary forms they produced, on the one hand, and the transformations in practice and genre required by contemporary political demands.

STORIES OF OFFICIALS AND OFFICES

The *Shiji* and *Hanshu* occasionally state that the Chancellery experienced a general decline in power and prestige over the course of Western Han. The previous chapter discussed one such narrative from the "Account" of Gongsun Hong: the "Account" follows a mention of Gongsun's "guest lodge" with a passage characterizing later chancellors as powerless and Gongsun's lodge as an "abandoned mound."[11] Another description comes in the *Shiji* "Account of Chancellor Zhang [Cang]," which at one point states that chancellors serving after Shentu Jia were mere placeholders, failing to achieve anything of note or make a name for themselves among contemporaries.[12] The validity of such statements, not to mention their barely suppressed pathos, is open to debate and interpretation, even if it is undeniably true that many of the chancellors from later in the reign of Wudi served for short periods or met tragic ends.

My focus here, however, will be less on historic accuracy and more on the nature of the account and its narratives. Note, for instance, that Shentu Jia takes center stage in an "Account" whose title at least implies a focus on Zhang Cang. In fact, far from an account of one single official, the "Account of Chancellor Zhang" is a complicated collection of meditations on the offices of imperial counselor and chancellor and the means by which people gained appointment to those posts. A discussion of the "Account" thus provides a good starting point for charting changing discussions of offices over the last century of Western Han. Such a diachronic perspective is possible due to the fact that the "Account" in its current form was clearly completed by somebody other than Sima Qian, detailing as it does the careers of chancellors who served through the time of Yuandi, who reigned long after Sima's death. Moreover, and most important for our purposes, the "Account" includes two different appraisals, one commenting on the chancellors serving through Jingdi's reign and a second discussing those serving under emperors Wudi through Yuandi. Comparison of the two shows a subtle but palpable shift toward depicting offices as more clearly defined, autonomous institutions whose duties could be matched to the competencies of their incumbents.

Such an interpretation might seem surprising, since narratives in both the pre-Wudi and post-Wudi sections of the "Account" emphasize the unexpected, surprising paths that led people to the Chancellery. Chance and fate, it seems, were important factors both for Sima Qian and for the unknown author of the second half of the "Account." The two sections, however, describe luck in rather different ways. The first presents a series of stories in which people suddenly and fortuitously realize the worth of the future imperial counselors and chancellors, and these realizations propel them on their path to high office. The opening story of Zhang Cang, for instance, starts with a brief discussion of his youth, beginning with his early interest in the calendar and service under Qin as a secretarial official.[13] After siding with Gaozu during the post-Han civil war, but then committing an undisclosed legal infraction, Zhang was sentenced to execution by beheading. Upon removing his robe and leaning over the chopping block, he revealed his prodigious body, "fat and white as a gourd." Precisely at that moment, another member of Gaozu's band saw Zhang and marveled at the "magnificent soldier." He quickly alerted Gaozu, who immediately pardoned and released Zhang.

Interestingly, Zhang's physical stature reappears in the "Account" much later, after the description of his service as chancellor. When Zhang died, his son Zhang Kang inherited his noble title, which upon Kang's death passed on to Kang's son and Zhang Cang's grandson, Zhang Lei. Lei, however, was convicted of acting disrespectfully at a funeral, causing the nobility to be eliminated.[14] The "Account" then compares Zhang's height to others in his lineage: "In the beginning,

Zhang Cang's father did not reach five *chi* [less than four feet] in height. Then Cang was born. He measured more than eight *chi* [over six feet] tall and became a noble and chancellor. Cang's son was the same height. As for the grandson Lei, who was over six *chi* [four and a half feet] tall, he was brought up on legal charges and lost his noble title."[15] The impressive physical stature of Zhang Cang was hardly foreseeable, since his father was so short, and yet somehow tied to his success, since his short grandson could not keep the family's nobility. The "Account" thus sandwiches the story of Zhang Cang's official career between two stories about his body that convey different if inextricably linked messages. While the concluding comparison of heights among Zhang family members suggests that Zhang Cang's rise to the chancellor post and a nobility was somehow preordained, it by no means guaranteed success: after all, if the bystander had not recognized the promise suggested by Zhang's body, he would have been executed. His fortune was decided by a perhaps unfathomable combination of both preternatural ability and the support of those who helped propel him on to an official career and, ultimately, the Chancellery.

Zhang Cang's story is not the only biography that falls between these two passages about the chancellor's body. Also included are stories about other men who served in succession as imperial counselor prior to Zhang's appointment, with the "Account" describing the path that brought each of them to that post. We read, for instance, of the service that two brothers, Zhou Ke and Zhou Chang, rendered to Gaozu, which resulted in their successive appointments as imperial counselor. While in office, Zhou Chang showed a willingness to criticize the emperor for misguided actions, especially his desire to remove the heir apparent and install the son of a favorite consort as his new successor. Meanwhile, a man named Ren Ao had long supported Gaozu: both men hailed from Pei, and Ren Ao once attacked local Pei officials who had detained Gaozu's wife, the future Empress Lü. Perhaps not surprisingly, Ren Ao gained promotion to the imperial counselor post when Empress Lü was in power after Gaozu's death. Only after Ren Ao does Zhang Cang reenter the narrative, when the "Account" mentions that Zhang succeeded Cao as imperial counselor before gaining promotion to chancellor. Significantly, Zhang Cang was the first to be promoted from imperial counselor to chancellor.

The first half of the "Account of Zhang Cang" is thus less a description of Zhang Cang's life and more an analysis of the imperial counselor and chancellor positions and the means by which people gained appointment to those posts. This narrative pattern continues even after the story of Zhang, as the "Account" goes on to describe Shentu Jia and his ascent from imperial counselor to chancellor. The first appraisal to the "Account" sums up the differences between these early imperial counselors and chancellors:

> The Grand Archivist states: "Zhang Cang was refined in his study of the pitch pipes and calendar, and served Han as a famous minister. However, he lent no credence to proposals from Master Jia, Gongsun Chen, and others to put the first month of the year, robes, and colors into proper alignment, but instead clarified and put into practice the Zhuanxu calendar of Qin. How could this be? Zhou Chang was strong as a tree. Ren Ao was employed for an old favor. Shentu Jia can certainly be called a stubborn and principled person, but without any technique or learning he should most probably be distinguished from Xiao He, Cao Shen, and Chen Ping."[16]

The appraisal to the "Account" thus expresses some puzzlement at Zhang Cang's ascent and his status as a "famous minister," despite the fact that he ignored calls to reform the calendar and move it away from the old Qin system. Meanwhile, the appraisal implies, Zhou Chang and Ren Ao form an odd pairing: the former strongly (and inflexibly) stood up to Gaozu's plans, while the latter gained appointment due to honor and appreciation given to him by Gaozu and Empress Lü. Shentu Jia, meanwhile, was not nearly as skilled in specific techniques as previous chancellors but still managed to attain the position. The appraisal thus presents a series of conundrums, emphasizing the particular, even idiosyncratic characteristics of each imperial counselor and chancellor without offering definitive conclusions regarding whether they deserved or did not deserve the posts. Even Zhang Cang, whose physical stature might have indicated future success, did not achieve that success without the help of others, and when he became chancellor he did not actually enact reforms that his own training and expertise in calendrics might have supported. As a result, while the first section of the "Account" clearly traces the appointment history of the imperial counselor and chancellor positions, by highlighting the incommensurable experiences and capacities of the incumbents, as well as their contradictory records, its appraisal denies the integrity and unity of that history. There was neither a consistent nor a standard relationship between an official post and its incumbents, who indeed did not act in a predictable fashion.

A rather different perspective emerges in the second half of the "Account." That portion, added by an unknown author possibly during the reign of Chengdi, discusses the lives of eight chancellors: Tian Qianqiu, Wei Xian, Wei Xiang (no relation), Bing Ji, Huang Ba, Yu Dingguo, Wei Xuancheng (Wei Xian's son), and Kuang Heng.[17] We need not concern ourselves with the details of all of their stories, some of which give little more than a name. It is worth pointing out, however, that physical appearance, and especially the art of physiognomy (*xiang*), plays an important part in several of the accounts, suggesting some connections but also differences with the discussion of Zhang Cang's body in the first half of the "Account." For instance, after assessing Wei Xian, a physiognomist judged that he would become chancellor and that his second son would receive his noble title. Such an outcome was difficult to imagine, as Wei Xian pointed out, since even if he were to achieve the post of chancellor his eldest son would be entitled to inherit his nobility.[18] The physiognomist was nonetheless proven correct, since Wei Xian's eldest son was convicted of a crime, causing the second son, Wei Xuancheng, to receive the nobility and eventually gain appointment as chancellor. Before that happened, however, the narrative in the "Account" relates that the same physiognomist also accurately predicted the rise of Wei Xiang and Bing Ji, and thus showed impressive "acuity of observation."[19] The author then applauds the physiognomist yet a third time. After a description of Wei Xianchang's career, father and son both became chancellor and the entire world praised both of them. The author concluded, "How could this not have been due to fate [*ming*]? This is what the physiognomist understood first."[20]

Compared to the first half of the "Account," then, the second half invokes chance and fate in more explicit and unproblematic terms. The lack of detail only highlights this characteristic. Recall that Sima Qian contemplated the interplay between natural, particular endowments and those who recognized them, even while pointing out the contradictions between what these endowments might portend and the actual historical record. By contrast, the second half of the "Account" offers a much simpler story, highlighting an especially perspicacious physiognomist, one talented in identifying those fated to enjoy official success. The appraisal to the second half of the "Account" makes this contrast clear:

> The Grand Archivist states: When we deeply ponder those men of service who wandered through various offices all the way to becoming

> enfeoffed nobles, there are really very few. So it was that many reached the offices of imperial counselor but were quickly dismissed. This is because all of them believed that as counselor they were just one step below the chancellor, and in their hearts they hoped to be so fortunate as to see the chancellor die, some even secretly slandering out of a desire to replace him. Some, however, remained imperial counselor for a long time and never achieved [the highest office], while others served for just a short time and then became chancellor, rising to a noble title. Truly this was a matter of fate!
>
> The Imperial Counselor, Lord Zheng Hong, remained in his office for several years but did not achieve the appointment. Lord Kuang Heng, however, was in the office for less than a year, and when Chancellor Wei Xiancheng died he immediately replaced him. How indeed could this achievement have been attained by clever stratagem? Many had the talents of a worthy or a sage, but those who met with difficulties and did not gain the post were legion.[21]

According to the appraisal, gaining appointment to these high offices was largely out of the control of any individual candidate, who had no choice but to submit to the inexplicable processes of fate. How else can we explain the fact that so many talented men who were clearly qualified and could have served with distinction failed to gain an appointment? Rather than noting the highly particular, even incommensurate abilities of each of the men, as in Sima Qian's appraisal, the appraisal to the second half of the "Account" glosses over the individual competencies of the men in favor of the power of "fate" as an explanation for career success. Moreover, note that the second appraisal primarily discusses not individual candidates but the actual offices of imperial counselor and chancellor. By focusing on the role fate played in helping people "wander through various offices" and achieve the highest posts, the appraisal took for granted the institutional structure within which the offices were embedded. In effect, chance and luck supported rather than undermined the autonomy of offices and their hierarchical organization.

TABLING OFFICIAL CAREERS

The Tang commentator Sima Zhen (fl. early eighth century CE) dismissed the biographies in the second half of the "Account of Chancellor Zhang" as superficial and poorly written.[22] They probably do not compare to the more nuanced and provocative narratives in the first half of the "Account." Yet, setting aside literary judgment, these biographies and the final appraisal provide important insight into depictions of officials, offices, and official careers at the imperial court in late Western Han. By ascribing all career success to fate, the final appraisal seems to have assumed if not embraced a notion of officialdom that placed high offices in hierarchical order and organized them into clearly defined slots from which officials were promoted or demoted. Of course, the author of the second half of the "Account" was by no means the first person to understand offices in this manner. However, neither does he seem to have been out of step with evolving notions of offices and their depiction in late Western Han. Indeed, the collection of biographies in the "Account of Chancellor Zhang" was part of a larger vogue, manifested in a range of texts, for depicting offices and their hierarchical structure.

Prominent among these different textual forms are two tables depicting high officialdom: the "Chronological Table of Generals, Ministers, and Famous Officials Since the Establishment of the Han" (Han xing yi lai jiang xiang ming chen nian biao), included in the *Shiji*, and the *Hanshu* "Table of the Many Offices and Ministerial Posts." Both are important sources for studying officialdom as a whole as well as the careers of individual Western Han officeholders. Of course, earlier sources had also depicted the entire bureaucracy; recall that the early Western Han text from Zhangjiashan entitled "Statutes on Salary Grades" (Zhi lü) listed many, perhaps even all of the offices in the empire according to salary rank. The tables in the *Shiji* and *Hanshu*, however, do not mention salary ranks. Instead, they depict the holders of specific high offices in the capital, not throughout the empire, in chronological fashion. Even while they share this characteristic, the two tables exhibit important differences in format and representational style, since the vision of hierarchical and autonomous offices found in the *Hanshu* "Table of the Many Offices" is largely absent from the *Shiji* "Chronological Table." Studying such differences presents interpretive difficulties, not least among them the question of how the tables, originally written on bamboo strips, were transferred to the printed page.[23] We cannot hope to solve such problems here. It is nonetheless still worthwhile to call attention to certain features of the *Shiji* and *Hanshu* tables, especially their distinct formats and information.

The *Shiji* "Chronological Table" is a particularly rich source for such comparisons, since it contains internal inconsistencies that point to the likely existence of multiple authors and to different emphases and modes of representing officials and their careers. Commentators have long recognized that Sima Qian could not have completed the "Chronological Table," since it covers appointments made long after his death.[24] The table is divided into four horizontal rows, while each year occupies a vertical column. The columns begin in 206 BCE, when Gaozu was crowned king of Han, and end in 20 BCE, during the reign of Chengdi. The four categories that occupy the rows of the "Chronological Table" are as follows: "Records of Major Events" (Da shi ji), "Position of Chancellor" (Xiang wei), "Position of General" (Jiang wei), and "Position of Imperial Counselor" (Yushi dafu wei) (see figure 5.1).

Incidents detailed in the "Records of Major Events" include installation and deaths of emperors as well as some empresses and regional kings, the naming of imperial heirs, major insurrections, visits to imperial temples and altars, invasions by the Xiongnu, and omens of various kinds. The "Position of Chancellor" row provides the dates when chancellors were appointed,[25] while continuous numbers in each table cell follow this record of appointment, thus indicating the number of years each chancellor was in office. The "Position of General" row also details the appointment of individual people, but not to one single position. The table lists any appointment to a high military post, but when a person receives appointment to the irregularly filled office of grand commandant (*taiwei*), the cells number the years that the incumbent held the office. In a few instances, a general was promoted to the position of chancellor. Finally, the "Position of General" row also details some of the military exploits and victories of the generals. The "Position of Imperial Counselor" row does not number the years that incumbents held the post, and up through the entry for 51 BCE simply gives the names of people appointed without their title or previous office.

In sum, before the changes that occur in the latter half of the "Chronological Table," the organization of and information within the table emphasizes a hierarchy of offices, with comparatively more detailed information (title, date of appointment) given for the chancellor at the top. At the same time, the rhetorical thrust of the table rests on the interplay between "Major Events" listed in the top row and the appointment of key officials. This function is particularly evident in years when the "Records of Major Events" row lists invasions by the Xiongnu. In such years or in the immediately following year, numerous generals led the military response to the Xiongnu attack.[26] Other columns invite more subtle connections. For example, included

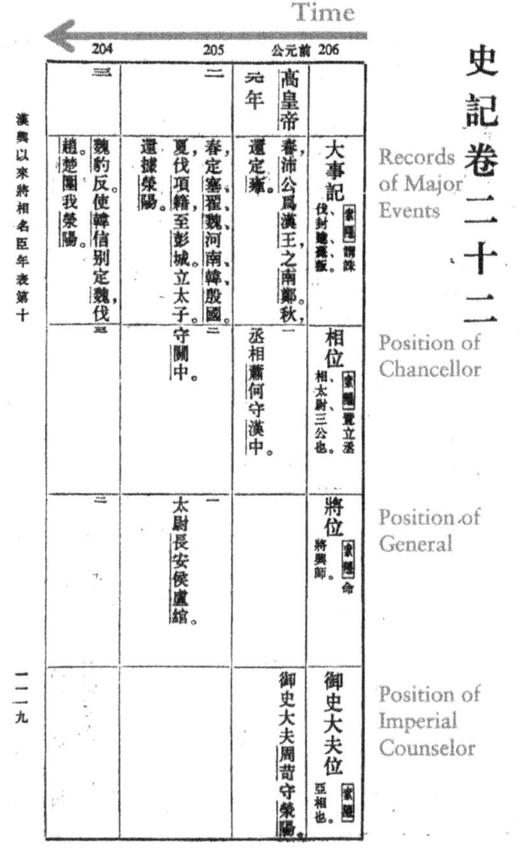

Figure 5.1. Shiji "Chronological Table of Generals, Ministers, and Famous Officials Since the Establishment of the Han," with categories indicated.

in the "Major Events" for 135 BCE was the death of Wudi's grandmother, Empress Dowager Dou, while in the same column we read in the "Position of Minister" row that Tian Fen (d. 131 BCE) was appointed chancellor.[27] The column thus hints at the disagreements between the empress dowager and Tian Fen that had earlier resulted in Tian's dismissal as supreme commander, a conflict described in the *Shiji* "Account" of Tian Fen.[28] The "Chronological Table" matched changes in the careers of individual officers to dynastic events deemed of particular significance and relevance for understanding these changes.

This pattern changes significantly in the lower half of the table, starting in entries for the Taichu reign period (104–101 BCE), and then especially for entries after 91 BCE.[29] Columns for the years 91 to 20 BCE contain a greatly reduced number of events: only seven for the sixty-nine-year period, all of them, with one exception, falling within entries recorded for the reign of Xuandi.[30] On the other hand, the table continues to regularly note the appointment and dismissal of chancellors, generals, and imperial counselors. A conspicuous change in entries for the "Position of Imperial Counselor" row starts after 51 BCE. Entries prior to 51 BCE give only the name of the person serving as imperial counselor as well as his noble title, if he possessed a nobility. Then, in 51 BCE, "Superintendent of Transport Chen Wannian became imperial counselor."[31] These post–51 BCE entries for imperial counselor also give the dates of appointment, while the same information appears in the "Position of General" row only after 91 BCE. Prior to 91 BCE, only the chancellor row lists appointment dates. Unlike the earlier years, then, the later years of the "Chronological Table" begin to trace the trajectory of officeholders in greater and more consistent detail and in a manner seemingly independent of the "Major Events."

There are parallels between this decoupling of official careers from major events in the second half of the "Chronological Table" and the differences in narrative style between the two halves of the *Shiji* "Account of Chancellor Zhang." The "Account" and the table are entirely different forms, of course, and there is no way for the table to discuss fate, which was so central to the appraisal to the second half of the "Account." If that appraisal, however, meditated on the path of "men of service who wandered through various offices," then the "Chronological Table" began to do something similar in its lower half. After all, the later biographies and appraisal in the "Account" and the later entries in the table downplay or ignore the contingencies, whether the competencies of particular officials or the influence of events, that contributed to the success of individual officials. In its place, they focused on a pared-down hierarchy of offices navigated by officeholders. In other words, the later sections of the "Account" and the "Chronological Table" offer some of the earliest representations we have of official "careers," a move that necessarily lent greater emphasis to representing the institutional structure in which such careers unfolded. This pattern developed further and became much more sophisticated in the *Hanshu* "Table of the Many Offices and Ministerial Posts." That "Table" was completed, if not started, by Ban Gu's sister, Ban Zhao (?48–?116 CE).[32] I cannot attempt a detailed study of the *Hanshu* "Table" here, not least due to its length and the huge number of officials mentioned: more than five hundred in total.[33] A few of its features, however, help illustrate one trajectory in an evolving style of representing and discussing offices, one that also resonated in some late Western Han and early Eastern Han literary compositions and poems.

First, the *Hanshu* "Table" refrains from including "Major Events" but does include many more offices, detailing all of the top ministerial posts as well as the governor of the capital (*jingzhaoyin*) and other offices in charge of administering the territory around Chang'an. Moreover, the "Table" carefully details in a single category all of the different titles used for the same office over the course of Western Han. For example, one row includes the titles director of guests (*dianke*), *taixing ling*, and superintendent of state visits (*da honglu*), all of which experienced important changes in responsibilities, as we saw in chapter 3. No doubt due to the nature of the format, the "Table" ignores these distinctions in favor of creating historical continuity for the different offices. The *Hanshu* "Table" also significantly changed two of the categories found in the *Shiji* "Chronological Table." It included the senior tutor (*taifu*), grand tutor (*taishi*), and grand protector (*taibao*) in the first category, along with the chancellor. It also split the supreme commandant (*taiwei*) and marshal of state (*da sima*) from the larger group of generals (*jiang*), which were then placed below the imperial counselor. At the top of the hierarchy of the *Hanshu* "Table" was the storied "Executive Council" (San gong), discussed in some detail in chapter 4, which comprised the chancellor, supreme commander, and imperial counselor. Compared to the *Shiji* "Chronological Table," the *Hanshu* "Table" expanded the number of high court offices, emphasized that all of them existed and persisted from the very inception of the dynasty, and enshrined the peerless status of the offices that composed the Executive Council (see figure 5.2).

Second, even though the *Shiji* "Chronological Table" began to trace the ascendance of officeholders up a hierarchy of offices by noting their previous posts, the *Hanshu* "Table" more consistently notes previously held posts and introduces an entire vocabulary of promotion and demotion that is largely absent from the *Shiji* table: officials were "promoted" (*qian*), "demoted" (*bian*), or "dismissed" (*mian*),

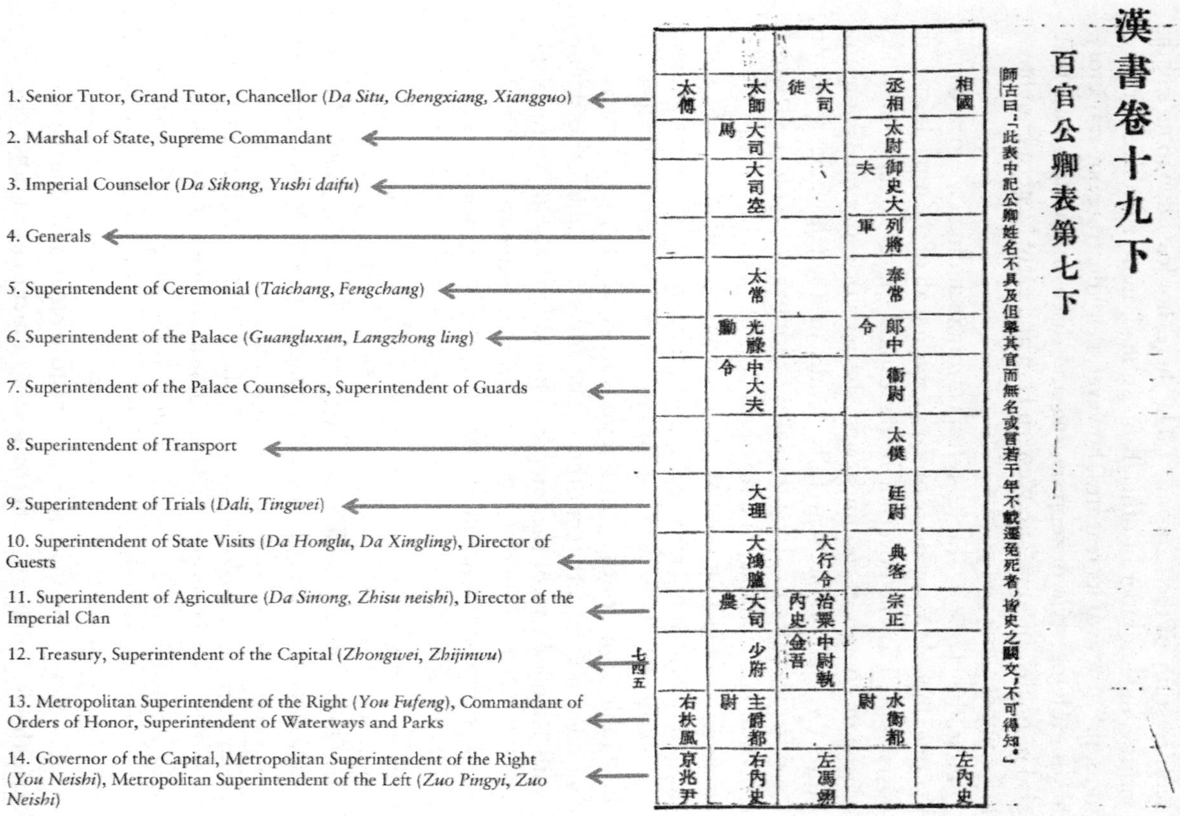

漢書卷十九下

百官公卿表第七下

師古曰：「此表中記公卿姓名不具及但舉其官而無名或官若干年不載遷免死者，皆史之闕文，不可得知。」

相國	丞相	大司徒	太師	太傅
	太尉		大司馬	
	御史大夫		大司空	
	列將軍			
	奉常		太常	
	郎中令		光祿勳	
	衛尉		中大夫令	
	太僕			
	廷尉		大理	
	典客	大行令	大鴻臚	
	宗正	治粟內史	大司農	
		中尉執金吾	少府	
	水衡都尉		主爵都尉	右扶風
左內史		左馮翊	右內史	京兆尹

七四五

1. Senior Tutor, Grand Tutor, Chancellor (*Da Situ, Chengxiang, Xiangguo*)
2. Marshal of State, Supreme Commandant
3. Imperial Counselor (*Da Sikong, Yushi daifu*)
4. Generals
5. Superintendent of Ceremonial (*Taichang, Fengchang*)
6. Superintendent of the Palace (*Guangluxun, Langzhong ling*)
7. Superintendent of the Palace Counselors, Superintendent of Guards
8. Superintendent of Transport
9. Superintendent of Trials (*Dali, Tingwei*)
10. Superintendent of State Visits (*Da Honglu, Da Xingling*), Director of Guests
11. Superintendent of Agriculture (*Da Sinong, Zhisu neishi*), Director of the Imperial Clan
12. Treasury, Superintendent of the Capital (*Zhongwei, Zhijinwu*)
13. Metropolitan Superintendent of the Right (*You Fufeng*), Commandant of Orders of Honor, Superintendent of Waterways and Parks
14. Governor of the Capital, Metropolitan Superintendent of the Right (*You Neishi*), Metropolitan Superintendent of the Left (*Zuo Pingyi, Zuo Neishi*)

Figure 5.2. Office categories in the Hanshu "Table of the Many Offices and Ministerial Posts."

and the date on which they died (*zu* or *hong*) is recorded.[34] The *Hanshu* "Table" also describes when officials ran into legal trouble that brought punishment, ranging from fines and removal from office to death.[35] Also listed are previous positions held by incumbents, the length of time they held that office, and if they held an office in an "acting" (*shou*) capacity. As an illustration, following are the appointments detailed in the "Table" for 80 BCE:

80 BCE (1st year of Yuanfeng)

Gu Shenghu served as the metropolitan superintendent of the left. In his second year he was convicted of releasing people who had plotted rebellion and was executed in the marketplace.

Zhao Chongguo, the leader of the gentlemen of the palace, was made superintendent of waterways and parks. In his sixth year he was promoted.

Hu Xin served as superintendent of the capital.

Du Yannian, [who sat on the] Advisory Council, was made superintendent of transport. In his fifteenth year he was dismissed.

The position of superintendent of the palace was combined with the general of the right.

Zhang Anshi, the superintendent of the palace, was made general of the right and superintendent of the palace. In his sixth year he was promoted.

In the ninth month on the day Gengwu, the metropolitan superintendent of the right, Wang Su, was made imperial counselor. Three years later he was promoted.[36]

Such entries make for dry reading, which no doubt partially provides an explanation for the fact that most scholars have focused on the first section of the *Hanshu* "Table," essentially a long preface that describes the history and duties of each office along with subordinate posts. The actual table has usually been consulted in order to confirm or supplement information provided in other sections of the *Hanshu*.

Not all of the entries listed in 80 BCE provide the previous office held by the new incumbents; specifically, we are not given the office held by Hu Xin prior to his appointment as superintendent of the capital. Usually, however, the previous post is listed, which, along with the promotions and dismissals, allows us to trace the rise and fall of officials in the hierarchy. In this vein, note the entry that describes the superintendent of the palace (*guangluxun*) combining with the general of the right (*you jiangjun*) position. Similar information appears in the immediately following entry for Zhang Anshi, but the "Table" still takes care to underscore the changes to the superintendent of the palace in that office's own category. In effect, the "Table" thus provides not just a description of careers of officers but also the histories of offices. The offices themselves exist independently of any individual incumbent, and the "Table" clearly emphasizes this idea throughout. By noting criminal convictions and the resulting demotions or removals from office, the "Table" also subtly suggests that promotion was the result of successful fulfillment of duties and good behavior. The *Hanshu* "Table" thus carefully depicted the highest echelons of officialdom, comprising the imperial court's officials, as an autonomous institution with processes and norms that were apparently divorced from political events and required incumbents to adhere to standards inherent in each post.

THE *ADMONITIONS OF THE MANY OFFICES* (BAI GUAN ZHEN): BUREAUCRATIC VOICE AT THE IMPERIAL COURT

If the narratives and tables explored above began to represent offices in a particular way starting in the late Western Han, the principles behind them were not necessarily new. Several pre-imperial texts emphasized that officialdom should be an autonomous and hierarchical institution that operated independent of both political events and the backgrounds and personal networks of individual incumbents, who were to be promoted and demoted based on qualifications and performance. Discussion of the courts of legendary sage rulers at times took on this theme: the "Canon of Shun" (Shun dian) chapter of the *Shangshu*, for instance, describes Lord Shun appointing qualified men to high office. The *Han Feizi* advocated promoting officials based solely on the results of their work.[37] The related ideals of clearly defined official responsibilities and assessment proved especially attractive in the context of intense political fights at the late Western Han court. "Discrete duties," however, was not merely a convenient slogan in factional struggles nor an ideological justification for institutional reform. It also found support in changing representational styles in forms such as the narratives and tables examined above, both of which shifted toward depicting offices as more autonomous entities, governed by clear rules and historically constant norms that endured beyond the tenures of individual officeholders. In short, people at the late Western Han court engaged in political struggles and advanced reforms in an environment in which the very principles undergirding the offices and institutions surrounding them were being reformulated and represented in new ways.

Why were these new modes of representation attractive? In the 8 BCE reforms and the *Hanshu* "Table" alike, the presence of hoary titles such as imperial counselor, grand protector, and the like suggest the influence of classical models of officialdom; those same titles are also found in the *Documents* (Shangshu) and *Rites of Zhou* (Zhouli). Even if a "love for antiquity" movement undoubtedly gained greater prominence in the courts of late Western Han rulers, the mere presence of such a trend does not entirely explain why classical models of officialdom were attractive to would-be reformers. Such models of imperial institutions also offered people at court new ways of thinking about their own place in the empire and their own role within the institutions they populated. This point finds dramatic illustration in a now highly fragmented text entitled *Admonitions of the Many Offices* (Bai guan zhen). The text was compiled by several different figures in Eastern Han, though most of the early accounts credit the late Western Han polymath Yang Xiong with writing the first of these office admonitions and note that Yang's work was inspired by an admonition from the *Zuozhuan*.[38] However, Yang departed from his *Zuozhuan* model in order to invoke normative and historically constant duties and performance standards that pertained to individual administrative posts. In other words, the admonitions were transformed into poems written in the voice of a depersonalized *office*, not an office's incumbent. Correspondingly, the admonitions were designed to criticize not only or even primarily the ruler but rather officeholders who failed to live up to the standards described in the poems.

The admonition in the *Zuozhuan*, entitled "Admonition of the Overseer of Hunts" (Yu ren zhen), appears as a quote in a larger speech by a minister to the lord of Jin.[39] The Jin minister describes the poem as a critique solicited by a late Shang minister named Xin Jia, so even while the poem describes legendary events during the preceding Xia period, its object of critique was presumably the last Shang king.[40]

Admonition of the Overseer of Hunts

Vast and far-reaching were Yu's tracks!
He demarcated the Nine Provinces,
Laid out and opened up the nine paths.
People had their chambers of rest and shrines,
Beasts had their luxurious grasses.
Each had their proper abodes,
Their qualities and functions kept separate.
When Yi of Yi was on the throne,
He rushed out to the beasts of the plains.
Forgetting the concerns of state,
And thinking only of dogs and stags.
His footsteps cannot be followed,
His actions did not elevate the house of Xia.
I, your manager of beasts, in charge of the plains,
Dare to notify my lord's servant.[41]

As the spaces added to this translation are meant to indicate, shifts in content naturally divide the "Admonition of the Overseer of hunts" into three different sections. The first opens with grand acclaim for the work of the legendary sage king Yu, using language also seen in the *Shijing*,[42] before moving on to three rhymed couplets. These couplets build upon the opening encomium, describing a perfect spatial division between humans and animals as well as a corresponding division of function between the two, all of which resulted from Yu's demarcation of the nine provinces. The next section moves on to describe the destructive actions of Hou Yi, who transgressed the boundaries established by Yu when he "rushed out to the beasts of the plains." In so doing, of course, Hou Yi neglected his state duties back in the human realm of his court. The second section thus contrasts Yu's rule of perfect division and order with the later ruler Hou Yi's indulgent disruption of that order.

The final section, just a single couplet in length, makes two moves that render it the rhetorical key to the entire poem. First, it establishes the authority of the poem's voice: being "in charge of the plains," its criticisms against excessive hunting are supported by the imprimatur of its office, which was responsible for managing the hunting grounds of the king. Second, the phrase "dare to notify" (*gan gao*) demonstrates the voice's adherence to administrative protocol. "Dare to notify" appears regularly in transmitted and excavated texts alike.[43] Its appearance in the "Admonition of the Overseer of Hunts" signals the poem's self-conscious adaptation in order to bolster its message:

the poem was not a one-off emission from an idiosyncratic individual but a regularized critique conforming to the duties of office and patterns of bureaucratic practice.

Many of these characteristics are found in poems included in the *Admonitions*, as demonstrated by the following example, the "Admonition of the Master of Works" (Sikong zhen), attributed to Yang Xiong:[44]

Admonition of the Master of Works

Spreading out were Kun's numina,[45]
According with Heaven it gave rise to principles.
The five zones were divided and established,
Demarcated into myriad realms.

Only then was established an office of the Earth,
The Minister of Works took this as his charge.
Vast and wide were the Nine Provinces,
Capital residences filled up districts.
Leading lines were set by the many shepherds,[46]
Then stitched together by the regional lords.

Magnificent were the talented and worthy men,
Protective and supportive were the royal ministers.
The ministers matched their offices,
Offices matched their ministers.
A one-in-nine tax was put into practice,[47]
The seven levies evenly distributed.[48]

In the past when the age went into decline,
Ranked salaries bypassed worthy men.
The corrupt filled the court,
Outwardly respectful, they offended Heaven.[49]

The wrong people asserted power,
And the wrong policies were promulgated.
Flows of money purchased favor,
And reed-wrapped gifts sealed the deals.[50]
The royal route thus in waste,
What ruler would not topple over?

I, the Master of works, am in charge of the land.
And dare to report to those attending at the side.

The poem generally conforms to the "Admonition of the Overseer of Hunts." Both admonitions, for instance, begin in high antiquity before moving to a later period of decline. Moreover, the "Admonition of the Master of Works," as in its *Zuozhuan* model, concludes with the same invocation of official duties and the "dare to report" statement.

While these overall patterns in "Master of Works" clearly reflect the influence of "Overseer of Hunts," differences in representation and above all voice distinguish the former from the latter. Note, for instance, their contrasting descriptions of the legendary sage king Yu. On a basic level, whereas "Overseer of Hunts" explicitly mentions Yu by name, "Master of Works" does not, even though the latter frequently invokes stories and texts associated with Yu. Specific lines from "Master of Works" consciously invoke the opening couplet from "Overseer of Hunts" that describes Yu's work, without actually using Yu's name: "Vast and far-reaching were Yu's tracks / He demarcated the Nine Provinces" in "Overseer of Hunts" becomes "Vast and wide were the Nine Provinces" (second stanza, "Master of Works") and "Demarcated into myriad realms" (first stanza, "Master of Works"). While these lines allow Yu to fade into the background of the admonition without entirely disappearing, the opening couplet of "Master of Works" invokes not "Yu's tracks" but "Kun's numina." Instead of a legendary sage's accomplishment, we read of patterns as well as boundaries and offices that arose from principles modeled on Heaven (*tian*). To the extent that "Master of Works" retained a role for Yu, it is one not of charismatic action but rather of disembodied fulfillment of a cosmic order.

Compared to the *Zuozhuan* "Overseer of Hunts" admonition, this emphasis on disembodied and historically constant offices encourages a different interpretation of poetic voice in the final "dare to report" statements. Specifically, in the Han admonitions, the voices behind the poems evaluate and critique not the behavior of the ruler but their own behavior as officials. Many admonitions achieve this aim by invoking historical examples of failed officials in the past. As a result, the voices of the poems trace a history of the office in question as a constant position and implicitly claim that their own actions and behavior, in contrast to the negative historical examples, measure up to the requirements and demands of the office. This rhetoric is seen quite clearly in the following admonition, also usually attributed to Yang Xiong:[51]

Admonition of the Superintendent of Guards

Boundless and vast is supreme Heaven,
Sublime and lofty its residence.
It installs stations in mountain defiles,
Marking out defensive borders.[52]

Boundary after boundary, enclosure after enclosure,
Blocking the unlawful.
Guard towers stand sentinel over the walls,
Prepared for invading troops.[53]
The realm is thus stable,
The people have their center.
Each safeguards a position,
Forever maintained without fail.
In past times there were many guards,
And offices obtained their proper people.
With halberds in hand they sang out,[54]
While interior and exterior held strong.
While Lord Huan of Qi was apprehensive,
The palace guards received no command.[55]
The gates did not have their proper people.
At doors they abandoned their duties.
Cao Mo brandished his sword,
And thus succeeded in his scheme.[56]
Jing Ke grasped the head of his dagger,
And the sentries did not notice him.[57]
The Second Emperor was careless with where he stayed,
And so met defeat at Wangyi Palace.[58]
When Yan Le forged the imperial order,
Those holding the halberds did not prevent him.[59]
The Superintendent of Guards commands the sentries,
I dare to report to the one enforcing the regulations.

Starting with the example of Duke Huan of Qi, the "Admonition of the Superintendent of Guards" refers to a series of historical instances in which security personnel failed in their duties, resulting in either the humiliation or death of the rulers they were supposed to protect. The situations are by no means comparable, and indeed the *Shiji* story about Jing Ke is a famously nuanced meditation on the complicated welter of factors that allowed the humble assassin to almost kill the First Emperor. The "Admonition," however, presents a rather simple explanation for all of these security breaches: "The gates did not have their proper people." In place of historical circumstance and the efforts of determined attackers, "Superintendent of Guards" attributes all security lapses to improper personnel. The "Admonition of the Secretariat" (Shangshu zhen), also attributed to Yang Xiong, presents a similar message:[60]

In the past Qin esteemed craftiness,
Its offices had the wrong people.
Seals were used to send secret documents,
And Fu Su took his life.[61]

Whether gates or offices, the central question was the same: How could appointed officials be properly fit to the responsibilities of their bureaucratic post? In this vein, it is perhaps significant that the "Admonition of the Superintendent of Guards" paired "The gates did not have their proper people" with the line "At doors they abandoned their duties." The parallel between "people" (*ren*) and "duties" (*zhi*) suggests a more complicated process than a simple insertion of qualified personnel into the appropriate bureaucratic slots. Rather, a two-way connection bound together officeholders and offices. This point is made most clearly in the "Admonition of the Master of Works," which includes the following couplet, describing conditions in high antiquity: "The ministers matched their offices, / Offices matched their ministers." In the ideal bureaucratic order articulated in the admonitions, the distinction between "office" and "official" dissolved, the norms and duties of the former resonating with the particular competencies of the latter.

The poetic voice of the admonitions, particularly as expressed in the final couplet, underscores this point. By reporting to the ruler on the performance of historic holders of an office, the admonitions effectively invoked normative standards and duties inherent in each of the offices they describe, irrespective of the different incumbents in any specific period. In doing so, the admonitions implicitly criticized those officials who did not fulfill the standards. At the same time, the poetic voice of the admonitions demonstrated its own internalization of those same standards. By perfectly communicating the cosmic and historical origins of offices and the historical instances when other, less perfect officeholders failed to measure up, authors of admonitions could demonstrate their own (potential?) perfection as an official. This is not to claim that admonition authors necessarily wanted to serve in the positions that their poems described; indeed, in the case of Yang Xiong, who famously never sought a particularly high office at court, the exact opposite might be said. Rather, the significant point is that authors of Han and post-Han admonitions expressly shifted the content and poetic voice of the *Zuozhuan* "Admonition of the Overseer of Hunts" in order to cast the poems as poetic embodiments, in both content and form, of a historically constant bureaucratic ideal.

In making this claim, the admonitions were not too dissimilar from a much more famous literary project at the late Western Han court: an imperial bibliography, begun in 26 BCE. That year,

Chengdi ordered several learned men to collate texts collected from around the empire.[62] The venerable Liu Xiang then put them in order by title and wrote summaries of each text, which he presented to the throne. Xiang died before completing his work, so his son Liu Xin continued the project. Xin eventually wrote the work *Seven Summaries* (Qi lüe), which divided all of the collected and collated texts into seven categories, with seven different essays summarizing each category. The "Treatise on Arts and Letters" (Yi wen zhi) chapter of the *Hanshu* was based on this work of Liu Xiang and Liu Xin, both of whom were contemporaries of Yang Xiong at the imperial court in Chang'an.[63] The important point for us is that descriptions in the "Yi wen zhi" both of smaller groups of texts and of the seven larger categories connect the texts collected in the imperial library to the duties of ancient offices.

According to the late Western Han bibliographers, textual production and the creation of literary forms were part and parcel of bureaucratic action. For instance, the "Yi wen zhi" bibliographic category "Military Specialists" (Bing jia), comprising some five subcategories, is said to have "probably issued from the official duties of the ancient military majors and the martial preparations of the royal officials."[64] Similarly, the "Treatise" describes the texts included under "Recipes and Techniques" (Fang ji) as follows: "They are all tools for producing life, uniformly maintained by royal officials."[65] In this manner, the "Yi wen zhi" locates the practices and ideas described in categorized texts as the outcome of specific aspects of work conducted by ancient officials. This claim is most consistently seen in the sections listing texts placed under the larger category of "Various Masters" (Zhu zi). Perhaps the most elaborate of such explanations is found after the list of texts classified under "Specialists in the [Traditions of Master] Mo" (Mo jia):

> The stream of Mo specialists probably issued from the maintenance of ancestral shrines. By thatching the roofs and using oak for the rafters, they thereby esteemed frugality. By supporting the *sanlao* and *wugeng* elders, they thereby practiced impartial love. In selecting men of service according to a grand archery competition, they thereby esteemed worthies. In their ancestral sacrifices they strictly revered their fathers, and thereby privileged the spirits. By according with the four seasons in their actions, they thereby acted against the idea of fate. By using the principles of family reverence to govern all under heaven, they thereby esteemed unity.[66]

The statement thus links not just the general Mo tradition but also specific ideas associated with Mo Di and his disciples to different tasks performed at the ancestral shrines. Some of the connections drawn might seem more obvious than others, but the claim advanced in the passage is clear enough: the responsibilities of people in charge of the ancestral shrines gave birth to the central ideas articulated and celebrated by Mo Di and his successors.

The explanation summing up the larger category of "Various Masters," however, does not emphasize the bureaucratic origins of the different "specialties" (*jia*). Indeed, we do not read of offices but rather of the decline of the "Way of kings" (*wang Dao*) during the Eastern Zhou, when the Zhou royal house began to lose political sway in the face of challenges from increasingly powerful regional states. The masters are said to have developed along with this decline ("[the masters] all arose when the Way of kings had faded") and with a concomitant need to develop persuasive techniques that allowed speakers to "attain concord with the various lords," since these lords had replaced the Zhou king as the dominant power holders.[67] The "Treatise" thus manifests a tension. On the one hand, the bibliographers recognized that knowledge of the various textual categories they had created were rooted in comparatively recent manuscript traditions, which arose in response to the political concerns and conditions of their day. On the other, they strove to draw connections between the textual evidence available and the practices of ancient offices, including, for instance, the link between Mohist ideas and duties at the ancestral temple.[68] Given the specific emphasis in the *Admonitions of the Many Offices* on speech as part of an official's duty, it is doubly interesting that the "Treatise" explains the "various masters" as arising from a demand for effective techniques of political persuasion that arose after the "Way of kings" declined. In so doing, the "Treatise" plainly allowed that persuasive speech and the ideas expressed by the masters were necessary responses to political chaos and had to be adjusted in order to fit contemporary demands. This idea is the precise opposite of the admonitions and their aesthetics of bureaucratic voice, however, which argued that speech and action were preconfigured requirements, rooted in the ancient, prescribed duties of an unchanging office. In other words, by tightly linking political persuasion to rigidly defined official duties, the admonitions presented one possible resolution of the contradiction in the "Treatise" between ancient offices and decidedly less ancient persuasive speech. The question of precisely how a minister matched his office and an office matched its minister, then, as well as the relationship in the context of government service between historical contingency and timeless constants, were incredibly important problems at the late Western Han court, driving political reform efforts as well as new modes of textual representation.

In this light, it is worth pointing out that Yang Xiong and other authors of admonitions did not write these poems only from the perspective of government ministry directors, such as the master of works, superintendent of guards, and other top offices detailed in the *Hanshu* "Table of the Many Offices and Ministerial Posts." Recall, for instance, that Yang wrote an "Admonition of the Secretariat," describing an office in charge of handling official documents, located within Weiyang Palace, that during late Western Han at least was often headed by imperial family members or others who enjoyed a close relationship with the ruler.[69] Composers of admonitions during the Eastern Han, meanwhile, wrote an "Admonition on the Consort Clans" (Waiqi zhen) and an "Admonition on the Palace Attendant" (Shizhong zhen).[70] Just as the reforms of 8 BCE sought to subsume members of the imperial Wang family within an institutional structure governed by rank and duty and applied to all of officialdom, the admonitions suggest a parallel trend in the world of literary production: the application of an aesthetics of bureaucratic voice, of discrete duties, to a broadly conceptualized imperial court, from palaces to capital bureaus.

When reformers in 8 BCE cited the creation of discrete duties as an important goal to be realized by their reform plans, they invoked not merely an ideological justification but a whole mode of representing offices that began to gain prominence in late Western Han. At first glance, the narratives about chancellors and imperial counselors in the second half of the *Shiji*'s "Account of Chancellor Zhang" would hardly seem to support any notion of carefully defined officially responsibilities since the stories emphasized the role of luck in career success. There is no reason to assume, however, that notions of luck are incompatible with a bureaucratic ideal.[71] The contrast between the first and second halves of the *Shiji* chapter suggests as much. Sima Qian's earlier stories highlighted the complex sets of factors that helped people gain appointment as chancellor. His appraisal focused on distinguishing (and judging) the vastly different talents and predilections of these high officials. By contrast, the second half of the chapter focused almost entirely on the importance of physiognomy and fate, with the appraisal wondering how a few people who "wandered through various offices" eventually managed to travel all the way up the bureaucratic hierarchy. As the appraisal put it, even though many people had sage-like talents, only the very lucky managed to gain promotion. Curiously, then, this focus on luck simultaneously cast the ascendance of qualified individuals as the norm, even if it was a norm that was rarely or inconsistently achieved.

The relationship between these narratives and the tables is not obvious. Given their rather dry, almost administrative descriptions of official appointments and promotions, the tables seem rather different from the narrative flourishes in the "Account of Chancellor Zhang." At the same time, changes within the *Shiji* table of officials, as well as contrasts between the *Shiji* table and its later *Hanshu* counterpart, show a transformation in representation and rhetoric that is not too distant from the contrasts between the two halves of the "Account of Chancellor Zhang." The lower half of the *Shiji* table began to move away from any discussion of official careers in relation to contemporary events. What emerged, especially in the *Hanshu* "Table of the Many Offices and Ministerial Posts," was a mode of representation that removed all historical contingency from the careers of officeholders. Instead, the *Hanshu* table confronts us with a smoothly operating system of hiring, promoting, and dismissing according to well-established and historically constant principles. I would emphasize that both the second half of the *Shiji* chapter and the second half of the *Shiji* table were written in late Western Han, perhaps during the reign of Chengdi, a period that saw many different kinds of reforms, often based on classical principles. Neither the narratives nor the table, however, evinces any clear affiliation with such principles, even while they point us toward the growing importance of a bureaucratic model that explicitly valued discrete duties.

In contrast, *The Admonitions of the Many Offices* could by almost any measure be understood as classicist texts. After all, they were first written by Yang Xiong, an acknowledged and influential master of classical texts and knowledge in late Western Han. And the admonitions were clearly modeled on a poem found in the *Zuozhuan*, a tradition of the *Annals* (Chunqiu) that by the reign of Chengdi was beginning to enjoy increased status at the imperial court. Authors of admonitions, however, did not slavishly imitate the *Zuozhuan* model. Rather, they borrowed the bureaucratic language and formality of the admonitions but shifted the object of critique from the ruler to office-holders. In the process, they championed a picture of officialdom in which offices had discrete duties and charted a history in which such clear official responsibilities had inhered in high capital offices since high antiquity. The very act of writing an admonition, then, was not to lodge complaints to the ruler but to give voice to the immutability of the office described and, of course, express the poet's perfect understanding of the conventions and duties of the office. As we saw in the discussion of the *Hanshu* "Treatise on Arts and Letters," bibliographic work in the late Western Han did something similar, since the prefaces to the bibliographic categories clearly linked textual production to the duties of ancient offices, though the "Treatise" never quite resolved the internal tensions that this narrative produced. In other words, a new vision of the offices of the imperial court emerged in relation not just or even primarily to the adoption of a certain ideological program but rather as part of a much broader and more interesting exploration of new modes of literary production and representation.

Conclusion

When Gaozu prevailed in the post-Qin civil war and established the Western Han, he and his supporters by no means completely recreated the Qin Empire that preceded them. Surely the Qin model was attractive: by eliminating his rival kingdoms, replacing them with a Qin-directed central government that reported directly to the capital, and taking the title emperor (*huangdi*), the First Emperor of Qin provided an almost irresistible touchstone for imperial order. Even if our sources caricature Gaozu and his band as uncouth country bumpkins, it is undeniable that the founding ruler of Western Han could not claim the royal pedigree of the First Emperor of Qin. Moreover, scholarly consensus rightly recognizes that Gaozu did not command sufficient military strength or economic resources to fulfill the Qin ideal of a universal empire. As we have seen, however, Western Han emperors and their advisers managed to quell challenges to Han imperial authority and by the mid- and late Western Han effectively established a centralized and unified imperial system.

To an extent that is perhaps not recognized enough, however, there was nothing inevitable or fated about this eventual triumph of the Han and its Liu ruling household. Unexpected fits and starts and moments when the whole system almost collapsed caution against smooth narratives of Han success. It is precisely these fits and starts that forced important changes in practice, changes that raised questions about the nature of Han imperial power and transformed the imperial court. These unanticipated events and changes paired with longer term demographic and territorial expansion in order to create an imperial court that, by the end of Western Han, was both much larger and more defined in spatial and institutional terms.

From its very opening days the Han, at least in theory, disbursed material goods and gifts of all kinds according to a set of sumptuary regulations. Many of these regulations drew equivalencies between salary ranks, held by officials, and the orders of honor given to Han subjects. Particularly during and after the rebellion of 154 BCE, however, such equivalencies were drawn between Han and non-Han subjects, including those of the insurrectionist kingdoms. During this same period, court attendants, guards, minor officials, and eventually even court consorts began to be organized according to "equivalent" ranks keyed to the salary ranks of Han officials. Only over time were these applied more systematically to people working at the imperial court, perhaps as late as the last century of Western Han rule. Equivalencies transformed from a way to secure material ties and loyalty to a Han throne into a pattern that helped organize court institutions. If no other realm could compare to the Han court, it necessarily required greater articulation, for defending court privileges and patterns necessarily required that they be defined, and the salary ranks provided one means to do just that. Even while Western Han emperors asserted that no other realm could possibly "equal" the Han court, the same language of comparison and equivalencies paradoxically integrated the Han court into the larger administrative structure of the empire.

A request from a leader of the Xiongnu to attend the annual court audience of 51 BCE was perhaps even more unexpected than the royal rebellions of a century earlier. The request required a rapid response from the emperor and his officials, who sought to determine the proper protocol for such an unprecedented event. During the resulting debate, officials advanced different understandings of the Han court's relationship to foreign groups. Even if the emperor's final decision to carve out a special ritual status for the Xiongnu leader was driven by several different considerations, some of them political and diplomatic in nature, retrospective accounts of the debate and the 51 BCE court ceremony cast the entire series of events as a clash between the emperor and his classically minded officials. Such a characterization ultimately supported calls in the *Hanshu* for further court ceremonial reform. In sum, even if the creation of sumptuary and ritual categories was a primary concern of rulers in the opening days of Western Han, their transformation over subsequent decades and centuries, and especially a growing focus on the establishment of categories and how to properly fill them, was driven by events and developments that rulers and officials could hardly have anticipated.

Another way to understand this dynamic is to say that imperial expansion, and the contingent events that occurred along the way, highlighted problems and raised questions that allowed or even required the imperial court to be transformed institutionally and represented according to new rhetorical formulations.[1] Certainly such a process seems to have been under way in discussions of the court as a space. By expanding and walling off Shanglin Park and building a whole slew of palaces and manufacturing facilities within it, Wudi eventually raised the question where exactly the legitimate court spaces were and who should be allowed into them. In their answers, and by associating morally proper officials with Weiyang Palace (not the park), late Western Han writers helped create new understandings of court spaces. No less important to this process of refashioning spatial symbolism at court, however, were legal regulations regarding the "forbidden zones," areas deep within imperial palaces that eventually came to represent the most privileged people in the empire. Moral critique and law thus combined to create a new and much more clearly articulated understanding of who belonged in precisely which spaces of the court.

This process of greater articulation and division was not limited to court spaces. Whether in politically driven fights over offices (the 8 BCE reforms) or the creation of new forms of writing and literary production (e.g., the tables of officials, admonitions, and bibliographic work), the idea of discrete duties spread to all aspects of court life and institutions, particularly during the reign of Chengdi. The growing power of Chengdi's maternal relatives, members of the Wang family, must have made a court with finely articulated divisions rather attractive. After all, since Wang uncles especially enjoyed a monopoly on important court titles and offices (e.g., the marshal of state and director of the Secretariat) and commanded a broad patronage network that perhaps extended even to the commanderies, would-be reformers opposed to Wang power sought to make even the innermost areas of the court conform to a universalized vision of clearly defined and immutable responsibilities.

This vision of "discrete duties" can hardly be ascribed only to an ideological program, for it was reflected in a range of texts, from official biographies to tables and admonitions. The rise of the admonitions is particularly illustrative in this regard, not least because the late Western Han admonitions transformed from critiques of rulers into critiques of officials. In addition, the admonitions extended the idea of discrete duties to all areas of the court and empire. Recall, for instance, that one of the poems was written from the voice of the director of the Secretariat, one of the offices held by members of the Wang family! Moreover, as the admonitions genre continued to develop, the positions they described spread both externally, to areas ever more distant from the capital, and internally, ever deeper into the court. Witness the fact that Yang Xiong purportedly wrote an "Admonition of the Village Elders" (Guo sanlao zhen), while an Eastern Han author composed an "Admonition of the Imperial Consort Clan" (Waiqi zhen).[2] In other words, the aesthetics of discrete duties eventually spread to the entire empire, even as it seems to have originated in institutional and political developments at the imperial court.

This final point thus brings us back to the 148 BCE board game discussed in the introduction. Recall that the game presented a vision of the empire as a series of circles, crossed by recommendations and relationships, all of which centered around the emperor at the imperial center. Eventually that understanding gave way to a vision of empire divided into little boxes, as in the late imperial promotion games. Such a fundamental change in cultural convention and vision cannot be ascribed to any one factor or short-term time period. A good case could be made for the late Western Han, however, when those at the center of court life and politics began to draw a stunning array of boundaries and boxes that separated the Han court from rival powers, distinguished palace halls from pleasure parks, and defined discrete offices while elevating them above illegitimate and messy political alliances. We cannot point to a specific moment when "court" (*chao*) as a term came to represent the entire Han dynasty or entire historical eras. We can say, however, that it happened during a period when court-based conventions were applied to the empire as a whole. In short, experiences and struggles at the late Western Han imperial court were central to developing new understandings of the entire empire, especially the offices that composed its administrative structure.

This is why the early imperial court matters: it was not just a backdrop for political struggle but provided new language and models, most of them not designed by the rulers, that could be projected on the empire as a whole. From a dizzying array of perspectives Western Han writers began to imagine and conceptualize what it meant to be a "member" of the imperial court, and it was those ruminations that set a foundation for understanding what it meant to be an imperial subject. Court rituals, spaces, and offices allowed people at the capital to reimagine their own place in the empire. The "court" as a category correspondingly became filled with social and institutional meanings that were entirely absent at the beginning of Western Han. It is probably no accident that during the Han period another significant and similar shift occurred to a different word: *guan* 官. In the pre-imperial period and most of the Western Han, *guan* referred only to an official post in the government, an "office." A different word, *li* 吏, was the most common term for "official." By the Eastern Han period, however, *guan* meant both office *and* official.[3] On the level of language and representation, imperial subject and imperial institution became fused together. Complicated interactions between a series of policy and institutional transformations, unanticipated events, and a rich landscape of cultural work, all of which converged at the imperial court, was necessary in order for such a significant change to occur.

This dynamic encourages us to pause and consider the larger problem of the origins and establishment of the Chinese bureaucracy, which one historian of the pre-imperial and early imperial eras characterized as one of China's key contributions to "world culture."[4] On some level, this might be true, but it of course depends on how one defines *bureaucracy*. After all, specialized administrative techniques, the keeping of records and accounts, and registries of land and people—all features of any system plausibly defined as bureaucratic—occur in ancient Near Eastern cultures that predate the earliest written records from China.[5] Though the roots of China's bureaucratic institutions are deep and began to develop many centuries before Qin unification in 221 BCE, as a broad set of administrative techniques they are not necessarily unique or pioneering in world historical terms, even if we allow for particular differences and distinct characteristics in the Chinese case.[6] Moreover, as the 148 BCE board game demonstrates, even if bureaucratic administration had existed in China for many centuries prior, the principles we might associate with bureaucracies—or, as the anthropologist David Graeber has put it, the "fictions" of consistency, meritocracy, and clearly defined hierarchies—did not seem to hold particular sway in representations and understandings of the empire.[7] In other words, even if there were bureaucratic techniques, there was not necessarily a bureaucratic ethos that enjoyed wide currency. Rather, the underpinnings and assumptions of imperial Chinese bureaucracy spread only after they developed at the imperial court, and not according to the designs of any individual ruler or even a set ideological program. This bureaucratic rhetoric does indeed seem to have been powerful and long-lasting; eventually, it even provided a basis for board games. If we are going to identify China's contribution to "world culture" in the realm of bureaucratic administration (admittedly a fraught enterprise), this rhetoric of bureaucracy, and the complicated institutional and social world of the imperial court from which it emerged, is a most fitting candidate.

NOTES

INTRODUCTION

1. For a description of these and other goods from the tomb, found near the town of Kongjiapo in Hubei and numbered eight (M8) by the archaeologists, see Hubei Sheng Wenwu Kaogu Yanjiu Suo and Suizhou Shi Kaogu Duibian 2006; and Harkness 2011, 27–29. The "grave contract" recovered from the tomb states that the occupant was an "armory supervisor" named Bi who hailed from the nobility (*guo*) Tao. That nobility's holder died in 140 BCE after serving as chancellor (*chengxiang*) from 147 to 143 BCE. See *Hanshu* 16.614; Loewe 2000, 353.

2. The asterisk after *rishu* indicates that the title was not found on the manuscript itself but rather assigned by modern editors. For details on this convention, which this book follows, see Richter 2013, 12–13. Kalinowski (2010) and Harkness (2011, 11–72) surveyed the existing daybook finds.

3. Some studies have characterized the diagram and the explanatory text in astrocalendrical terms or as a divination board. See, e.g., Yan Changgui 2008. As far as I am aware, Li Ling (2011) is the only study to analyze the diagram and text as a board game. Of course, we need look no further than the Ouija board (or, indeed, Monopoly and Life) for a reminder that the line between divination and game boards is thin at best, a point acknowledged in Kalinowski 2012–13, 343n36.

4. The phrase *huan yu* (serving the emperor), is unattested in received literature. The translation adopted here partly reflects information from the text that follows. The phrase *huan huangdi zhe* (those who serve the emperor) is found throughout the early Western Han legal statutes and ordinances excavated from Zhangjiashan tomb 247. See chapter 1. The photograph of strip 357 in the excavation report shows no trace of text, while the report's transcription notes only that the graphs are missing.

5. Hubei Sheng Wenwu Kaogu Yanjiu Suo and Suizhou Shi Kaogu Duibian 2006, strips 352–58 (third register), 100 (photograph) and 174 (transcription). As the photographs show, the manuscript compilers divided the text into two sections via a dot above the graphs on strip 355, which starts the section on "holding office" (*ju guan*).

6. Archaeologists have excavated many dice sets from Han tombs. For one example, see Shandong Sheng Zibo Shi Bowuguan 1985, 241 (photograph) and 242 (transcription).

In this book, "early imperial" refers to the period from Qin unification in 221 BCE to the fall of Eastern Han in 220 CE. "Late imperial" refers to the Ming (1368–1644) and Qing (1644–1911) periods. Li Ling (2011) noted connections between the 148 BCE diagram and late imperial promotion games but did not emphasize the differences.

7. For the late imperial promotion games, see Morgan 2004; Lo 2004.

8. Kalinowski 1998–99, 156.

9. See *Xunzi jian shi* 1996, "Wang zhi," 9.98; *Han Feizi jiao shi* 1996, "Er bing," 12.204.

10. The diagram, entitled "The Constants of Government Service" (Zheng shi zhi chang), was found among the strips recovered from the Qin tomb near Wangjiatai in Jingzhou, Hubei. See *Wenwu* 1 (1995): 37–43. Full transcriptions and photographs of the Wangjiatai strips have yet to be published. For a discussion of "The Constants of Government Service," see Wang Mingqin 2004. "The Way to Act as a Good Official" was among the Qin manuscripts from the Shuihudi tomb. See Shuihudi Qin Mu Zhujian Zhengli Xiaoau 1990, 81–5 (photographs) and 167–76 (transcription). For the excavation report, see Xiaogan Diqu Di Er Qi Yigong Yinong Wenwu Kaogu Xunlian Ban 1976.

11. In this sense, the 146 BCE excavated game evokes the importance of "agreement in judgment," a concept developed by Wittgenstein (1889–1951) in reference to mathematical logic but also, by extension, all rules governing everything from games to grammar. Wittgenstein's basic idea was that rules were inseparable from actual practice, which in a process of unending instantiation gave rise to shared agreements about correct rule enactment. For a detailed discussion with reference to Wittgenstein's *Remarks on the Foundations of Mathematics*, see Minar 2011, 290. Thanks to Roy Chan for this reference. For a rare focus on the role consensus and agreement, as opposed to coercion, played in forming the early empires, see Sanft 2014.

12 For a recent discussion that emphasizes the role of "ideology" (in this case, "Legalism" and "Confucianism") in the Western Han, see Zhao 2015. I do not deny the importance of ideas in shaping and reforming government institutions, but rather doubt, for at least two reasons, that we have sufficient evidence to demonstrate that a set ideological or intellectual program guided government reform in early China. First, many scholars have demonstrated that early texts do not support the existence of set philosophical "schools" of ideas with coherent programs (see, e.g., Csikszentmihalyi and Nylan 2003; Goldin 2011). Second, political theorists remain divided about the definition of "ideology" and the links between ideology and political action. For an overview, see Martin 2015, which argued that ideology in contemporary politics is little more than a theorization and justification of extant political alliances. If we accept that definition of "ideology," then I do not think we can clearly understand the role of "ideology" in a world for which we usually do not have enough sources to understand the complexities of political

positions and alliances, which were themselves highly unstable and required constant renewal. See the discussion in chapter 4; for an analysis of similar problems in the context of the late Roman republic, see Hölkeskamp 2010. Moreover, early Chinese thinkers tended to conceptualize intellectual debate using metaphors of lineage, connection, and consensus, further obscuring our ability to identify positions in political debates. For a detailed discussion that treats such irenic characterizations of early thought with some skepticism, see Brashier 2011, 18–34.

13. Max Weber outlined several reasons for bureaucratic expansion, from the creation of standing armies to the emergence of communication technologies that knit together large geographic areas. See "Bureaucracy," in Gerth and Mills 1946, 212–14. Some of these developments date to China's early imperial period, but many started centuries before imperial unification in 221 BCE. Regardless, the mere existence of such factors in the early Chinese case tells us little about their links to specific institutional developments. For one critique of Weber's characterization of ancient China, see Creel 1964. For a more recent and sympathetic application of Weber's ideas about bureaucracy to the early imperial period, see Zhao 2015. More important for the arguments in this book is the fact that the conceptual, normative, and rhetorical underpinnings and consequences of bureaucratized government are absent from Weber's analysis and from the work of most social scientists and historians. On this point, see Herzfeld 1992.

14. Many of these insights are in David Knechtges's translations of *Selections of Refined Literature* (Wenxuan), with three volumes published thus far. Knechtges (1976) provided an early and important discussion of Han dynasty rhapsodies. For a discussion of the rhapsodies as political criticism, see Knechtges 1999. For a summary of Knechtges's work, with citations as well as references to other studies of court rhetoric and literature, see Kern 2009.

15. See, e.g., Kern 2003b; Kern 2014.

16. See Nylan 1999a; Kern 2001. For a different view, see Lewis 1999b.

17. Japanese scholarship has been particularly important in this field. See the summary in Yoneda Kenshi 2000. Important scholars of institutional history writing primarily in Chinese include Yan Gengwang, Zhu Zongbin, An Zuozhang, Xiong Tieji, Yan Buke, Gan Huaizhen, Chen Suzhen, and Hsing I-tien.

18. Note that the *Hou Hanshu* "Treatise on the Many Offices" (Bai guan zhi) is an earlier work than the *Hou Hanshu* itself, since Sima Biao (240–306 CE) completed the former over a century before Fan Ye (398–446) compiled the latter. See Beck 1990, esp. 196–226.

19. This point received emphasis throughout Yoneda Kenshi 2000. Much of Michael Loewe's work on Han government has supported this idea. See, e.g., Loewe 2000, which does not cover Eastern Han, and Loewe 1981, which stresses the different models of rulership that dominated in Western versus Eastern Han.

20. See Loewe 1967, 1:9. Other scholars, based on recently excavated documents, have offered bolder claims. For instance, drawing upon materials

excavated near Liye, Hunan, and elsewhere, Pines et al. (2013, 22) stated that the Qin state was almost "modern," insofar as it established an "intrusive bureaucracy, whose tentacles penetrated the entire society." Fukuyama (2011, esp. 110–19) offered a similar characterization. For an earlier exploration of these ideas, see Creel 1964. Liye was a frontier outpost, so the documents there might reflect intensive practices designed to secure borderlands. For treatments of Qin that de-emphasize, in different ways, the dominant emphasis on centralized bureaucratic control, see Sanft 2014; Nylan forthcoming.

21. See, e.g., essays in Nylan and Vankeerberghen 2015; Chin 2014; Blitstein 2015. In contrast to the other two works, which focused on late Western Han, Blitstein analyzed texts produced from the late fifth to early sixth centuries at the Jiankang courts of the "Southern Dynasties." Moreover, all of these scholars studied links between literature and institutions in very different ways. For instance, Chin analyzed the impact of imperial expansion on Western Han literary practices, while Blitstein focused on cultivated literary knowledge in Jiankang as a form of political power.

22. For studies of the Ming court, see Robinson 2008. For two different perspectives on the Qing court, see Bartlett 1991; Rawski 1998.

23. From Map's *Of Courtier Trifles* (De Nugis Curialium), cited in Llewellyn-Jones 2013, 3.

24. On this point, see Blitstein (2015, 42n5), focusing on the fifth- and sixth-century Southern Dynasties courts at Jiankang. Blitstein expanded upon points made in Twitchett (1992), noting that the court as a physical space was paired with the notion of a court as a collection of people bound together by shared codes of etiquette and defined duties. As Blitstein put it, the "court of Jiankang" was correspondingly a "physical and symbolic space," simultaneously "unified and fragmented." Something similar could be said of the early imperial Chinese court, with the important caveat that we cannot assume a consensus about the nature of the norms and duties that bound it together. Indeed, if anything, they changed significantly over the course of Western Han. It was the forging of these social and institutional norms that created what we call the "Han court." Such norms included more than just court ritual codes and regulations, though they are an important part of the story. See chapters 1 and 2, as well as Gan Huaizhen 2003, 79–116.

25. It was arguably central to the work of sociologist and historian Norbert Elias (1897–1990), the influential and perhaps inadvertent founder of the field. "Inadvertent," since Elias was at least initially not interested in the court per se but in its critical but unrecognized role in forming modern nation-states. He articulated this argument in *The Civilizing Process* ([1969] 2000) (*Über den Prozess der Zivilisation* [1936–39]). However, Elias also emphasized the capacity of court protocol and space to uphold royal power in a manner that did not require "harder" forms of political control, his ideal type being the court of Louis XIV at Versailles (see also Elias [1969] 2006). The most thorough analysis and critique of Elias, focusing particularly on his (mis)treatment of Versailles, comes in Duindam 1994. For a concise overview

of Elias's work, including its complicated publication history, see D. Smith 2009.

26. See Duindam 2003, 10.

27. This fact received cross-cultural, comparative attention in Knechtges and Vance 2005.

28. R. Smith 2007, 163. The volume in which Smith's essay appears (Spawforth 2007) is one of the few to take a serious look at monarchical courts in ancient empires, including the Han (Van Ess 2007). Several of the articles in the book address the gap between representation and institutional practice, but Smith's highlighted the problem in the clearest terms.

29. The precise spaces indicated by both *chao* and *ting* remain debated. It is not clear that in pre-imperial texts *chao* referred to a roofed space and *ting* to an attached, outdoor "courtyard," even though that became the standard understanding beginning in the Han period. For example, see *Zuozhuan*, Lord Zhao 28.4 (4:1297) which describes three people sharing a meal in a *ting* during the winter, when cold temperatures might not have encouraged outdoor eating (cf. Durrant et al. 2016, 3:1693). For a detailed discussion, see Lu Zhongfa 2005. Note that the distinction between *chao* and *miao* ("temple") is unclear in many sources: the former is an orthographic variation of the latter in early bronze inscriptions, while the "Palaces and Villas" (Gong di) chapter of the *Erya* (late third century BCE?) defines *miao* as a building with eastern and western wings but does not mention specific sacrificial or religious functions. A parallel case is *gong*[a] ("palace"), which in both pre-imperial and early imperial sources could mean "palace" or "temple" (See Kern 2009, 156–60). Li 2001–2, 3–14, argued that *gong*[a] in Western Zhou bronze inscriptions also could refer to administrative offices. *Lai chao* is found throughout the *Annals* (Chunqiu). For *bu ting*, which in the *Zuozhuan* seem to imply rebellious intent on the part of vassal lords, see *Zuozhuan* Lord Yin 10.3 (1:68-9; Durrant et al. 2016, 1:57) and Lord Cheng 12.2 (2:856; Durrant et al. 2016, 2:796n243, 797). In the *Odes*, see "Han yi" (#261) for *bu ting*, while "Chang wu" (#263) speaks of groups "coming to court" (*lai ting*) in obeisance (Waley and Allen 1996, 277, 283). This positive sense of *ting*, however, is not found elsewhere. Moreover, in most texts *ting*, unlike *chao*, does not take an object.

30. The "Duo shi" chapter of the *Documents* includes the following line: "From the Xia some were recommended for consideration at the king's court, while some served the many officials." The precise relationship between court and officials in this passage is unclear. See *Shangshu zhuzi suoyin* 1995, 42/38/24; Gu Jiegang and Liu Qiyu 2005, 3:1519n9.

31. See, e.g., *Guoyu* (compiled ca. third century BCE?), "Yue yu" chapter (*Guoyu zhuzi suoyin* 1999, 8.7/124/4); *Yu Liaozi*, "Zhan quan" chapter (*Bingshu zhuzi suoyin* 1992, B12/27/17); *Shiji* 6.628, 129.3271. Note that both *Shiji* passages distinguish the *langmiao* from the "court" (*queting* or *chaoting*), while the latter passage implicitly contrasts the "plans" (*mou*) of the *langmiao* from the formal court debates. Neither the *Guoyu* nor the *Yu Liaozi*, however, clearly distinguish the *langmiao* from the court.

32. See, e.g., *Hanshu* 45.2168, in which Wu Pi (fl. 122 BCE) blurs the boundaries between *Han ting*, *chaoting*, and "All Under Heaven." *Shanyu ting*, referring to the court of the leader of the Xiongnu confederation, also appears regularly in the *Hanshu*. Importantly, the few instances of *Qin ting* in early texts use *ting* in its spatial sense: for instance, the story of Shen Baoxu, who "stood in the court of Qin [*Qin ting*] and cried day and night" (*Shiji* 66.2177). These observations thus support the argument by Wang Zijin (2011) that "Han court" (Han chao), as a term indicating the entire Han polity, does not seem to have emerged until during and after the reign of Wudi (r. 141–87 BCE). They do not, however, support Wang's tendency to read later commentators as transparently reflecting Han-period concepts or his claim that *chao* came to mean "nation" (*guojia*) during late Western Han.

33. The *Duduan* (compiled ca. 190 CE) claims *chaoting* referred to the emperor's location at any given time, allowing speakers to equivocate regarding where the ruler made his capital. In other words, it casts "the court" as a term with *no* specific spatial referent, a meaning that did not exist until the Han period (see *Duduan, juan* 1 in *Yakuchū Seikei Zakki, Dokudan* 2000, 212). For *Han chao* as a term for the empire and a historical period, see *Lun heng* (comp. ca. 70 CE), "Chao qi" chapter (*Lunheng jijie* 1962, 1:284).

34. Bastid-Bruguière (2013) emphasized the word *chao* always had a weaker social valence than equivalent terms in European languages (court, *cour*, *corte*, etc). This study does not contradict Bastid-Bruguière's point but emphasizes that such a social valence, however weak, nonetheless *did* eventually emerge in Chinese during the first centuries of imperial rule, and that this development was closely linked to institutional, social, and rhetorical changes at court.

35. For a similar point made in the Roman imperial context, see Paterson 2007.

36. Ch'ü 1972.

37. According to the imperial census of 2 CE, the *registered* population of Chang'an and its surrounding metropolitan region numbered 682,000. For a detailed discussion of this figure, see Nylan 2015b, 46n64. On the basis of administrative documents excavated from a tomb near Yinwan, Jiangsu, dating to after 11 BCE, the number of officials serving in the central government in Chang'an has been estimated at around 30,000 (Loewe 2004, 70). The little information that exists suggests what we might assume: a general increase in the size of central government bureaus in the capital over the course of Western Han. For instance, according to the *Han jiu yi*, a now fragmented compilation by Wei Hong (25–57 CE), the number of personnel working under the chancellor (*chengxiang*) had increased from 15 in the opening days of Western Han to 382 by 117 BCE. See Sun Xingyan and Zhou Tianyou (1990) 2008, 68; Bielenstein 1980, 8. Of course, not all of these officials, probably not even a majority, would have had regular access to all imperial palaces and high ministerial bureaus. Conversely, no doubt many did who are not included in this figure. Such problems are a good reminder that the categories of "courtier" (whatever that word might mean, for there is no clear equivalent in classical Chinese) and "official" overlap significantly but

are not necessarily coterminous. "The court" and "central government" are not the same thing, but our sources are so overwhelmingly biased in favor of the latter that it is quite difficult to understand the social and institutional life of the former as a distinct entity.

38. Loewe (1981) emphasized this point. As many scholars have highlighted, debates about state sacrifices proved contentious throughout Western Han, arguably reaching a height during the last few decades of the dynasty, which witnessed several major attempts to reform sacrificial practice. On this topic, see Tian Tian 2015a, 2015b as well as the discussion in chapter 2. For an episodic history of imperial ancestral sacrifices from Qin through Eastern Han, one that highlights the gaps and connections between ritual theory and practice, see Brashier (2011, 102–83).

39. Bielenstein 1980, 143. As Loewe (2004, 113) put it, active participation on the part of the emperor in governing the empire was "exceptional rather than normal." For a critique of "despotism" and "autocracy," especially on the application of these terms to Japanese and Chinese politics and history during nineteenth-century imperialist struggles, see Hou Xudong 2008.

40. See Loewe 1981.

41. On this point, see Liu Qingzhu 2004.

42. Loewe (1999a, 989–90) pointed out that the years 221 to around 202 BCE saw the "rapid succession" of three forms of government: the Qin established an "emperor" in charge of territory organized into commanderies and counties (*jun xian*); Xiang Yu (d. 202 BCE) installed a puppet ruler with the title *di*, while taking the title "overlord king" (*bawang*) with eighteen subordinate but autonomous kingdoms; and Gaozu combined the emperor-commandery model with the semi-autonomous regional kingdoms. For recent studies of the commanderies and counties, see Kamiya Masakazu 2009; You Yifei 2013. The latter persuasively argued that some early Western Han kingdoms eliminated the old Qin commanderies contained within their borders (You Yifei 2013, 201–78).

43. This is the impression given by the early Western Han statutes and ordinances excavated from Zhangjiashan. See Chen Suzhen 2011, 83–94.

44. The sole exception was the southern kingdom of Changsha, which was ruled by a non-Liu household member until 157 BCE.

45. See Tatemi Satoshi (2012, esp. 21–22), which provides a table and discussion of different rebellions, attempted coups, and other intrigues regarding imperial succession throughout Western Han.

46. For the kings in late Western Han, see Vankeerberghen 2015.

47. When Xiao He, Gaozu's top official and most trusted adviser, received his title and ranking as the highest of all nobles, some supporters complained the rank was unjustified since Xiao had not achieved military merit. Gaozu rebuffed these complaints, but the story shows Xiao was the exception proving the rule: only supporters with successful military service became nobles. See *Shiji* 53.2015; *Hanshu* 39.2008.

48. These responsibilities became increasingly important over the Western Han, and from the reign of Wendi (r. 180–157 BCE) included payments

of gold for brewing sacrificial wine. See Tatemi Satoshi 2009. On the wine payments in particular, for which 106 nobilities were revoked in 112 BCE on charges of submitting insufficient or low quality gold, see Loewe 2004, 294.

49. The numbers of nobilities in this table are taken from Loewe (2004, 290, 391–93). Loewe based his tables and lists on information from the three *Hanshu* tables of nobilities (those given to royal sons, for merit, and for favoritism).

50. Loewe 2004, 315.

51. These ministerial-level posts are collectively called the "Nine Ministers" (*jiuqing*) in our sources, though the term is misleading because fully ten ministerial posts were ranked at fully 2,000 bushels, just below the chancellor and imperial counselor.

52. See n40 above.

53. Fukui Shigemasa 1988, 10. See also Loewe 2004, 114. As Fukui demonstrated, by late Western Han emperors mostly solicited recommendations in response to natural disasters or other disturbing events. Only one type of recommendation, for candidates deemed *xiaolian* (i.e., men with a sense of "family responsibility and integrity"), were given annually, starting from around the late 130s BCE. Most commonly these men were appointed as "gentlemen-at-arms" (*lang*), from which they might hope to gain promotion to higher posts. Bielenstein (1980, 134–35) estimated that by the last century of Western Han these *xiaolian* recommendations yielded 250 to 300 candidates per year. For an overview of all recruitment practices, see Loewe 2004, 119–54.

54. *Hanshu* 19a.727.

55. As Liu Pak-yuen ([1986] 1998) discussed in detail, the superintendent of guards was in charge of security at the perimeters of palace complexes; the superintendent of the Imperial Household managed security within the complexes themselves; and the director of the Lesser Treasury guarded the more private areas in which the emperor and imperial consorts resided. A system of registries kept track of who was allowed entry into different areas.

56. In a 202 BCE edict, Gaozu ordered that sons of nobles who settled in the capital region instead of returning home would receive twice the length of tax exemption (*Hanshu* 1.54). Over time many prominent families were also required to relocate to the Chang'an region and settle in towns established around imperial burial sites. The importance of these "mausoleum towns" in solidifying Han power can hardly be overemphasized (see *Shiji* 99.2719-20; Yoshinami Takashi 1976).

57. Perhaps the most impressive of such studies is the Song dynasty antiquarian Cheng Dachang's (1123–1195) *Yonglu* (Records of the Yong Region) (see Cheng Dachang 2002). Cheng never visited the old Chang'an region, but many of his descriptions are remarkably close to the archaeological record.

58. For an overview of archaeological evidence for Chang'an, see Liu Qingzhu and Li Yufang 2003. For Weiyang Palace, see Zhongguo Shehui Kexue Yuan Kaogu Yanjiusuo 1996. For Gui Palace, see Zhongguo Shehui Kexue Yuan Kaogu Yanjiusuo and Nihon Nara Kokuritsu Bunkazai Kenkyūjo

2007. No comprehensive excavation report of Changle Palace exists, but see these articles: Liu Zhendong and Zhang Jianfeng 2006; Zhongguo Shehui Kexue Yuan Kaogu Yanjiusuo 2006; Zhongguo Shehui Kexue Yuan Kaogu Yanjiusuo 2011. Liu Rui (2007 and 2011) argued, contrary to maps provided by excavators, that Changle Palace did not extend north of an east-west Chang'an avenue running between Bacheng Gate and Zhicheng Gate. According to Liu, foundations unearthed north of this avenue were likely part of Mingguang Palace, which he further argued could not have been located so far in the northwest corner of the city.

59. Beard 2015, 33 and *passim* emphasized that Rome did not begin to transform into the marbled splendor we imagine today until perhaps the mid-first century BCE, all the while noting the difficulty of discussing early architecture and public works projects, since later writers tended to exaggerate their grandness and significance (e.g., the sixth century BCE drainage system later called the Cloaca Maxima, or "Great Drain").

60. This point receives detailed treatment in Tang Xiaofeng 2015.

61. One partial exception might be the *Huainanzi* (comp. 139 BCE), since that text was compiled at the royal court of Liu An and presented to the imperial court. The rhetorical patterns in that text are quite complicated, however, and it certainly provided no systematic descriptions of a "court." For the political background to the *Huainanzi*, see Vankeerberghen 2001; Major et al. 2010, 1–13. Our earliest fully extant description of the imperial court and its institutions is *Duduan*, composed by Cai Yong (133–192). While *Duduan* offers a significant amount of valuable information about the court, some of its definitions are extremely laconic and belie the many changes to court institutions that occurred over the course of the two Han dynasties (see n36 above). For a close study of portions of the *Duduan* describing official court documents, along with detailed analysis of their composition, transmission, and management, see Giele 2006.

62. Dubs (1938) first formulated the "victory of Han Confucianism" model. For more than two decades, scholars have pointed out from multiple perspectives that it is probably not appropriate to translate *ru* as "Confucian." As Nylan (1999b, 18–19) put it, *ru* could mean (a) "classicist," referring to people who had mastered old precedents, rituals, and music; (b) a "Confucian" who self-identified as an adherent of the way of Confucius; and (c) a potential or actual "government official." See also Zufferey 2003; Nylan 2009, esp. 735–41.

63. See, e.g., Nylan 1999a; Cheng 2001; Brashier 2011, esp. 6–18; Chin 2014; Tian Tian 2015b.

64. The Tang historian Liu Zhiji (661–721) identified fifteen different people who were said to have added material after the periods covered by Sima Qian (Loewe 2000, 486). For detailed overviews of the evidence for different *Shiji* authors and the early transmission of the text, see Lü Shihao 2009; Klein 2010, 384–445; Van Ess 2015. Van Ess's essay includes a table (497) summarizing the different theories of authorship for twenty-seven chapters or major passages added to the *Shiji* after Sima Qian died.

65. Hulsewé 1993a, 129–30.

66. On these problems, see Giele 2010.

67. The first is a cache of wooden documents, probably dating to the reign of Wang Mang, found near the Front Hall (Qian dian) of Weiyang Palace. See Hsing I-tien 2000. The second is a collection of some sixty thousand bone tags recovered from the remains of a building, probably a kind of storehouse, in the northwest quadrant of Weiyang Palace. For theories regarding the tags' function, see Barbieri-Low 2001, 3–5. For archives and the emergence of private libraries in Western Han, see Nylan 2011 (34n11, 37–47). On libraries and textual loss in early and medieval China, see Drège 1991.

68. On this point, see many of the essays in Nylan and Vankeerberghen 2015.

CHAPTER 1

1. *Shiji* 57.2079; *Hanshu* 40.2062. The accounts of Zhou Yafu are almost exactly the same in the *Shiji* and *Hanshu*. On the *shangfang*, see *Hanshu* 19a.731; Barbieri-Low 2001, 65–67.

2. The term for central government used here is *xian guan*. For discussions of the term, including this specific passage, see Loewe 2008, esp. 519–27. According to Loewe, despite statements in commentaries, the term probably does not refer to the emperor.

3. *Shiji* 57.2079; *Hanshu* 40.2062.

4. At the same time, concerns about posthumous insurrection are not necessarily out of the question. For analysis of examples from a later context, see Bokenkamp 2007, 60–94.

5. The *Shiji* implies Jingdi was of two minds regarding Zhou Yafu. On the one hand, Zhou was the son of one of Gaozu's most important generals and led the effort to eliminate the Lü clan and install Jingdi's father, Wendi, as emperor. Zhou also played an important role in suppressing the 154 BCE rebellion of the kingdoms. Jingdi thus owed his throne to the efforts of Zhou Yafu and his family. On the other, Jingdi's mother, the powerful Empress Dowager Dou, hated Zhou since he refused her plea in 154 BCE to rush to Liang and aid her favorite son, King Xiao, when his kingdom was attacked. Zhou had also opposed Jingdi's plan to ennoble an uncle (at the request of the empress dowager) and recently surrendered leaders of the Xiongnu, stating that bestowing such titles to people who had performed no meritorious acts went against precedents established by Gaozu. After Zhou retired in 147, Jingdi was apparently all too happy to pursue his vulnerable former chancellor when the opportunity arose. See *Shiji* 2076–79.

6. For state funerals, see Loewe 1999b. On routes in and around Chang'an used to parade the clothing and other effects of deceased emperors, see Jiao Nanfeng 2010.

7. *Shiji* 106.2834; *Hanshu* 35.1915.

8. According to the *Shiji*, after a man pilfered a jade ring from a shrine to Gaozu he was investigated for breaking the "statutes" (*lü*) prohibiting stealing "imperial goods [*yu wu*] from the imperial ancestral shrines" (*Shiji*

102.2755). The *Hanshu* version of this story does not refer to a statute (*Hanshu* 50.2311).

9. *Hanshu* 63.3731. More precisely, the passage states that Empress Xu offered "chariots, robes, and imperial goods." The language shows the extent to which, by Han times, words associated with chariots had come to signify luxury goods enjoyed by the imperial household. This is even true of the word *yu* (imperial), which also means "to drive a chariot."

10. *Xinyu*, "Zi zhi" chapter (*Xinyu zhuzi suoyin* 1995, 7/11/29). See also L'Haridon and Feuillas (2012, 54–55), which noted that some editions eliminate the negative in the final sentence, making it "With commoners, they use it to craft their implements."

11. Scholars have long debated the role of sumptuary rules, particularly with regard to the regional kings. The Zhangjiashan statutes demonstrate conclusively that sumptuary regulations certainly existed, but material evidence for their actual enforcement is spotty. In an exhaustive analysis of all excavated Western Han royal tombs, Liu Rui and Liu Tao (2010) argued that there is no archaeological evidence that Western Han kings followed a consistent set of regulations in the orientation, design, and siting of royal mausoleums.

12. This shift in Western Han discourse about the regional kings reflects other court discussions and debates about ritual. For instance, as Joachim Gentz has shown, the rise of the *Gongyang* interpretive account of the *Annals* (Chunqiu) tacked between emphasizing ritual regulations and, when they failed or did not apply, a moral judgment based on those regulations. The *Gongyang*'s message was thus "three-dimensional" and could simultaneously "bolster the ruler's legitimacy" and "guide, moderate, and . . . restrict the ruler" (Gentz 2015, 116–17).

13. *Shiji* 106.2834; *Hanshu* 35.1915.

14. Based on current evidence, the Zhangjiashan statutes and ordinances seem to have been enforced only within the commanderies under Han control. The regional kingdoms probably used their own laws, though quite likely there was overlap between their legal systems and that of the Han.

15. On this point, see Loewe 2010b, 297.

16. For a detailed overview, including discussion of salary lists from Eastern Han, see Bielenstein 1980, 125–26.

17. The equivalent salary ranks receive detailed treatment in Yan Buke 2009, esp. 408–68.

18. For a translation of the "Statutes on Salary Ranks," one section of a larger collection of legal regulations entitled "Statutes and Ordinances of the Second Year [of Empress Lü]" (Er nian lü ling), hereafter *ENLL*, see Barbieri-Low and Yates 2015, 2:962–81. References to the Zhangjiashan manuscript strip numbers for *ENLL* are keyed to the sequence in Zhangjiashan Ersiqi Hao Han Mu Zhujian Zhengli Xiao Zu 2006. The very last entry in the "Statutes on Salary Ranks" lists the household assistants (*jia cheng*), with a rank of 300 bushels, of four imperial princesses otherwise unattested in early texts. It is impossible to know why these attendants appear at the end of the statutes. Some have argued that the princesses were

children of Empress Dowager Lü, who was in charge of the government at the time, which would support the interpretation of Barbieri-Low and Yates that the empress revised the "Statutes on Salary Ranks" in order to support officials under the empress dowager's command. As Barbieri-Low and Yates noted (1082–83n427), however, not all scholars agree that the princesses were her children.

19. *ENLL* #451–64; Barbieri-Low and Yates 2015, 2:969–77.

20. Inner coffins refer to the coffins that actually held the body of the deceased. They were often deposited in one or several outer coffins, which also had space for interring funerary goods.

21. *ENLL* #283–84; translation follows, with some modification, Barbieri-Low and Yates 2015, 2:767.

22. *ENLL* #284; Peng Hao et al. 2007, 209n10; Barbieri-Low and Yates 2015, 2:775n14.

23. *ENLL* #289; Barbieri-Low and Yates 2015, 2:769. It remains unclear whether all people holding honors regularly received coffins and robes for their funerals, or whether the regulations were enacted only when a particular order holder received such a gift.

24. *ENLL* #291; Barbieri-Low and Yates 2015, 2:769.

25. For the former, see Yan Buke 2009, 370–406. For the latter, see Yoshinami Takashi 2003. Barbieri-Low and Yates (2015, 2:620n7) followed Yan Buke's interpretation, that *huan huang di* refers to people serving the emperor "privately" in the palace without a salary rank.

26. On the princesses, see Bielenstein 1980, 107; Barbieri-Low and Yates 2015, 2:666n65.

27. *ENLL* #295; Barbieri-Low and Yates 2015, 2:771.

28. *Hanshu* 97a.3935.

29. See, e.g., the description of Shusun Tong's court audience ceremony, designed for Gaozu, in which "civil officials" (*wen guan*) faced west while generals and nobles faced east (*Shiji* 99.2723).

30. Note that the "Wang zhi" chapter of the *Liji* (compiled first century CE?) uses the word *shi* ("looked to"), not *bi*, to describe a series of equivalencies between different orders of honor, salaries, officials, and sacrificial duties (*Liji jijie* [1989] 2007, 1:347).

31. Cf. Yan Buke 2009, 370.

32. The difference between *zhonglang* and *langzhong* is not entirely clear. Loewe (2000, 760, 764) rendered both as "gentlemen of the palace." A note by the early third-century CE commentator Su Lin interprets *zhonglang as xingzhong lang* (gentleman of the inspection zone) (*Hanshu* 2.86), but mention of an "inspection zone" for early Western Han is surely anachronistic (see chapter 3). The *Hanshu* refers to *langzhong* much more frequently than *zhonglang*, though both positions receive mention in the *Hanshu* "Table of the Many Offices and Ministerial Posts" (Bai guan gong qing biao) (*Hanshu* 19a.727), and we do read regularly of officials serving as a "leader of the gentlemen of the palace" (*zhonglang jiang*). While the *Hanshu* "Table of the Many Offices" gives 600 bushels and 300 bushels as the respective salary ranks of the *zhonglang* and *langzhong*, in this passage at least they seem to be treated in equal fashion.

33. This office of the director of the kitchens is otherwise unattested in early texts, though Ying Shao's (ca. 140–before 204 CE) commentary stated that the director of the kitchens was one of five "directors" (*shang*); others included the director of robes (*shang yi*) and the director of mats (*shang xi*). Ru Chun (fl. mid-third century CE) stated that *shang* (director) was reserved for offices in charge of items owned by or directly associated with the emperor. See *Hanshu* 2.85.

34. *Hanshu* 2.85.

35. *Hanshu* 19a.727.

36. *Hanshu* 19a.727.

37. *Hanshu* 19a.726.

38. *Hanshu* 19a.797.

39. For a more detailed discussion of this point, see Yan Buke 2009, 238–47.

40. See *Hanshu* 19a.741.

41. See, e.g., Loewe (1986, 144) which mentioned the administrative changes but did not include sumptuary regulations among Jingdi's postrebellion reforms.

42. *Hanshu* 5.145.

43. For a more detailed description, see Habberstad 2014, 86–88.

44. Regarding the changes to administrative officials in the kingdoms, the "Annals of Jingdi" mentions only the change from *chengxiang* to *xiang*. See *Hanshu* 5.148.

45. No doubt the most famous is the story of Shusun Tong's court audience ceremony (*chao*; see *Shiji* 99.2723), analyzed in greater detail in chapter 2. For less grand examples that still emphasize the critical role of performance and comportment, see the *Shiji* "Account of Master Li and Lu Jia" (Li Sheng Lu Jia liezhuan), which describes advisers upbraiding would-be rulers for receiving their advice while reclining or with legs crossed (*Shiji* 97.2692, 2697).

46. See *Shiji* 8.343, 347, 348.

47. *Shiji* 8.381. Statements elsewhere attribute Gaozu's success to making generals and supporters realize they would all "share the benefits" if Han prevailed. See, e.g., *Shiji* 97.2695.

48. On loyalty in pre-imperial times, with an emphasis on the rise during the Zhanguo period of reciprocal rather than hierarchical relations between rulers and ministers, see Pines 2002.

49. Chavannes 1895–1905, 2:404.

50. *Shiji* 9.393–94.

51. A similar phrase is found in the "Commentary on the Appended Phrases, Part Two" (Xi ci xia) chapter of the *Changes* (Yijing). Perhaps significantly, the particular section of the "Xi ci xia" that contains this phrase describes actions taken by the legendary sage emperors Huangdi, Yao, and Shun when they came to power. Specifically, the three rulers "unblocked the [process of] transformation" (*tong qi bian*), an action that resonates with the cyclical transfer of political power described here in the appraisal. See Lynn 1994, 78.

52. *Shiji* 8.394.

53. The appraisal to the "Annals of Emperor Gaozu" states that Han took as its power the color red, which was linked to a cycle of powers organized under the *wuxing* rubric. As the *Hanshu* appraisal concludes, with this action Han "accorded with the power of fire" and "achieved a heavenly concordance" (*Hanshu* 1b.82). As many scholars have noted, Han did not actually take red as its color or fire as its power when Gaozu first came to the throne. Rather, debates about which power Han should take continued for most of the first century of Western Han rule. This larger story about the development of the *wuxing* and other cyclical understandings of historical and natural processes provides one way to interpret the *Shiji* appraisal. See, e.g., Loewe 2011, 275–86. As Loewe noted, some commentators associated the appraisals with the ideas of Dong Zhongshu, who wrote a response to an imperial rescript that associates Xia, Shang, and Zhou with loyalty, respect, and refinement, respectively (*Hanshu* 56.2518). Moreover, the appraisal resonates with other sections of the *Shiji* as well as other Han texts that saw a cyclical relationship between qualities of "substance" (*zhi*) and "refinement" (*wen*), perhaps inspired by a famous *Analects* passage (*Lunyu* 3.5). For one example, see the *Liji* (comp. first century CE?), "Biao ji" chapter, (*Liji jijie* [1989] 2007, 51.1309–11). For a summary and analysis, see Chen Suzhen 2011, 190–98. Neither Loewe nor Chen, however, addressed the *Shiji* appraisal's final statement about sumptuary regulations.

54. "Heavenly concordance" (*tian tong*) concludes the appraisal to the "Annals of Gaozu" (*Hanshu* 1b.82).

55. *Shiji* 8.394.

56. The idea might not be far-fetched, for "reverence" (*jing*) and "refinement" (*wen*) were both used regularly to describe ideal types of comportment when performing ceremonies, including ritual audiences and funerary offerings. On *jing*, see Csikszentmihalyi 2009; on *wen*, see Kern 2001.

57. Court audiences are noted regularly in the *Annals* (Chunqiu). The phrases "yellow canopies" (*huang wu*) and "pennants on the left side" (*zuo dao*) are unattested in pre-imperial texts. The *Mozi* describes several auspicious signs foretelling King Wen of Zhou's victory over the Shang, including the statement "The earth produced a *sheng huang*." Early commentators gave different interpretations of *sheng huang* (literally "chariot team in yellow"), but most understood it as an auspicious horse-like creature, associated with legendary rulers, that conferred immortality. See *Mozi*, "Fei gong xia" chapter (*Mozi jijie* 1996, 5.142). Ying Shao offered the same interpretation in his commentary to the song "The Rising and Setting Sun" (Ri chu ru), which was performed in the imperial suburban sacrifices and included in the *Hanshu* "Treatise on Rites and Music" (*Hanshu* 22.1059–60).

58. Note, for instance, that the list of Qin kings appended to the *Shiji* "Basic Annals of the First Emperor" (Qin Shihuang ben ji) regularly indicates where the kings were buried. According to the list, the first Qin ruler to be buried in a "mausoleum" (*ling*) was King Huiwen (r. 338–311 BCE) (*Shiji* 6.288), though some would date the first emergence of mounds over Qin tombs somewhat earlier. In general, archaeologists date the emergence

of tomb mounds to the late Chunqiu period, making Qin a relatively late adopter of the custom. See Liu 2012.

59. Cf. Loewe (1999b, 48), which emphasized the strict enforcement of injunctions against using a yellow canopied chariot.

60. *Shiji* 7.326.

61. For a detailed discussion see Brindley 2015, 193–220.

62. *Shiji* 97.3637.

63. *Shiji* 58.2081. Liu Yi is also occasionally called Liu Sheng (see *Hanshu* 48.2264).

64. *Shiji* 58.2082.

65. *Shiji* 17.824–26.

66. *Shiji* 58.2082.

67. *Shiji* 58.2083.

68. *Shiji* 58.2083.

69. *Shiji* 58.2086.

70. *Shiji* 58.2089.

71. *Hanshu* 47.2220.

72. Loewe 2000, 316.

73. *Shiji* 59.2096; *Hanshu* 53.2414.

74. *Shiji* 59.2096; *Hanshu* 53.2414.

75. *Hanshu* 53.2417.

76. *Hanshu* 53.2417.

77. *Shiji* 59.2096.

78 *Shiji* 59.2104.

79. See, for instance, the *Shiji* chapter "Account of Yuan Ang and Chao Cuo" (Yuan Ang Chao Cuo liezhuan) (*Shiji* 101.2737–47), which calls attention to the fact that Yuan Ang cited ritual regulations in order to take down his enemies, even though his own comportment was hardly beyond reproach. For a more detailed discussion, see Habberstad 2014, 132–35.

80. For consideration of this question in reference to another *Shiji* chapter, see Nylan 2015a.

81. *Hanshu* 70.2436.

82. See *Xunzi*, "Ai gong" chapter (*Xunzi jian shi* 1996, 31.409; Hutton 2014, 336).

83. See Liu Rui and Liu Tao 2010.

CHAPTER 2

1. Some Xiongnu advisers reportedly supported the audience as a strategy to secure Han support against Jihoushan's enemies (*Hanshu* 94b.3797).

2. Changping was a few dozen miles north of Chang'an (Ru Chun (fl. mid-third century CE) claimed 50 *li* in his *Hanshu* commentary), across the Wei River but still south of the Jing River.

3. Chiyang Palace was north of the Jing River. The important point here seems to be that the *shanyu* stayed overnight closer to Chang'an than did Xuandi. The *shanyu* and his entourage thus would have observed the

emperor's procession as it reached the slope of Changping, before the entire party continued south to view the emperor's passage over the Wei River Bridge.

4. *Danghu* were Xiongnu "high functionaries," but their role and duties are unclear (Hulsewé and Loewe 1979, 197n712).

5. *Hanshu* 8.271.

6. See, e.g., Yu 1967, 45; di Cosmo 2002, 206; Li Dalong 2014, 46–47.

7. For instance, the *Hanshu* account of Dayuan (Ferghana) ends with a description of the area west of Wusun to Anxi (Persia), noting that while the region had traditionally been under the sway of the Xiongnu, "when the *shanyu* Huhanye came for his court audience with Han, later all held Han in high esteem" (*Hanshu* 96a.3896). Translation follows, with some changes, Hulsewé and Loewe 1979, 137–38.

8. Just five years later, in 46 BCE, Han territory actually began to shrink when Yuandi (r. 49–33 BCE) decided to abandon the rebellious Hainan Island, which first came under Han control in 110 BCE. See *Hanshu* 64b.2830–35. For a discussion of the political and policy background to the Hainan debate, see Loewe 2012–13, esp. 390–92.

9. Generally speaking, during the Han period addressing somebody by given name (*ming*) rather than a courtesy name (*zi*) emphasized a speaker's higher social rank or indicated that the speaker wished to denigrate the addressee. See Brashier 2014, 77–82.

10. For a detailed study, see Okayasu Isamu 1987.

11. See chapter 3, n28.

12. Bodde 1975, 135–61. Bodde argued that the "presentation of accounts" (*shang ji*) probably continued to occur in the tenth month, even after the 104 BCE calendar reforms moved the court audience to the first month.

13. Commentators have offered different interpretations for *jiu bin*. The rendering "nine ranks" here follows Wei Zhao's (204–273 CE) commentary, which interprets the phrase as referring to nine different ranks as they are recorded in the *Rites of Zhou* (Zhouli) (*Shiji* 99.2723).

14. *Shiji* 99.2723.

15. *Shiji* 23.1159.

16. *Shiji* 58.2082.

17. According to his account in the *Shiji*, after his son died in Chang'an at the hands of Wendi's (180–157 BCE) son, the king of Wu, Liu Pi, stopped attending the court audience on the pretext of illness. A furious Wendi bound and interrogated an envoy from Wu before eventually giving Liu Pi special dispensation to not travel to Chang'an for the court audience. *Shiji* 106.2823–24.

18. Wang Yue (obtained *juren* degree in 1705) and Xu Kefan (fl. ca. early eighteenth century) offered this interpretation in their "Du Shiji shi biao." See *Er shi wu shi bu bian* 1937, 1:14.

19. On the evidence in received texts for written regulations governing the court audience, see Hulsewé 1955, 37, 66–67n44. A collection of Western Han legal manuscripts from tomb 336 at Zhangjiashan contained a text entitled "Statutes on Court Ceremonial" (Chao lü), but transcriptions and

photographs remain unpublished. For a short discussion, see Peng Hao 1993, 171.

20. *Hanshu* 78.3282.

21. Mao #304 ("Chang fa"). Translation partially follows Waley and Allen 1996, 321. The translation of the first couplet, however, follows commentary provided by Yan Shigu, who glossed *sui* as *bian* (throughout). Xiang-tu is understood to have been the grandson of the Shang founder. See *Hanshu* 78.3282.

22. *Hanshu* 78.3282.

23. On the "tributary orders," see Chin 2014, 14–18. Okayasu Isamu (1987), focusing entirely on the meaning of the ritual terminology used in the actual audience, did not discuss the proposal by Huang and Yu.

24. *Hanshu* 78.3282. The final line refers to Hexagram 15, Modesty (Qian), from the *Changes* (Yi). The judgment statement and commentary on the judgment statement of Hexagram 15 extol the virtues of modest action by the ruler. See Lynn 1994, 229–30.

25. *Hanshu* 78.3282.

26. It is unclear from Xiao Wangzhi's statement whether treating the *shanyu* as a guest meant that he *necessarily* had to be put above the regional kings. However, given the opinion expressed by Huang and Yu immediately prior, the opposition is clear enough: Huang and Yu argued that the foreign *shanyu* was coming in submission and had to be put in a ritual position that reflected his greater distance, while Xiao argued that the *shanyu* had to be treated in a manner that avoided ritual obligations. Xiao implies, without stating outright, that putting the *shanyu* above the kings was one way to express that the leader was not being treated like a vassal.

27. Immediately prior to describing the debate, the "Account" notes that after Xiao was demoted from imperial counselor (*yushi dafu*) to senior tutor to the heir apparent (*taizi taifu*), Huang Ba replaced him in the imperial counselor position and eventually went on to become chancellor (*chengxiang*). Early in Xuandi's reign, Xiao was among the more strident critics of the Huo clan, which had monopolized power at court in the years after Wudi's death. When Xuandi came to the throne, Xiao was among the officials he promoted to circumvent Huo family members and ultimately assert control over the government (*Hanshu* 78.3273). Huang Ba and Yu Dingguo, by contrast, were not among those critics of the Huo clan. Indeed early in his career Yu was promoted by Huo Guang, the powerful Huo patriarch and head of government in the opening years of Xuandi's reign (*Hanshu* 71.3042). Despite these possibly different orientations toward the Huo clan and its elimination, no doubt the most consequential event in the early years of Xuandi's reign, the *Hanshu* does not provide evidence of a sustained rift between Xiao and Huang and Yu.

28. In support, Xiao cited a policy enacted in 97 BCE, late in the reign of Wudi, that allowed people convicted of a capital crime to pay 500,000 cash to lower their degree of punishment and thus escape death. According to Xiao, the scramble to secure such a large amount of money resulted in increased theft and disorder, which at times became so severe that military action was necessary to restore calm (*Hanshu* 78.3278).

29. *Hanshu* 78.3278.

30. *Hanshu* 78.3279.

31. Here, "central states" should probably be understood as the Han capital, or perhaps the empire. *Hanshu* 78.3280.

32. The phrase is found throughout the "Account of the Xiongnu," but for the struggle between Jihoushan and his rivals over the "court of the *shanyu*," see *Hanshu* 94b.3796.

33. *Hanshu* 94a.3790. This rival, named Xianxianchan, was connected to Jihoushan, being related to the wife of Jihoushan's father-in-law.

34. *Hanshu* 94a.3796.

35. Loewe 2004, 167.

36. Loewe 2004, 312.

37. See, e.g., *Shiji* 26.2057, 27.2068.

38. *Hanshu* 3.96.

39. For an overview of the sources, see Dubs 1944, 126–28. Brashier (2011, 114–23), provided a detailed discussion of the "wine-tribute scandal" and its place in the history of ancestral sacrifice during the Han.

40. *Hanshu* 6.187.

41. For instance, Chancellor Bing Ji reportedly warned his son that failure to be "reverent and careful" (*jing shen*) when performing ritual duties at the imperial ancestral temples would cost him his noble title (*Hanshu* 74.3148). See Tatemi Satoshi (2009) for a detailed discussion.

42. On the director of the Imperial Clan, see Bielenstein 1980, 41–43; Tatemi Satoshi 2012.

43. The evidence is limited. When Zhou Bo conspired to suppress the Lü clan and install Wendi on the throne, the director of guests managed to confiscate Lü Lu's seal and on the authority of that seal turn control of the Northern Army over to Zhou (*Shiji* 9.409; *Hanshu* 3.102). The *Hou Hanshu* "Treatise of the Many Offices" (Bai guan zhi) states that the superintendent of state visits disbursed ribbons and seals for the kings (*Hou Hanshu* 30.3583), but there is no evidence that he did so in early Western Han. See Kumagai Shigezō 2001, 79, 97.

44. *Hanshu* 12.145.

45. Only the *Shiji* records this change (*Shiji* 12.446). See Kumagai Shigezō 2001, 92–93.

46. Presumably these included both the mansions in Chang'an and those near Ganquan, which Wudi had constructed in 104 BCE.

47. *Hanshu* 19a.730.

48. *Hanshu* 19a.735.

49. *Hanshu* 94b.3798.

50. The twelve imperial annals of the *Hanshu* record only one gift of weapons: two swords in 76 BCE to the king of Guangling, Liu Xu (d. 54 BCE) (*Hanshu* 7.231). We cannot assume the *Hanshu* annals include all instances of imperial gifts, but since Liu Xu's swords made their way into the annals we can conclude that there was no proscription per se against recording gifts of weapons. More likely such martial items were simply much less common than the many gifts of rank, money, clothing, and so on that are

recorded in the annals; certainly the sheer number of weapons given to the *shanyu* in 51 BCE was anomalous. Note that the "Jin li" chapter of the *Rites* (Yili; comp. third century BCE?), probably the most important ritual text during Western Han, describes only gifts of robes and chariots from the Son of Heaven to his vassal lords.

51. The *Zi zhi tongjian* (1084 CE) gives the two opinions of Huang and Yu and Xiao, while ignoring, without comment, the unanimous "all" (*xian*) from the *Hanshu* "Annals." See *Xin jiao Zizhi tong jian zhu* 1974, *juan* 27, 2:885–86.

52. The word *wang* ("king") should be understood as referring to Xuandi, hence the translation "ruler." An alternative reading would understand *fei* as modifying the entirety of the sentence, thus "The *shanyu* is not added to the first-month calendar or treated as a ruler's guest." This interpretation, however, was convincingly refuted in Okayasu Isamu (1987, 34). As readers might have noticed, in the "Account of Xiao Wangzhi," Xiao calls the *shanyu* an "adversarial kingdom" (*di guo*). Here, however, the compiler of the "Annals" has replaced the phrase *di guo* with "guest of the ruler" (*wang zhe suo ke*). Elsewhere in his article (34–35), Okayasu presented convincing evidence that the statements should be understood as synonyms. However, Okayasu further pointed out that the "Bu chen" chapter of the Eastern Han text *Bai hu tong* quotes a line from the "Great Commentary of the *Documents*" (*Shangshu* dazhuan): "Those to whom the calendar is not applied are not treated as vassals by the ruler." "Adversarial realm," "guest," and "nonvassal" all seem to be synonyms. In this vein, note that the appraisal to the "Account of the Xiongnu" (yet a fourth source for the 51 BCE audience!) paraphrases Xiao Wangzhi's opinion, stating that Xiao said it would be "appropriate to use guest ritual [to receive the *shanyu*]" (*Hanshu* 94b.3833). The important point is that the compiler of the "Annals" changed the ceremonial action required of this guest status: now a foreign guest was supposed to be situated below the kings.

53. *Hanshu* 8.270.

54. *Hanshu* 8.270. The "Account of Xiao Wangzhi" also includes this edict.

55. Elsewhere in the *Hanshu*, Ban Gu paired Xuandi with Wudi as two rulers dedicated to "strengthening the authority of the ruler" (*Hanshu* 10.345).

56. See, e.g., the statement in Liu Xiang's memorial on ritual reform, from the "Treatise on Ritual and Music," which claimed that Liu's proposals would transform the unfinished work of Shusun Tong into a more timeless model (*Hanshu* 22.1034).

57. We know little about the schools called Xiangxu, which the *Mengzi* (late fourth–early third century BCE) in one passage characterized as referring to two different educational institutions (*xiang* and *xu*) from different historical periods. See *Mengzi*, "Teng wen gong shang" chapter, *Mengzi ben yi* 1996, 5.3, 147; *Mencius* 3A/3, in Lau 1970, 98–99.

58. *Analects* 9/19; translation follows Leys 1997, 41.

59. *Hanshu* 22.1035.

60. This emphasis on a copious but disordered collection of texts in imperial archives is hardly unique to the "Treatise on Ritual and Music." For

just one of many examples in Han writings, see the first lines of the *Hanshu* "Treatise on Arts and Letters" (Yi wen zhi) (*Hanshu* 30.1701).

61. For an analysis of Western Han legal history emphasizing new legal interpretations that regulated interpersonal relations, see Goldin (2012, esp. 6n16), which states that this process of "Confucianization" occurred "along specific ideological lines."

CHAPTER 3

1. *Hanshu* 82.3370. The adviser who offered this advice was Wang Feng (d. 22 BCE), Chengdi's maternal uncle, director of the Secretariat (*shangshu*), and effective head of the government. Wang Feng also said that the imperial family could escape the flood by boat.

2. Ying Shao (ca. 140–before 204 CE) identified Sishang as a town near the Wei River, which ran in a northeasterly direction north of Chang'an.

3. *Hanshu* 9.306–7.

4. Wang Zijin and Lü Zongli 2011, esp. 50–51, also distinguished between the flood, which seemed to have prompted Chengdi's edict, and the description of the girl Chen in the "Annals," but were probably too optimistic regarding the capacity of the story to illustrate the "social consciousness" of late Western Han Chang'an.

5. Note that the Heng Gate, located in the northwest corner of Chang'an, was one of the city's closest gates to the Wei River. In order to reach Weiyang Palace, Chen would have had to walk south from the gate for several kilometers, traveling between the eastern and western markets and the guard station that overlooked them, as well as between Gui Palace and villas and residences occupied by powerful residents. Chen's journey thus took her through the most important and exclusive areas of the capital.

6. *Hanshu* 27c(1).1474.

7. *Hanshu* 27c(1).1474–75.

8. As the "Treatise on the *Wuxing*" makes clear in the conclusion to this story, the "low people" were Chengdi's maternal relatives, the powerful men of the Wang clan. For a close analysis of the politics surrounding the Wang clan and the impact those politics had on institutional arrangements at and normative conceptions of the imperial court, see chapter 4. Sources suggest that the rhetorical point of the story of Chen Who-Carried-the-Bow became even clearer in the decades after Ban Gu compiled the *Hanshu*. For example, Xun Yue (148–209 CE), in his *Records of the Former Han* (Qian Han ji), made no mention of Chen's entry through the "side gate" attached to the Imperial Workshop (Shangfang). Rather, he wrote that Chen "entered into a hall gate in the female quarters of Weiyang Palace." By explicitly placing the point of entry in the female quarters of the palace, Xun more clearly emphasized the danger of consort families such as the Wang.

9. The dangerous connotation of Chen's name is clear enough without reference to other sources, but the "Treatise on the *Wuxing*" provided a more specific explanation, stating that the name Carried-the-Bow made the incident "akin to the omen of the mountain mulberry bow of the Zhou

household" (*Hanshu* 27c[1].1475). This omen refers to the story of Baosi, the favored consort of King You of Zhou. As described in Liu Xiang's (79/78–8 BCE) *Lie nü zhuan*, Baosi's mother was a young child consort of King You's father who became impregnated by a magical serpent. The king cast out Baosi, but she was adopted by a couple who sold mulberry bows and woven bamboo quivers. A common ditty at the time warned that the mulberry bow and quiver signaled the downfall of Zhou. The king tried to kill the couple, but they escaped. Eventually, Baosi grew up to be a beautiful woman who caught King You's attention after he came to the throne. Her famously extravagant and wicked behavior ultimately caused the collapse of the Western Zhou. See *Lie nü zhuan*, "Nie bi" (Depraved and Favored) chapter, *juan* 7 (*Lie nü zhuan zhuzi suoyin* 1994, 7/64/20–65/14; Kinney 2014, 138).

10. *Shiji* 6.256.

11. The best discussion of Shanglin Park's borders is Wang Shejiao 1995. Li Lingfu (2009, 46–47), compiled written and material evidence (mostly excavated seals) to argue that there were at least seven and possibly as many as twelve Qin imperial parks near Xianyang. The relationship between these parks is unknown, but none of the Qin seals Li identified contains the word *Shanglin*, which Li allowed might have been only a "general designation" for all of the Qin imperial parks south of the Wei River. See also Xu Weimin 2011, 161–66.

12. See *Shiji* 7.315. The *Shiji* passage suggests total devastation, but it strains credibility to think that every one of the many Qin palaces and temples in the Xianyang area burned to the ground.

13. For instance, archaeological evidence suggests that the Front Hall (Qian dian) of Weiyang Palace was none other than the Qin structure called Zhangtai, which had been one of the main audience halls used by Qin rulers for official ceremonies. See Zhongguo Shehui Kexue Yuan Kaogu Yanjiusuo 1996, 265.

14. The Southern Song scholar Cheng Dachang (2002, 24) emphasized this fact in his *Yonglu*.

15. Yong, an old cult site used by Qin rulers, housed a temple dedicated to the Five Lords (Wu di) that was in use from the reign of Gaozu.

16. For a map, see Tian Tian 2015b, 268.

17. For this argument, see Meguro Kyōko 2011. For a map indicating the First Emperor's progresses, see Tian Tian (2015b, 265), though Tian Tian highlighted differences in the frequency and duration of the First Emperor's and Wudi's journeys. Geertz (1983) explained the importance of royal progresses in establishing territorial control. Chang (2007) examined the topic in the Qing context.

18. In Taishan, the mansions were built in 110 BCE (*Shiji* 28.1398; *Hanshu* 25a.1236). The *Hanshu* records Wudi receiving accounts there in 106 BCE and 98 BCE (*Hanshu* 6.196, 6.204). See also Tian Tian 2015a, 192. The mansions at Ganquan were built in 104 BCE (*Shiji* 28.1402, 25b.1245), and according to the *Hanshu* Wudi held court audiences there in 97 BCE (*Hanshu* 6.205) and 87 BCE (*Hanshu* 6.211) and convened foreign dignitaries there in 94 BCE (*Hanshu* 6.206). See also Tian Tian 2015a, 170.

19. Meguro Kyōko 2011, 67. See also Tian Tian 2015b, 268.

20. See *Hanshu* 27a.1337.

21. For archaeological evidence of the imperial mint in Shanglin Park, see Jiang Baolian and Qian Jianming 2004.

22. See Luo Qingkang 1988.

23. For retrenchment in late Western Han, see Loewe 1974.

24. *Shiji* 8.385–86.

25. *Hanshu* 75.3175.

26. In fact, Yi Feng elided a much longer and more complicated history of palace construction. Ganquan in particular was an old Qin site that even Wendi visited on at least two different occasions (see *Hanshu* 4.119, 123). Wudi did, however, greatly expand Ganquan. For more details, see Yao Shengmin 2002.

27. *Hanshu* 75.3176.

28. The secondary literature on the imperial sacrifices in general and their reform in late Western Han in particular is vast. The foundational study came in Loewe 1974, 154–92. Lewis (1999a, 50–80) examined the *feng* and *shan* sacrifices and their symbolic importance during mid–Western Han. In several articles and a book, Marianne Bujard (1997, 2000, and 2008) cast debates over sacrifices as contests between classicists at the Han court and magicians (*fangshi*). Tian (2015b) emphasized political contingencies along the way to Wang Mang's 5 CE reforms of the state sacrifices, and noted that even if advocates of reform shared certain ideas, sharp divisions remained between classicists and there is little evidence of a unified reform plan. For a fuller treatment, see Tian Tian 2015a.

29. For one exception, see Tang Xiaofeng (2015), which traced the evolution of space in the capital based on archaeological evidence.

30. *Shiji* 10.430.

31. *Hanshu* 4.127.

32. Most of the content in the "Basic Annals of Wudi" is a reproduction of the "Treatise on the *Feng* and *Shan*." Very likely, a later author and not Sima Qian himself compiled the former.

33. *Shiji* 28.1389.

34. *Hanshu* 6.183.

35. *Hanshu* 6.198, 96b.3905.

36. *Hanshu* 8.271.

37. On this "ethics of thrift" and its emergence in late Western Han texts, especially the rhapsodies, see Chin 2014, 77–96.

38. For "nurturing life" culture and self-cultivation discourse, see Lo 2001; Csikszentmihalyi 2009.

39. See *Lüshi chunqiu ji shi* 1996, 1.3 ("Zhong ji"), 14–15; Knoblock and Riegel 2000, 69. Related messages are found throughout early texts. On the problem of pleasure in early texts, see Nylan 2001.

40. *Xunzi jian shi* 1996, 11 ("Wang ba"), 150; Hutton 2014, 108, lines 352–69.

41. See *Mengzi* (comp. ca. early third century BCE?), "Liang hui wang xia" chapter (*Mengzi ben yi* 1996, 2.2, 37–38; *Mencius* 1/B, in Lau 1970,

61–62). For a related idea, see *Lüshi chunqiu* (comp. 239 BCE), "Ting yan" chapter (*Lüshi chunqiu ji shi* 1996, 13.13, 13; Knoblock and Riegel 2000, 289). An anecdote from the *Han Feizi* (comp. ca. late third century BCE?) presents yet a third perspective on parks, arguing that they should be tightly regulated, though not for the ruler's enjoyment or self-cultivation practice. Rather, they were to provide resources that could be disbursed to meritorious subjects. See *Han Feizi*, "Wai chu shuo, you xia" chapter (*Han Feizi jiao shi* 1996, 33, 659).

42. My punctuation and translation here departs slightly from that of Swann (1950, 297), which rendered the *duo* as "[but this was] too much." Swann's translation interprets the passage as describing a situation in which the superintendent of agriculture could not handle administering both the salt and iron offices and minting coins. My translation takes a different perspective, linking this passage to a prior statement about establishing the metropolitan superintendents of left and right (*zuo you fu*). As Swann herself noted (297n568), these superintendents were created "probably to bring large taxable fields under metropolitan control." Rather than describing an administrative adjustment occasioned by excessive duties in a single office, the passage seems to be tracing the establishment of a series of new offices (first the superintendents, then the superintendent of waterways and parks) designed to increase the amount of wealth controlled by the imperial center.

43. *Shiji* 30.1436.

44. For an overview of evidence for Shanglin palaces and structures mentioned, see Xu Weimin 1991. Xu identified forty-seven park structures in early sources.

45. *Shiji* 53.2018.

46. *Shiji* 53.2018. According to the *Shiji*, an adviser warned Xiao He that the emperor was growing suspicious of his chancellor, since Xiao was popular among the people of the capital region for instituting fair and reasonable policies. The adviser told Xiao He to engage in land profiteering in order to smear his own reputation a bit and thus allay Gaozu's fears that Xiao's popular support constituted a threat. Xiao followed the advice, and in his retort about the park request Gaozu pointed out the hypocrisy of simultaneously profiting from the people and making demands on their behalf from his "personal park."

47. For this point, see Loewe 2000, 73. Van Ess (2015, 491) suggested that Chu Shaosun's portrait of Dongfang Shuo might have been designed to show Wudi's softer and compassionate side. See also Knechtges 1970–71.

48. *Shiji* 126.3205.

49. *Hanshu* 65.2849.

50. In the *Mengzi* story, King Xuan complained, "The people still find [my park] large." See above n42.

51. *Hanshu* 65.2849–50.

52. *Hanshu* 65.2856–57.

53. Note that before quoting Dongfang Shuo's statement to Wudi about the crimes of Dong Yan, the *Hanshu* account takes care to describe Dongfang setting aside his weapons before moving forward into the hall where the emperor was located (*Hanshu* 65.2856).

54. For a concise overview of modern rhapsody studies, see Chin 2015, 74–77.

55. See Kern 2003b, 423–24; Rouzer 2001; Chen 2010.

56. The discussion here relies heavily on translations by Knechtges. While many scholars have focused on the Western Han rhapsodies discussed here, most have emphasized their representations of imperial power. My analysis, however, explores poems about Shanglin Park and the imperial hunt as specific reactions to moral conundrums that imperial largesse based on park resources posed to court officials (not just the emperor).

57. Knechtges 1987, 102n329, n330.

58. Knechtges 1987, 109–13.

59. Rouzer 2001, 47.

60. *Hanshu* 87a.3550; Knechtges 1987, 129–31.

61. *Hanshu* 87a.3550–51; Knechtges 1987, 131.

62. Including, for instance, women from "Didi," understood as a "Chinese transcription of a Central Asian place name" (Knechtges 1987, 106n401).

63. For this interpretation, see Knechtges 1987, 130n228. Received texts provide many descriptions of tattooed foreigners, often specifically identified as Yue. See Brindley 2015, 164–68.

64. Knechtges 1976, 76–77. For the case of Qu Yuan, see Zikpi, 2014. For Wu Zixu, see Johnson 1981.

65. *Hanshu* 87a.3552; Knechtges 1987, 133.

66. Knechtges 1987, 135.

67. After Wendi eliminated the ban on private minting of coins, Jia Shan submitted a letter opposing the policy change (*Hanshu* 51.2337). The central government did not reestablish a monopoly on coinage until 113 BCE, however, long after Jia's proposal and no doubt long after his death.

68. A work entitled *Jia Shan* in eight fascicles (*pian*) is included in the *Hanshu* chapter "Treatise on Arts and Letters" (Yi wen zhi), which was based on the late Western Han bibliographic project at the imperial archives headed by Liu Xiang (*Hanshu* 30.1726). Liu Xiang thus might have had a hand in editing and compiling Jia Shan's work. The relationship between "Sublime Sayings" and the text *Jia Shan*, however, is unclear. See *Hanshu* 51.2327.

69. On this trend, see Nylan forthcoming.

70. Jia Shan's text reads, "By taking the beauty of his palaces and chambers as far as this, the First Emperor made it so that his successors were unable to assemble even a group of huts as they set up residence" (*Hanshu* 51.2328). As Xiao stated, if Gaozu did not build structures of "majesty and beauty," his successors would have nothing to build upon. For Jia Shan, the Qin example demonstrated that excessive "majesty and beauty" made it impossible to continue a founder's legacy.

71. *Hanshu* 51.2332.

72. *Hanshu* 51.2336.

73. Jia Shan's formulation thus contrasts with the description of imperial parks in the *Han Feizi*, which described them as among the tools available for the ruler for advancing the government's interests.

74. See *Hanshu* 65.2863.

75. *Hanshu* 65.2842.

76. The nephew was Lord Zhaoping, son of Wudi's younger sister. See *Hanshu* 65.2852.

77. In commentarial notes to the *Hanshu* "Table of the Many Offices and Ministerial Posts" (Bai guan gong qing biao), Yan Shigu wrote that the forbidden zone (*jin zhong*) was located within the Yellow Gates. See *Hanshu* 19a.731. See also Bielenstein 1976, 24.

78. See Liu Pak-yuen 1983, 177–91. The most detailed study of this system based on received texts is Liu Pak-yuen (1986) 1998. Liu outlined palace security in the Western Han: the walls and grounds of Weiyang Palace were secured by guards under the the commandant of the guards (*weiwei*); buildings within the palace were guarded by the *guangluxun*; the inner areas of the palace within the Yellow Gates were patrolled by guards under the director of the lesser treasury (*shaofu*).

79. Aoki Shunsuke 2007.

80. Watanabe Masatomo 2010.

81. For a reference to the *jin zhong* in Shanglin Park, see *Shiji* 101.2740; *Hanshu* 49.2271.

82. See, for example, Llewellyn-Jones (2002, esp. 25–30), which discussed the imperial harem in Achaemenid Persia. According to Llewellyn-Jones, the root meaning of the word *haram* in Arabic is "taboo" or "forbidden." In Persia, the word referred to a personal area that only people with privileged access could enter: it was "not necessarily a defined space" (30). Llewellyn-Jones suggested that the harem of Achaemenid rulers was in reality a space whose perimeters could change but nonetheless served as a private and restricted refuge for the ruler, away from the official business of government. Women were not necessarily confined to secluded and secure spaces within the palace; many were able to move about the empire and wield substantial political power at court.

83. According to comments attributed to Cai Yong (132–192 CE), the taboo was supposedly in deference to Wang Jin, the father of Wang Zhengjun, Yuandi's empress, mother of Chengdi, and aunt of Wang Mang. See *Hanshu* 7.217. The *Hanshu*, however, still refers to a *jin zhong* in stories about figures after Empress Yuan, and taboos were not systematically observed in the Han.

84. The *Hanshu* "Table of the Many Offices and Ministerial Posts" (Bai guan gong qing biao) mentions one conviction for "leaking" information in 27 BCE (*Hanshu* 19b.827). In 77 BCE, the "Table" also mentions an official convicted of leaking secret documents (*Hanshu* 19b.796).

85. *Shiji* 6.257.

86. *Hanshu* 66.2900.

87. See Loewe 2012–13, 372–73, for a discussion of Shi Xian and his role in political struggles during the reign of Yuandi.

88. Commentators have provided different explanations for *sima zhong*. Ying Shao and Yan Shigu (581–645) both argued that it referred to a gate, entry through which was highly restricted (see *Hanshu* 9.286). Ru Chun (fl.

mid-third century CE) wrote in rather unclear terms that it referred to a zone within a military encampment (see *Hanshu* 69.2994).

89. *Hanshu* 69.2994.

90. *Hanshu* 81.3353.

91. *Hanshu* 81.3354.

92. For instance, Wang Guowei's (1877–1927) characterization of capital cities as "political and cultural symbols" expressed an idea not too distant from Xiao He's justification for building Weiyang Palace (for the quote from Wang, see Liu Qingzhu 2006). The idea has even framed the interpretation of archaeological evidence. One of the lead archaeologists of the Han Chang'an site has written that Xiao He's statement was the "guiding concept" behind the construction of the buildings that composed Weiyang Palace. See Liu Qingzhu (1995) 2006.

93. On this point, see Nylan 2015b, 13.

94. Tang Xiaofeng 2015, 69.

CHAPTER 4

1. *Shiji* 6.236.

2. A wooden document recovered from the Qin-era well found near Liye, Hunan, lists dozens of new titles and terms to be used by Qin officials in place of old terms. One of the more well-known items on the list states that "the 'royal hounds' shall be called the 'imperial hounds.'" See Liye strip 8–461; Chen Wei 2012, 155–60.

3. In particular, the "Offices of Zhou" (Zhou guan) and "Royal Institutions" (Wang zhi). See *Hanshu* 99b.4136.

4. *Hanshu* 99b.4128.

5. For a more detailed discussion of early emperors and their changing sources of authority, see Loewe 1981.

6. *Hanshu* 73.3126.

7. The count encompasses only references to establishing or eliminating offices or changing office titles after Gaozu became emperor. It thus does not include descriptions in the "Table" of Han offices as they existed at the beginning of Western Han, since almost all of those offices were inherited unchanged from the Qin.

8. *Hanshu* 19a.727.

9. The "inner court vs. outer court" understanding of early politics remains more or less standard in scholarship written in Chinese and Japanese. Key early works include Lao Gan (1948) and Nishijima Sadao ([1965] 1983). In English-language scholarship, an early and forceful articulation of the idea came in Wang 1949. A recent and equally forceful invocation is found in Lewis 2005, 63–64. See also Zhao 2015, 82.

10. *Hanshu* 64.2775.

11. See Bielenstein 1980, 154–55; Liu Pak-yuen 1983, 171–318.

12. The commentary, by Yan Shigu (581–645), comes in the "Account" of Gongsun Hong. Yan glossed *ge* as *he* (*Hanshu* 58.2621). Recall from chapter 3 that the *Hanshu* describes Wudi, in response to criticism from Dongfang

Shuo, admitting Dong Yan through an eastern gate, which was renamed "Eastern Meeting Gate" (Dong jiao men).

13. *Hanshu* 58.261. This statement from the "Account" heightens a dramatic narrative, which concludes by stating that after Gongsun Hong's death, ineffective or powerless men became chancellors. As a result, "the guest lodge of the Chancellery became nothing more than an abandoned mound." Moreover, the "Account" notes that only two of the post–Gongsun Hong chancellors managed to avoid execution (*Hanshu* 58.2623).

14. The family-faction narrative of Western Han courtly politics can be traced all the way back to the *Hanshu*. The appraisal to the annals of Chengdi, for example, argued that the conditions for Wang Mang's ascension to the throne as founder of the Xin were set years before, when the Wang family managed to take control of the government (*Hanshu* 10.330). Even at the beginning of the Western Han, however, we have evidence for factional politics based on kin and friendship ties. For instance, the *Shiji* "Treatise on Ritual" (Li shu) states that during the reign of Jingdi officials devoted themselves to "nurturing relationships" at court rather than reforming ritual and policy (*Shiji* 23.1160). We should thus not assume that late Western Han was comparatively worse in this regard than earlier eras, even if the *Hanshu* argued that imperial consort families and their clients were especially powerful and corrosive during this period.

15. Liu Pak-yuen (1983) and Kamiya Masakazu (2009) emphasized this point from different perspectives.

16. See, e.g., *Mozi*, "Fei ru xia" chapter (*Mozi jijie* 1996, 9.250); *Guanzi*, "Ming fa" chapter (*Guanzi tong shi* 1996, 21.418); *Xunzi*, "Jun dao" chapter (*Xunzi jian shi* 1996, 12.170; Hutton 2014, 125, line 283); *Lüshi chunqiu*, "Huan dao" chapter (*Lüshi chunqiu ji shi* 1996, 3.17; Knoblock and Riegel 2000, 109); *Han Feizi*, "Nan yi" chapter (*Han Feizi jiao shi* 1996, 4.345). All these sources assume the desirability or explicitly praise the importance of clearly defined "discrete duties." Though Sima Tan praised "legal specialists" (*fa jia*) for their commitment to the concept, in fact many texts esteemed the clear and explicit division of official duties.

17. In the *Hanshu*, most instances of the term *fen zhi* appear in the treatises or in statements made by figures active during the reign of Chengdi. There are only two exceptions: a statement in Sima Tan's essay "Yao zhi" commending the "legal specialists" (*fa jia*) for "clarifying the discrete duties [of officials] so they do not infringe upon each other (*Hanshu* 62.2713), and a response by Gongsun Hong to a question posed by Wudi (*Hanshu* 58.2615). The only memorials self-consciously claiming to institute discrete duties via administrative changes come in the memorials submitted in support of the 8 BCE reforms.

18. Though the three proposals were approved as a unit (see below), scholars have typically treated them separately. The literature is extensive. Most work focuses on the Executive Council (Sangong) reform, which some scholars have characterized as a further step toward marginalizing bureaucrats and establishing authoritarian rule. See, e.g., Xu Fuguan ([1978] 2001, 151–55), refuted by Zhu Zongbin (1990, 55–61). Others have cast the Executive

Council reforms as part of a larger struggle between the "inner court" and "outer court," with Chengdi firmly supporting the latter in 8 BCE. The idea runs through much of the literature, but for an early example, see Yoshinami Takashi 1968. For the Inspectorate reforms, see de Crespigny (1981) 2007. The kingdom administration reforms have received less attention, but see Kamada Shigeo 1962, 162–63; Kamiya Masakazu 1974.

19. Note that Loewe (2000) used "imperial counselor" for both *yushi dafu* and *da sikong*, but Loewe has recently suggested replacing titles he translated as "superintendent" with "commissioner" (personal communication, August 7, 2011). Use of "Executive Council" for *Sangong* follows Giele 2006.

20. The *Hanshu* "Table of the Many Officers and High Ministerial Posts" does not give ranks for the chancellor or the imperial counselor (*Hanshu* 19a.724–25), prompting Bielenstein (1980, 7) to state that the ranks of these officials were unknown. The Zhangjiashan "Statute on Salary Grades" (Zhi lü), however, indicated a rank for the imperial counselor of 2,000 bushels but did not specify a salary grade for the chancellor (*ENLL*, strip 440). See Peng Hao et al. 2007, 258. The *Shiji* and *Hanshu* clearly show that the chancellor headed the government and ranked higher than the imperial counselor, who was his second-in-command. Moreover, beginning in early Western Han chancellors often served first as imperial counselors. See the list of chancellors in An Zuozhang and Xiong Tieji (1984–85) 2006, 26–29.

21. Note, however, the statement by Zhu Bo (6 BCE) to the effect that provincial shepherds were still considered one slight step below the ministers, despite their identical rank (*Hanshu* 83.3406). See also n55 below.

22. *Hanshu* 6.197.

23. For a description and analysis of the duties of the Inspectors, see de Crespigny (1981) 2007.

24. Evidence for this change is fragmentary but convincing. The *Hanshu* states that in 37 BCE Yuandi increased the grades of governors of "large commanderies," defined as having more than 120,000 registered households (*Hanshu* 9.294). According to the *Han jiu yi*, in 8 BCE the grades of these governors were reduced to 2,000 bushels, effectively reversing the policy of 37 BCE by lowering the rank of large commandery governors to that of all other governors. See *Han jiu yi*, *juan* 2, in *Han guan liu zhong*, compiled by Sun Xingyan (1753–1818), in Sun Xingyan and Zhou Tianyou (1990) 2008, 82. Bielenstein (1980, 187n12) wrote that Yuandi had increased the rank to "fully" 2,000 bushels, since "fully" 2,000 bushels was higher than 2,000 bushels.

25. For the rank of the commandants, see *Hanshu* 19a.742. In 37 BCE, commandants of large commanderies, like their immediate superiors, the governors, received an increase in salary grade to 2,000 bushels (*Hanshu* 9.294). Unfortunately, we have no record that the rank of commandant in the large commanderies was reduced in 8 BCE. Nevertheless, Bielenstein (1980, 183n26) speculated that the order of 37 BCE "may have been rescinded in 8 BCE." He is likely correct, since the thrust of Chengdi's policy was to equalize the ranks of all local administrators and make them

consistent with a system in which capital officials were highest in rank (see below).

26. *Hanshu* 10.312.

27. For the ranks of 186 BCE and 23 BCE, see Yan Buke 2009, 89–90. For those of 8 BCE, see Bielenstein 1980, 4; Fukui Shigemasa 1988, 280.

28. See, e.g., *Shiji* 10.436; *Hanshu* 5.138.

29. The equivalent ranks described in the "Table of the Many Offices and Ministerial Posts" might plausibly be understood as yet another type of gradation, but as discussed in chapter 1, it was a system of perhaps retroactive construction that applied only to officials at the imperial court.

30. The 600- and 1,000-bushels positions were conceived as one unit for purposes of privileges and benefits. According to *Hanshu* (19a.743), the 2,000-bushel officials received silver seals and green ribbons, whereas positions of 600 bushels "and above" received bronze seals and black ribbons. Fukui Shigemasa (1988, 281–83) marshaled the evidence from imperial edicts to demonstrate that many officials ranked at 600 and 1,000 bushels received the same sort and type of gifts and privileges, which usually did not compare with the largesse enjoyed by those ranked at 2,000 bushels or above.

31. Fukui Shigemasa 1988, 279–302; Loewe 2010a, 310–11. Note that officials at 2,000 bushels had the particular privilege of recommending candidates for office. Those who had served at that rank for three years or more could sponsor a son or brother as a gentleman-at-arms, allowing him to serve as an escort or guard in the imperial palaces. See Loewe 2004, 131–34.

32. Chengdi's motivation for eliminating the rank of 800 bushels in 23 BCE is less obvious. Undoubtedly the most important 800-bushel position at court was advisory counselor (*jian dafu*), whose duties are ill understood. The evidence at hand indicates that after 23 BC the advisory counselor was ranked at "equivalent" to 600 bushels. See Bielenstein 1980, 26.

33. As figure 4.1 indicates, we do not know the salary ranks of the chancellor and the kingdom officials prior to 8 BCE. For the chancellor, see n8 above. For the kingdom administrators, we know only that in 46 BCE Yuandi lowered the ranks of the kingdom ministers to below that of the governors (*Hanshu* 9.283). Kamiya Masakazu (1974, 25) asserted that the kingdom ministers and commissioners were demoted from "fully" (*zhen*) 2,000 bushels to 2,000 bushels.

34. As de Crespigny ([1981] 2007, 57–61), noted, during the time of Yuandi, subordinate officers had been established in the Inspectorate provinces. By raising the inspectors to the rank of "fully" 2,000 bushels, Chengdi helped complete a process by which the inspectors became more fully integrated as regular officers in the highest levels of the bureaucracy, assuming an institutional identity that was quite different from their initial role as imperial envoys.

35. In 6 BCE, the newly enthroned Aidi (r. 7–1 BCE), on the advice of his chancellor Zhu Bo, rescinded the reforms of the Executive Council and the Inspectorate, reinstituting the previous structure with the chancellor as the chief administrator and the regional inspectors at 600 bushels. The reforms of regional administration were retained, however, and in 2 BCE Aidi reversed his position and reinstated Chengdi's reforms.

36. The relationship between Chengdi and the Wang family was complex, and a full discussion must remain outside the bounds of this chapter. Chengdi was in a difficult position. He was expected to accord his mother proper respect, and probably felt a close affinity to her and her brother, Wang Feng (d. 22 BCE). After all, according to the *Hanshu* the trio were "united in their worry and fear" when Chengdi's father, Yuandi, considered removing Chengdi as heir (*Hanshu* 96.4016–17). However, as emperor he recognized the danger that the Wang family posed and actively worked to control its influence. See, e.g., the example of Wang Zhang (no relation). Early in his reign Chengdi met privately with Zhang to discuss Wang Feng's removal, but ultimately the emperor imprisoned Zhang after Wang Feng heard of their discussions (*Hanshu* 96.4020–23).

37. See *Hanshu* 86.3481 for He Wu and Zhai Fangjin's friendship. Wu and Fangjin jointly proposed each of the reforms in quick succession. They thus must have put forth the proposals with a shared understanding of the institutional problems that needed to be addressed, as well as the ideal structure of governance they hoped to realize.

38. The statement is found in He and Zhai's proposals. For instances of "discrete duties" in earlier pre-imperial texts.

39. Over the course of the Western Han, several systems had been established for identifying and promoting worthy candidates for office. Governors, kingdom ministers, the Nine Ministers in the capital, and regional inspectors were all required to make such recommendations. Evaluating and recommending officials thus came to be a key responsibility and privilege of high office. See Fukui Shigemasa 1988; Loewe 2004; de Crespigny (1981) 2007.

40. *Hanshu* 60.2667.

41. Kamiya Masakazu 2009, 322–25. This strategy was in contrast, Kamiya argues, to the approach of the Huo family during Zhaodi's reign and Shi Xian during Yuandi's reign, since both the Huo family and Shi Xian almost exclusively appointed supporters to positions at court. Kamiya details the career paths of eight officials specifically connected to recommendations from Wang family members and who served in regional administrative posts before achieving 2,000-bushel positions. To take one example, Wang Feng initially installed Xiao Yu as a subordinate in his own bureau, after which Xiao moved through various local and regional administrative positions, including prefect of Maoling, colonel of internal security, regional inspector of Jizhou, regional inspector of Qingzhou, and governor of Taishan (*Hanshu* 78.3289). Kamiya misses the example of He Wu, who was recommended by Wang Yin to be advisory counselor (*jian dafu*) and then was appointed to be regional inspector of Yangzhou (*Hanshu* 86.3482). He Wu, of course, eventually rose to become imperial counselor.

42. The official in question was Wang Zhang (no relation to the empress dowager's family). As the *Hanshu*'s description of this incident reveals, alliances must have been a commonly expected result of recommendations: "At this time the emperor's uncle, the Grand General Wang Feng, controlled the government. Even though Feng had recommended Wang Zhang, Zhang

objected to Feng's monopoly of power and did not form close attachments with him" (*Hanshu* 76.3238).

43. The example of Chen Tang, a military hero, is a case in point. Wang Feng and Wang Yin greatly esteemed Tang, but their younger brother, Wang Shang, despised him and had him exiled upon assuming the title of marshal of state (*Hanshu* 84.3418).

44. For example, after the emperor's uncles Wang Shang, Wang Li, and Wang Gen were detained for their excessively lavish lifestyles, they collectively appealed to the empress dowager for support, and their eldest brother, Wang Yin, managed a successful appeal for clemency (*Hanshu* 98.4025). In a related vein, Hölkeskamp (2010, 30–39) emphasized that patron-client alliances in the late Roman republic were prone to fracture and required continual renewal and reaffirmation.

45. Gu Yong (d. ca. 8 BCE) is an instructive example in this regard, since according to the *Hanshu* he actively attempted to curry favor with Wang Feng (*Hanshu* 85.3451–54) and later enjoyed good relations with Wang Tan. But when Tan was passed up to succeed Wang Feng as marshal of state and director of the government in favor of Wang Yin, Gu's stock took a tumble. Tan and Yin grew apart, and the latter directed some of his ire against Gu (*Hanshu* 85.3455–56).

46. *Hanshu* 86.3481, 84.3411.

47. Both Zhai Fangjin and He Wu studied under academicians (*boshi*) in Chang'an, with Zhai mastering the *Zuo* commentaries to the *Annals* (Chunqiu), and He, the *Changes* (Yi). Zhai gained notice for scrupulously adhering to the statutes as regional inspector; He was punctilious in preparing his reports. Moreover, He decided impartially the case against Dai Sheng, reversing his death sentence, even though Sheng had previously criticized He at court. For Zhai Fangjin, see *Hanshu* 84.8412, 99.3618; for He Wu, see *Hanshu* 86.3481–82.

48. *Hanshu* 86.3482, 3416. The construction of Chengdi's mausoleum at Changling had provided opportunities for speculation and graft among the rich and powerful families of Chang'an.

49. *Hanshu* 86.3485.

50. *Hanshu* 60.2679.

51. The only explicit example I have found comes from Wang Zhang (no relation), who died in prison after he submitted a statement to Chengdi urging him to get rid of Wang Feng. The statement included an accusation that Feng had installed his wife's younger sister, previously married to a man of low status, in the palace on the pretext that she would be able to bear Chengdi a son, when in fact Feng was acting purely to secure his own interests (*Hanshu* 98.4023).

52. The *Hanshu* says that He Wu submitted the Executive Council proposal while he was still serving as commissioner of trials (*tingwei*) from 10 to 8 BCE. After Zhang Yu agreed that the reform should be enacted, Chengdi established the Executive Council in the fourth month of the first year of Suihe. He Wu was no longer the commissioner of trials, having been

appointed imperial counselor two months prior; his title was simply changed to *da sikong* (*Hanshu* 83.3404–5).

53. Wang Gen had previously criticized Zhang Yu for requesting burial land near Pingling, Zhaodi's (r. 86–74 BCE) mausoleum. Chengdi ignored Gen's concerns, but thereafter Gen persistently criticized and slandered Zhang (*Hanshu* 81.3350). Given the bad blood between Zhang and Gen, Zhang possibly saw the Executive Council reforms as an opportunity to neutralize Gen in a manner that left Zhang's hands relatively clean. Indeed, we are told that Zhang so feared his sons would be harmed by Gen that he put in a good word for the Wang family to the emperor when other officials had blamed them for a series of portents (*Hanshu* 81.3351). The timing of these incidents is unclear, but the *Hanshu* dates the portents in question to the Yongshi (16–12 BC) and Yuanyan (12–8 BC) reign periods, which means Zhang put in that good word about the same time that he lent his support to the 8 BCE reforms. Zhang thus appears to have been simultaneously working defense and offense, acting cautiously and supportively toward members of the Wang family when necessary but exploiting opportunities to take them down when possible.

54. *Hanshu* 83.3405.

55. According to Kamiya Masakazu (2009, 311), between 8 BCE and 6 BCE, when Aidi rescinded the 8 BCE reforms of the Executive Council and the Inspectorate, no governor or kingdom minister managed to achieve a 2,000-bushel post in Chang'an, suggesting that the emperor and Executive Council could more effectively control who was placed in ministerial positions at the capital.

56. *Hanshu* 83.3406.

57. Note as well that in 8 BCE Wujiang Long was appointed to be provincial shepherd of Jizhou. Wujiang had initially received a post as advisory councilor under Wang Yin's sponsorship, but after he submitted a memorial requesting Chengdi to move Liu Xin (the future Aidi) to Chang'an, he was promoted to the newly created post of provincial shepherd (see *Hanshu* 77.3263–64). The promotion shifted a potential client of the Wang family to the direct oversight and evaluation of the emperor and his Executive Council.

58. Significantly, later in 8 BCE Wang Gen claimed illness and asked to retire. Chengdi allowed him to withdraw from active government service, increasing his sinecure by 5,000 households and providing him with a chariot and 500 catties of gold (*Hanshu* 98.4027). In 8 BCE, Wang Gen had just supported Aidi's successful installation as heir to the throne and perhaps saw an opportunity to remove himself while he could, since he had accepted bribes and built an opulent residence whose luxury rivaled that enjoyed by the emperor himself. Indeed, these offenses came under close scrutiny in memorials submitted against Wang Gen after Aidi came to the throne in 7 BCE (*Hanshu* 98.4028).

59. *Hanshu* 83.3405. As noted earlier, the chancellor Zhu Bo managed to convince Aidi, Chengdi's successor, to rescind the reforms. Zhu argued that they were disrupting the old promotional hierarchy whereby the imperial counselor gained experience before moving into the position of chancellor

and preventing the provincial shepherds from actually doing their job of inspecting the provinces (*Hanshu* 83.3405–6). In 8 BCE, Zhai Fangjin had managed to remove Zhu Bo from his position as General of the Rear (Hou Jiangjun), saying that Zhu had supported the emperor's uncle Wang Li, who had just been indicted (*Hanshu* 84.3419). Given this conflict between Zhu Bo and Zhai Fangjin, Zhu was more than likely one of the opponents of the reforms with links to the Wang family.

60. He Wu and Zhai Fangjin's call to reform the Inspectorate particularly emphasized this problem with the chain of command. Many scholars have noted the controversy inspired by the lower rank of regional inspectors vis-à-vis the governors and kingdom ministers, a controversy that arose when Wudi established the positions. De Crespigny ([1981] 2007) emphasized that the 8 BCE reform of the Inspectorate responded to these concerns and completely transformed Wudi's model. As the evidence assembled in this chapter reflects, however, the 8 BCE reforms cannot be cast solely as reactions against Wudi's policies. For a helpful overview of the gradual incorporation of ad hoc inspectors and monitors into the larger bureaucratic structure, see Liu Pak-yuen 2006.

61. Wudi established the deputy to the chancellor post in 118 BCE (*Hanshu* 19a.725). In 18 BC, Zhai Fangjin was promoted from deputy to the chancellor to governor of the capital (*jingzhao yin*) (*Hanshu* 19b.833), a position hardly distinguishable from a ministerial post, in that the governor was expected to participate regularly in court debates and policy discussions; see An Zuozhang and Xiong Tieji (1984–85) 2006, 534.

62. *Hanshu* 84.3412.

63. Bielenstein 1980, 8; An Zuozhang and Xiong Tieji (1984–85) 2006, 36–37. Bielenstein (1980, 84–85) noted that the only difference between the colonel of internal security and the regional inspectors was that (prior to 8 BCE) the former was higher in rank at 2,000 bushels and retained the staff of authority that allowed him to act in the name of the emperor. See also Kamada Shigeo 1962, 291–92; An Zuozhang and Xiong Tieji (1984–85) 2006, 498–505.

64. *Hanshu* 84.3414. In this particular case "precedent" outweighed rank: according to "precedent," the colonel of internal security, ranked at 2,000 bushels, held more authority than the deputy to the chancellor at "equivalent to" 2,000 bushels.

65. *Hanshu* 84.3413.

66. *Hanshu* 84.3414.

67. Following Yan Shigu's (581–645) interpretation, based on citation of the *Han Jiuyi* (*Hanshu* 84.3414).

68. A reference to the *Analects* (*Lunyu*) 17.12: "The Master said: 'The coward who assumes fierce looks—to borrow a crude image—is like a cutpurse who sneaks over the wall.'" *Analects* translation follows Leys 1997, 87.

69. *Hanshu* 84.3414.

70. This fact is no less true of contemporary political institutions. Historians and social scientists alike have emphasized the importance of path dependence in the development of institutions, as well as their "stickiness"

and the difficulties inherent in reforming them. See, e.g., Pierson 2004; Fukuyama 2011. For conjunctures in institutional change, see Sewell 2005.

CHAPTER 5

1. For Zhai Fangjin's memorials against Wang Li and his associates, see *Hanshu* 84.3419–20.

2. *Hanshu* 81.3356.

3. Excavated texts from the Juyan corpus refer regularly to officials "simultaneously carrying out" the duties of different offices at the same time. The *Hanshu* uses the same phrase once, in an account describing Wang Zun serving simultaneously as magistrate of two counties (*Hanshu* 76.3227).

4. Kong Guang was superintendent of trials (*tingwei*). See *Hanshu* 19b.841.

5. *Hanshu* 19b.841–42.

6. The "Table of the Many Offices and Ministerial Posts" admits as much (*Hanshu* 19a.726).

7. For an overview of Western Han military titles, see Loewe 2004, 176–207.

8. The man was Lian Cen (*Hanshu* 19b.838).

9. See Loewe 2004, 195–97.

10. Loewe 2004, 197.

11. *Hanshu* 58.2623; see chapter 4, n13.

12. *Shiji* 96.2685.

13. The "Account" describes Zhang Cang as being "in charge of writing on boards at the foot of the pillars," a phrase understood in one commentary as referring to a secretarial post (*Shiji* 96.2675).

14. *Shiji* 96.2682.

15. *Shiji* 96.2682.

16. *Shiji* 96.2685.

17. In his *Shiji suoyin*, the Tang scholar Sima Zhen (early eighth century CE) stated that Chu Shaosun wrote the biographies, but they were shortened when included in the *Shiji* chapter (*Shiji* 96.2686). Sima added, however, that a "later person" wrote the appraisal that concludes the biographies (*Shiji* 96.2689). In reality, we probably do not know precisely who wrote the biographies or when they were added to the *Shiji*. The fact that the biographies do not detail any of the chancellors serving under Chengdi, however, would strongly suggest that they were written during that emperor's reign.

18. *Shiji* 96.2686.

19. *Shiji* 96.2687.

20. *Shiji* 96.2688.

21. *Shiji* 96.2689.

22. *Shiji* 96.2689.

23. For an overview of the history of different manuscripts and editions of the *Shiji*, see Hulsewé 1993b. Detailed study of the tables can be found in Loewe 2004, 208–78.

24. Loewe (2004, 242–48) discussed the *Shiji* "Chronological Table" in detail and provided summaries of commentarial opinions about its style and

authorship. The discussion here does not touch upon the curious and wholly unique portions of the "Chronological Table" that are upside-down, not least because those passages were likely added after Western Han. On the upside-down passages, see Yi Ping 1989.

25. Sometimes the table provides months and stem-branch days, while elsewhere it says only that a given person "became chancellor" (*wei Chengxiang*).

26. See, for example, the columns for 158 BCE (*Shiji* 22.1129) and 126–123 BCE (*Shiji* 22.1136).

27. *Shiji* 22.1134.

28. *Shiji* 107.2843.

29. Commentators have generally assumed that Sima Qian stopped his work on the table up to entries for this period. Not all agree, however; there is not even consensus that Sima Qian wrote the first half of the table. On these problems, see Loewe 2004, 247–48.

30. The exception is an eclipse recorded in the "Major Events" row of the column for 42 BCE (*Shiji* 22.1152), during the reign of Yuandi. It is worth pointing out that except for the notation of the death of an empress and the installation of Empress Huo, the events given for Xuandi's reign are positive, perhaps causes for celebration, such as the naming of the imperial heir, trips to complete imperial sacrifices, and the discovery of precious treasures. The treatment of Empress Huo here is notable, since we read nothing else in the table of the disaster that befell her family after the powerful Huo Guang died. Moreover, Empress Huo, along with Wei Zifu, are the only two empresses listed by name in the "Chronological Table." Wei Zifu gave birth to Liu Ju (b. 129 BCE), Wudi's eldest son and heir apparent, who became embroiled in the disastrous "witchcraft" incident of 91 BCE. The explicit naming of these two empresses in the "Chronological Table" perhaps signaled these background political conflicts involving consort families, which the table otherwise does not discuss.

31. *Shiji* 22.1150.

32. We mostly do not know Ban Zhao's sources for the table, though Michael Loewe has demonstrated she likely had access to and consulted Western Han documents that were transferred to the Eastern Han capital of Luoyang. Moreover, Ban Zhao probably did not consult the *Shiji* "Chronological Table," so her efforts most likely were not a "response" to the *Shiji* table. See Loewe 2004, 255–56.

33. A count of the *Hanshu* "Table" yielded 508 discrete names, but this figure is only tentative. Many entries are highly laconic, providing nothing but given names along with a person's office title. In some cases we have but single-character names that could refer to the same person mentioned elsewhere in the table.

34. The *Shiji* "Chronological Table" does contain these terms, but more inconsistently. We read only twice in the entire "Chronological Table" that an officer was "promoted" (*qian*) (see *Shiji* 22.1121, 1131). The first is not even really a "promotion" since it refers only to the fact that in 198 Chancellor Xiao He received the new title of *xiangguo*. The term "dismissed" (*mian*)

is used only in the upside-down text, which was probably written long after Western Han. The word "demote" (*bian*) is entirely absent. In the *Hanshu* "Table" the word *zu* for "death" is used for all officials, but usually *hong* is used only for the highest-ranked officers: chancellors, imperial counselors, and generals. There are a few exceptions: *hong* notes the death of one director of the imperial clan (*zongzheng*) and two superintendents of ceremonial (*taichang*).

35. Usually, in cases of criminal activity, the "Table" says that an official "engaged in criminal activity" (*you zui*), was "imprisoned" (*xia yu*), or was "convicted" (*zuo*) of breaking a law. The "Table" sometimes specifies the broken laws as "ordinances" (*ling*). Of the fifty-one total "convictions" (*zuo*) given in the "Table," twenty (almost 40 percent) were committed by superintendents of ceremonial (*taichang* or *fengchang*). These include instances of superintendents being convicted of accepting nonlegal tender coins (*Hanshu* 19b.778), presumably as part of the money payments that nobles and kings were required to give to maintain the sacrifices in the ancestral temples, and providing "scanty offerings" (*fa ci*) for the sacrifices. I am unsure how to interpret the relative prevalence of infractions among the superintendents of ceremonial. At the very least, in the world of the "Table" the ritual regulations that the superintendents were expected to uphold appear particularly important, meriting more detailed exposition than crimes committed by other officials.

36. *Hanshu* 19b.795.

37. On tensions within pre-imperial texts between the ideals of rule by family line and by merit, see Allan 1981.

38. A detailed study of the authorship of the admonitions cannot be attempted here. Ban Gu's appraisal to Yang Xiong's autobiography, included in the *Hanshu*, states that Yang wrote admonitions of the provincial inspector posts (*zhou zhen*) based on the *Zuozhuan* admonition (*Hanshu* 87b.3583). The *Hou Hanshu* biography of the Eastern Han official Hu Guang (91–172 CE) gives a short history of the text entitled *Bai guan zhen*, stating that Yang Xiong composed twelve admonitions of the provincial inspector posts and fifteen "office admonitions" (*guan zhen*). Cui Yin (d. 92 CE), his son Cui Yuan (77/78–142/143), Liu Taotu (fl. ca. 110–25), and Hu Guang continued writing admonitions in the style established by Yang Xiong, and Hu compiled all of the poems together into a text entitled *Admonitions of the Many Officials* (Bai guan zhen), putting the poems in order by title and writing explanations for them (*Hou Hanshu* 80.1511). In his compilation of writings from the Han period, Yan Kejun (1762–1843) attributed different admonitions to Yang and the Eastern Han authors, primarily on the basis of attributions in the later collectanea (*lei shu*) by which most of the admonitions were transmitted. Yan also analyzed the different accounts of the text's authorship (*Quan Han wen, juan* 54.9). The admonitions have been almost entirely neglected in English-language scholarship and have received only spotty treatment in Chinese and Japanese. A major exception is work by Satō Tatsurō in four different articles. For a discussion of the authorship and compilation of the *Admonitions*, see Satō Tatsurō 2005.

39. *Zuozhuan*, Lord Xiang 4.7 (3:936–39; Durrant et al. 2016, 2:917–19). Schaberg (1997, 151–54) translated portions of this speech and analyzed it in detail.

40. The *Zuozhuan* is slightly ambiguous on this point, however, since it notes that "Xin Jia of Zhou" (not Shang) solicited the admonitions from officials. Nonetheless, it is hard to imagine that readers or even compilers of the *Zuozhuan* understood the "Admonition of the Overseer of Hunts" to be directed against King Wen of Zhou, the founding Zhou king to whom Xin Jia fled, at least according to stories circulating during the Western Han (see a fragment of Liu Xiang's *Bie lu*, cited in Pei Yin's *Shiji* commentary [fifth century CE], in *Shiji* 4.116).

41. *Zuozhuan* Lord Xiang 4.7 (3:938–39; Durrant et al. 2016, 2:919).

42. Two poems from the *Odes* (Shijing), "Xuan niao" (#303) and "Chang fa" (#304), contain the phrase "vast and far-reaching" (*mangmang*). In "Chang fa," it describes floodwaters in a line that prefaces mention of Yu's work "disposing" (*fu*) of the land.

43. The phrase *gan gao* is found throughout the *Zuozhuan*. The *Yili* describes the phrase being used by people in formal gift exchanges during wedding ceremonies. *Gan gao* appears but rarely in the *Shiji* and *Hanshu*, though a 7 BCE memorial by Wang Jia describes the phrase as a formal requirement in petitions. According to Wang, use of *gan gao* was necessary before a matter could be sent down to officials for review and investigation (*Hanshu* 86.3491). On petitions, see Giele 2006, 107.

44. The translation is based on the transcription in Satō Tatsurō 2002, 13. Yan Kejun attributed "Master of Works" to Yang Xiong (see *Quan Han wen* 1961, 54.4), an assessment that Satō Tatsurō supported. The *Chuxue ji* and a commentary to the *Guwen yuan*, however, attributed it to Cui Yin. Stanza divisions reflect my best attempts at rhyme patterns based only on the final word in each line, following the rhyme tables in Luo Changpei and Zhou Zumou (1958). I also referred to the Digital Etymological Dictionary of Old Chinese (edoc.uchicago.edu), which includes the phonological reconstructions of Karlgren, Baxter, and Schussler. In this particular poem, the same rhyme classes or "combined rhymes" (*he yun*), following Zhuo and Luo's tables, sometimes repeat across different stanzas. The last word in the first line of each stanza, however, is a break, making a pattern roughly as follows: ABBB / ABBBBB / CDDDDD / EFFFF / BBBBBB / GB. Needless to say, discerning Western Han rhyming patterns is a tricky business, both due to the vagaries of textual transmission and the fact that authors "did not write according to the kinds of prescriptions and constraints known from later regulated verse . . . [but] used rhyme considerably more freely" (Kern 2014, 138). For these reasons, combined with a lack of space and my own lack of expertise, thorough analysis of prosody remains impossible. Nonetheless, rhyme patterns in this poem seem to highlight the third and fourth stanzas, which is where the poem turns from a description of halcyon ancient times when "ministers matched offices / and offices matched ministers" to later ages when corruption reigned.

45. *Kun* (Field) is Hexagram 2 from the *Changes* (Yijing), associated with the earth. For "Kun's numina," see Knechtges 1982, 116n142.

46. The "shepherds" probably refer to central government officials responsible for the surveillance of delineated geographic areas. For the phrase "many shepherds" (*qun mu*), see the "Canon of Shun" (Shun dian) chapter of the *Documents* (Shangshu) (*Shangshu zhuzi suoyin* 1995, 2/2/17; Gu Jiegang and Liu Qiyu 2005, 1:127–28n16).

47. The *Mengzi* (comp. ca. early third century BCE?), "Teng wen gong shang" chapter describes Mencius suggesting a tax in the countryside, whereby people would be assessed one-ninth of their produce. See *Mengzi benyi* 1996, 5.3; 134; *Mencius* 3/A, in Lau 1970, 99.

48. The "seven levies" also appears in the fourth chapter ("Wen dao") of Yang Xiong's *Exemplary Figures* (Fayan). Commentators such as Li Gui (fl. 335 CE) have glossed it as the five grains along with silk and hemp. See Nylan 2013, 59.

49. The phrase is a direct quote from the "Canon of Yao" (Yao dian) chapter of the *Documents* (Shangshu) (*Shangshu zhuzi suoyin* 1995, 1/1/16; Gu Jiegang and Liu Qiyu 2005, 1:75–76n17).

50. The term *baoju* appears in several pre-imperial and early imperial texts, where commentators in some cases understand it as a reed wrapping that covered fish or meat. In other texts, the term more clearly refers to a gift or bribe. See, e.g., *Xunzi*, "Da lüe" (*Xunzi jian shi* 1996, 27.376; Hutton 2014, 305).

51. For a transcription, see Satō Tatsurō 2002, 23. Compared to those of "Admonition of the Master of Works," the rhymes in "Admonition of the Superintendent of Guards" seem to be more regular, approaching (without quite reaching) an ABCB pattern in each four-line stanza.

52. The establishment of "mountain defiles" (*shan xian*) in this couplet evokes a line from the *Changes* (Yijing) in the judgment commentary of Hexagram 29, *Kan* (Sink Hole): "Kings and nobles set up strategic spots [*xian*] in order to protect their realms." See Lynn 1994, 318.

53. The entire stanza recalls the following statement from the "Xici xia" chapter of the *Changes* (Yijing): "They had gates doubled and watchmen's clapper[s] struck and so made provision against robbers." See Lynn 1994, 79.

54. Some studies have argued that *ge* ("sang out") was perhaps a corruption of *qu* ("hurry forward"), an interpretation that Satō Tatsurō (2002, 23) allowed made the line more comprehensible. Nonetheless, she retained *ge*, arguing that the word could describe the harmonious state of the emperor's guard corps, an interpretation followed in this translation. Yan Kejun's transcription has *ge*, not *qu* (*Quan Han wen* 1961, 54.6).

55. Studies of the admonitions do not agree on the precise story referred to in this couplet. Zhang Zhenze (1993, 368n7) argued that a negative *wu* should be added before *shu ti* ("apprehensive"), since that wording is found in a story about Lord Huan from the *Guanzi*. That story, however, states that Lord Huan felt no apprehension because the civil rather than the martial had prevailed. The fact that the stanza is highlighting a dangerous breakdown in security, however, does not really fit with the tone of the *Guanzi* story.

56. A reference to a story in the *Shiji* chapter "Accounts of Assassin Retainers" (Ci ke lie zhuan). According to the story, during treaty negotiations

between Lu and Qi, when the Lu general Cao Mo threatened Lord Huan of Qi with a dagger and forced him to return land to Lu, "none of Lord Huan's attendants dared budge" (*Shiji* 86.2515).

57. The couplet refers to the *Shiji*'s famous story of Jing Ke's attempted assassination of the king of Qin and future First Emperor. Jing Ke hid his dagger in a map he presented to the king (*Shiji* 86.2534).

58. The Second Emperor committed suicide at Wangyi Palace after soldiers under Zhao Gao and his son-in-law Yan Le's command infiltrated the palace and executed the superintendent of guards (*Shiji* 6.274).

59. According to the *Shiji*, the Second Emperor's superintendent of the palace (*langzhong ling*) conspired with Zhao Gao and Yan Le in order to allow them entry into Wangyi Palace (*Shiji* 6.274).

60. Yan Kejun followed the *Yiwen leiju* in attributing the poem to Yang Xiong (*Quan Han wen* 1961, 54.4–5), but the *Guwen yuan* attributed it to Cui Yuan. See Satō Tatsurō 2002, 15.

61. Fu Su was the eldest son of the First Emperor. According to the famous story in the *Shiji* account of Li Si, after the First Emperor died his adviser Zhao Gao did not dispatch an envoy to deliver an official order prepared by the emperor on his deathbed that established Fu Su as heir. Rather, Zhao Gao convinced Li Si to go along with his scheme to install Hu Hai as the second emperor. The duo forged an imperial statement harshly critical of Fu Su, who, still oblivious of the First Emperor's death and the fact that he was the officially designated heir, immediately committed suicide. Zhao and Li thereupon installed Hu Hai as the Second Emperor (*Shiji* 87.2251).

62. *Hanshu* 30.1701.

63. For an overview of the two Liu men and their work, see Loewe 2015.

64. *Hanshu* 30.1762.

65. *Hanshu* 30.1780.

66. *Hanshu* 30.1738.

67. *Hanshu* 30.1746.

68. Cf. Lewis 1999b, 328–31, which noted that the masters texts were "the literary expression of the fragmentation of power" and were "equat[ed] . . . with political offices" but did not highlight the gap between these two narratives.

69. Members of the Wang family and Kong Guang all served as directors of the Secretariat.

70. The "Admonition on the Consort Clans" was written by Cui Qi (*Hou Hanshu* 80a.2619), the "Admonition on the Palace Attendant" by Hu Guang (Satō Tatsurō 2004, 52).

71. As noted in the introduction, Herzfeld (1992) argued that ideas of chance provided rhetorical support for modern "rationalized" bureaucracies, since they allowed injustices that might well be endemic to bureaucratic institutions to be explained away as cases of "bad luck."

CONCLUSION

1. Other authors have made similar points. Most important among them is Michael Loewe, who in his influential *Crisis and Conflict in Han China* (1974) identified a clash between a "modernist" vision of government devoted to activist interventions in society and a "reformist" understanding that emphasized restraint and retrenchment.

2. *Quan Han wen* 1961, 54.8; *Hou Hanshu* 80a.2619–22; *Quan Hou Han wen* 1961, 45.8. The author of "Waiqi zhen" was Cui Qi (d. ca. 140 CE).

3. Loewe 2014, 384.

4. Creel 1964, 155.

5. See, e.g., Nissen et al. 1993, cited in Graeber 2015, n145; Wang 2014, esp. 55–105.

6. Many studies, including Creel (1964) and Blakeley (1998, esp. 56–57), have pointed out that, long before Qin, the kingdom of Chu seems to have established a centralized government that did not rely on intermediating landholders or nobles and employed highly specialized techniques of administration. Li 2001–2 and Zhao 2015, meanwhile, emphasized the Western Zhou roots of bureaucratic government. For an in-depth exploration in comparative terms that focuses on writing and bureaucratic administration, see Wang 2014, esp. 53–237.

7. See Graeber 2015, 27 and *passim*.

GLOSSARY

General Terms

bi 比
bian 貶
biao 表

chao 朝
chehou 徹侯
chen 臣

dang 黨
de 德
Di 帝

enze 恩澤

fanchen 藩臣
fen zhi 分職
fu 賦
fu gu 復古

gan gao 敢告
ganzhi 干支
gong[a] 宮
gong[b] 功
gong qing 公卿
guan 官
guo 國

hong 薨
huan huangdi zhe 宦皇帝者
huang taihou 皇太后
huangdi 皇帝
huangwu 黃屋

ji 紀
jing 敬
jinzhong 禁中
jiuqing 九卿
jue 爵
juedi 角抵
junxian 郡縣

keli 客禮

lang 郎
langmiao 廊廟
li 吏
liehou 列侯
lü 律

mian 免
miao 廟

ni 擬

qian 遷

rishu 日書
rushu 儒術

sangong 三公
shang fa 賞罰
Shanglin Yuan 上林苑

shanyu 單于
shengguantu 陞官圖
shi 視
shi / dan 石
shou 守

tian tong 天統
Tianzi 天子
ting 廷 / 庭

wei[a] 位
wei[b] 威
wen 文
wu fu 五服

xian 咸
xianguan 縣官
xiaolian 孝廉
xie xingzhong yu 泄省中語
xing xing 行幸
xing zhong 省中
xingde 刑德
yang xing 養性

yi 儀
yu wu 御物
yue zhi 越制

zhen 箴
zheng chu 正處
zhi 質
zhi[a] 志
zhi[b] 秩
zhi[c] 質
zhi[d] 職
zhidu shu 制度史
zhong[a] 忠
zhong[b] 中
zhong chen 眾臣
zhuan 傳
zhuhou wang 諸侯王
zu 卒
zun jun yi chen 尊君抑臣
zuo dao 左纛

Text Titles

Bai guan gong qing biao 百官公卿表
Bai guan zhen 百官箴
Ci lü 賜律
Er nian lü ling 二年律令
Er ya 爾雅
Han Feizi 韓非子
Hanshu 漢書
Han xing yilai jiang xiang mingchen nian biao 漢興以來將相名臣年表
Hou Hanshu 後漢書
Lü shi chunqiu 呂氏春秋
Mengzi 孟子
Mozi 墨子
Shangshu 尚書
Shiji 史記
Shijing 詩經
Wei li zhi dao 為吏之道
Xin yu 新語
Xunzi 荀子
Yi wen zhi 藝文志
Zheng shi zhi chang 政事之常
Zhi lü 秩律
Zhi yan 至言
Zuozhuan 左傳

BIBLIOGRAPHY

Allan, Sarah. 1981. *The Heir and the Sage: Dynastic Legend in Early China.* San Francisco: Chinese Materials Center.

An Zuozhang 安作璋 and Xiong Tieji 熊鐵基. 2006 [1984–85]. *Qin Han guanzhi shi gao* 秦漢官制史稿. Jinan: Qi Lu shu she.

Aoki Shunsuke青木俊介. 2007. "Kan Chōan jō Biō kyū no kinchū—so no ryōiki teki kōsatsu" 漢長安城未央宮の禁中—その領域的考察. *Gakushūin shigaku* 45 (3): 35–62.

Barbieri-Low, Anthony. 2007. *Artisans of Imperial China.* University of Washington Press.

———, and Robin Yates. 2015. *Law, State, and Society in Early Imperial China.* Vols. 1–2. Leiden: Brill.

Bartlett, Beatrice. 1991. *Monarchs and Ministers: The Grand Council in Mid-Ch'ing China, 1723–1820.* Berkeley: University of California Press.

Bastid-Bruguière, Marianne. 2013. "Réceptions et fêtes dans les cours de Chine, du Japon, et de l'Europe au XIX siècle." Paper presented at Cité Interdite, Palais impériaux et Cours royales: Comparaison entre les symbols du pouvoir imperial et monarchique en Orient et en Occident. Université du Littoral Côte d'Opale, Boulogne-sur-mer, September 25–28, 2013.

Beard, Mary. 2015. *SPQR: A History of Ancient Rome.* New York: Liverwright.

Beck, J. Mansvelt. 1990. *The Treatises of Later Han: Their Author, Sources, Contents, and Place in Chinese Historiography.* Leiden: Brill.

Bielenstein, Hans. 1976. "Lo-yang in Later Han Times." *Bulletin of the Museum of Far Eastern Antiquities* 48.

———. 1980. *The Bureaucracy of Han Times.* Cambridge, UK: Cambridge University Press.

Bingshu zhuzi suoyin 兵書逐字索引. 1992. Edited by D. C. Lau. Hong Kong: Commercial Press.

Blakeley, Barry. 1998. "Chu Society and State: Image versus Reality." In *Defining Chu: Image and Reality in Ancient China*, edited by Constance A. Cook, John S. Major, and Barry B. Blakeley, 51–66. Honolulu: University of Hawaii Press.

Blitstein, Pablo. 2015. *Les fleurs de royaume: Savoirs lettrés et pouvoir imperial en China, Ve–VIe siècle*. Paris: Les Belles Lettres.

Bodde, Derk. 1975. *Festivals in Classical China: New Year and Other Observances During the Han Dynasty, 206 BC–AD 220*. Princeton, NJ: Princeton University Press.

Bokenkamp, Stephen R. 2007. *Ancestors and Anxiety: Daoism and the Birth of Rebirth in China*. Berkeley: University of California Press.

Brashier, K. E. 2011. *Ancestral Memory in Early China*. Cambridge, MA: Harvard University Asia Center.

———. 2014. *Public Memory in Early China*. Cambridge, MA: Harvard University Asia Center.

Brindley, Erica Fox. 2015. *Ancient China and the Yue: Perceptions and Identities on the Southern Frontier, c. 400 BCE–50 BCE*. Cambridge, UK: Cambridge University Press.

Bujard, Marianne. 1997. "Le 'Traité des sacrifices' du Hanshu et la mise en place de la religion d'État des Han." *Bulletin de l'Ecole française d'Extrême-Orient* 84: 111–27.

———. 2000. *La sacrifice au ciel dans la Chine ancienne: Théorie et pratique sous les Han occidentaux*. Paris: École française de l'extrême orient.

———. 2008. "State and Local Cults in Han Religion." In *Early Chinese Religion, Part One: Shang through Han*, edited by John Legerwey and Marc Kalinowski, 777–811. Leiden: Brill.

Chang, Michael. 2007. *A Court on Horseback: Imperial Touring and the Construction of Qing Rule, 1680–1785*. Cambridge, MA: Harvard University Asia Center.

Chavannes, Edouard. 1895–1905. *Les mémoires historiques de Se-ma-Ts'ien*. Edited by Ernest Leroux. Paris: N.p.

Chen, Jack Wei. 2010. *The Poetics of Sovereignty: On Emperor Taizong of the Tang Dynasty*. Cambridge, MA: Harvard University Asia Center.

Chen Suzhen 陳蘇鎮. 2011. Chunqiu *yu "Han dao": Liang Han zhengzhi yu zhengzhi wenhua yanjiu* 《春秋》與「漢道」: 兩漢政治與政治文化研究. Beijing: Zhonghua.

Chen Wei 陳偉. 2012. *Liye Qin jiandu jiaoshi* 里耶秦簡牘校釋. Wuhan: Wuhan daxue chubanshe.

Cheng, Anne. 2001. "What Did It Mean to Be a *Ru* in Han Times?" *Asia Major*, 3rd series, 14 (2): 101–18.

Cheng Dachang 程大昌. (1123–1195). 2002. *Yonglu* 雍錄. Punctuated and edited by Huang Yongnian 黃永年. Beijing: Zhonghua.

Chin, Tamara. 2014. *Savage Exchange: Han Imperialism, Chinese Literary Style, and the Economic Imagination*. Cambridge, MA: Harvard University Asia Center.

Ch'ü, T'ung-tsu. 1972. *Han Social Structure*. Seattle: University of Washington Press.

Chunqiu Zuozhuan zhu 春秋左傳注. (1981) 2009. Vols. 1–4. Edited and annotated by Yang Bojun 楊伯峻. Beijing: Zhonghua.

Creel, Herlee G. 1964. "The Beginnings of Bureaucracy in China: The Origins of the *Hsien*." *Journal of Asian Studies* 23 (2): 155–84.

Csikszentmihalyi, Mark. 2009. "Ethics and Self-Cultivation Practice in Early China." In *Early Chinese Religion, Shang through Han (1250 BC–220 AD)*, vol. 1, edited by John Lagerwey and Marc Kalinowski, 519–42. Leiden: Brill.

Csikszentmihalyi, Mark, and Michael Nylan. 2003. "Constructing Lineages and Inventing Traditions through Exemplary Figures in Early China." *T'oung Pao* 89 (1–3): 59–99.

de Crespigny, Rafe. (1981) 2007. "Inspection and Surveillance Officials under the Two Han Dynasties." 2nd edition. Accessed March 22, 2012. www.anu.edu/au/asianstudies/decrespigny/Inspection_1981_for_Internet.doc. Originally published in *State and Law in East Asia: Festschrift Karl Bünger*, edited by Dieter Eikemeier and Herbert Franke, 40–79. Wiesbaden: Otto Harrasowitz.

di Cosmo, Nicola. 2002. *Ancient China and Its Enemies: The Rise of Nomadic Power in East Asian History*. Cambridge, UK: Cambridge University Press.

Drège, Jean-Pierre. 1991. *Les bibliothèques en China au temps des manuscrits: Jusqu'au Xe siècle*. Paris: École française d'Extrême-Orient.

Dubs, Homer H. 1938. "The Victory of Han Confucianism." *Journal of the American Oriental Society* 58: 435–39.

———, trans. 1944. *The History of the Former Han Dynasty*. Vol. 2. Baltimore, MD: Waverly.

Duindam, Jeroen. 1994. *Myths of Power: Norbert Elias and the Early Modern European Court*. Translated by Lorri S. Granger and Gerard T. Moran. Amsterdam: Amsterdam University Press.

———. 2003. *Vienna and Versailles: The Courts of Europe's Dynastic Rivals, 1550–1780*. Cambridge, UK: Cambridge University Press.

Durrant, Stephen, Wai-yee Li, and David Schaberg, trans. 2016. *Zuo Tradition, Zuozhuan,* 左傳*: Commentary on the "Spring and Autumn Annals."* Vols. 1–3. Seattle: University of Washington Press.

Elias, Norbert. (1969) 2000. *The Civilizing Process: Sociogenetic and Psychogenetic Investigations.* Translated by Edmund Jephcott. Edited by Eric Dunning, Johan Goudsblom, and Stephen Mennell. Oxford: Blackwell. Originally published in 1936–39.

———. (1969) 2006. *The Court Society.* Translated by Edmund Jephcott. Edited by Stephen Mennell. Dublin: University College Dublin Press. Originally published in 1933.

Er shi wu shi bu bian 二十五史補編. 1937. Vol. 1. Shanghai: Kaiming shu dian.

Fukui Shigemasa 福井重雅. 1988. *Kandai kanri tōyō seido no kenkyū* 漢代官吏登用制度の研究. Tokyo: Sōbunsha.

———. 2005. *Kandai Jukyō no shiteki kenkyū: Jukyō no kangakuka o meguru teisetsu no saikentō* 漢代儒教の史的研究：儒教の官學化をめぐる定說の再檢討. Tokyo: Kyūko Shoin.

Fukuyama, Francis. 2011. *The Origins of Political Order: From Prehuman Times to the French Revolution.* New York: Farrar, Straus and Giroux.

Gan Huaizhen 甘懷真. 2003. *Huang quan, li yi yu jing dian quanshi: Zhongguo gudai zhengzhi shi yanjiu* 皇權, 禮儀與經典詮釋：中國古代政治史研究. Taipei: Ximalaya yanjiu fazhan jijinhui.

Geertz, Clifford. 1983. "Centers, Kings, and Charisma: Reflections on the Symbolics of Power." In *Local Knowledge: Further Essays in Interpretive Anthropology.* New York: Basic Books.

Gentz, Joachim. 2015. "Long Live the King! The Ideology of Power between Ritual and Morality in the *Gongyang zhuan* 公羊傳." In *Ideology of Power and Power of Ideology in Early China*, edited by Yuri Pines, Paul R. Goldin, and Martin Kern, 69–117. Leiden: Brill.

Gerth, H. H., and C. Wright Mills, trans. and eds. 1946. *From Max Weber: Essays in Sociology.* New York: Oxford University Press.

Giele, Enno. 2006. *Imperial Decision-making and Communication in Early China: A Study of Cai Yong's* Duduan. Wiesbaden: Harrassowitz.

———. 2010. "Excavated Texts: Context and Methodology." In *China's Early Empires: A Re-appraisal*, edited by Michael Nylan and Michael Loewe, 114–34. Cambridge, UK: Cambridge University Press.

Goldin, Paul. 2012. "Han Law and the Regulation of Interpersonal Relations: 'The Confucianization of the Law' Revisited." *Asia Major* 25 (1): 1–31.

———. 2011. "Persistent Misconceptions about Chinese Legalism." *Journal of Chinese Philosophy* 38 (1): 88–104.

Graeber, David. 2015. *The Utopia of Rules: On Technology, Stupidity, and the Secret Joys of Bureaucracy.* Brooklyn, NY: Melville House.

Gu Jiegang 顧頡剛 and Liu Qiyu 劉起釪. 2005. *Shangshu jiao shi yi lun* 尚書校釋譯論. Vols. 1–4. Beijing: Zhonghua.

Guanzi tong shi 管子通釋. 1996. In *Min guo cong shu*民國叢書. Vol. 12. 5th edition. Shanghai: Shanghai shu dian.

Guoyu zhuzi suoyin 國語逐字索引 1999. (A Concordance to the *Guoyu*). Edited by He Zhihua 何志華. Hong Kong: Commercial Press.

Habberstad, Luke. 2014. "Courtly Institutions, Politics, and Status in Early Imperial China." Ph.D. dissertation. University of California, Berkeley.

Hanshu: *Hanshu* 漢書. 1962. Compiled by Ban Gu 班固 (32–92 CE) et al. 100 *juan* (12 vols.). Beijing: Zhonghua.

Han Feizi jiao shi 韓非子校釋. 1996. In *Min guo cong shu* 民國叢書. Vol. 8. 5th edition. Shanghai: Shanghai shu dian.

Harkness, Ethan. 2011. "Cosmology and the Quotidian: Day Books in Early China." Ph.D. dissertation, University of Chicago.

Herzfeld, Michael. 1992. *The Social Production of Indifference: Exploring the Symbolic Roots of Western Bureaucracy*. New York: Berg.

Hölkeskamp, Karl-J. 2010. *Reconstructing the Roman Republic: An Ancient Political Culture and Modern Research*. Translated by Henry Heimann-Gordon. Princeton, NJ: Princeton University Press.

Hou Hanshu: *Hou Hanshu* 後漢書. 1965. Fan Ye 范曄 (398–446 CE) et al. 90 *juan*, 30 *zhi* (12 vols.). Beijing: Zhonghua.

Hou Xudong 侯旭東. 2008. "Zhongguo gudai zhuanzhi shuo de zhishi kaogu" 中國古代專制說的知識考古. *Jindai shi yanjiu* 4: 4–28.

Hsing I-tien 邢義田. 2000. "Han Chang'an Weiyang gong qian dian yi zhi chutu mu jian de xingzhi" 漢長安未央宮前殿遺址出土木簡的性質. *Da lu za zhi* 100 (6): 1–4.

Hubei Sheng Wenwu Kaogu Yanjiu Suo. 湖北省文物考古研究所 and Suizhou Shi Kaogu Duibian 隨州市考古隊編. 2006. *Suizhou Kongjiapo Han mu jian du* 隨州孔家坡漢墓簡牘. Beijing: Wenwu.

Hulsewé, A. F. P. 1955. *Remnants of Han Law*. Leiden: Brill.

———. 1986. "Ch'in and Han Law." In *Cambridge History of China*. Vol. 1: *The Ch'in and Han Empires, 221 BC–AD 220*, edited by Dennis Twitchett and Michael Loewe, 520–44. Cambridge, UK: Cambridge University Press.

———. 1989. "Founding Fathers and Yet Forgotten Men: A Closer Look at the Tables of the Nobility in the *Shih chi* and the *Han shu*." *T'oung Pao* 75 (1–3): 43–126.

———. 1993. "*Han shu* 漢書." In *Early Chinese Texts: A Bibliographical Guide*, edited by Michael Loewe, 129–36. Berkeley: Society for the Study of Early China and Institute of East Asian Studies, UC Berkeley.

———. 1993b. "*Shih chi* 史記." In *Early Chinese Texts: A Bibliographical Guide*, edited by Michael Loewe, 404–14. Berkeley: Society for the Study of Early China and Institute of East Asian Studies, UC Berkeley.

——— and Michael Loewe. 1979. *China in Central Asia: The Early Stage: 125 B.C.–A.D. 23: An Annotated Translation of Chapters 61 and 96 of the History of the Former Han Dynasty*. Leiden: Brill.

Hutton, Eric, trans. and ed. 2014. *Xunzi: The Complete Text*. Princeton, NJ: Princeton University Press.

Jiang Baolian 姜寶蓮 and Qin Jianming 秦建明, eds. 2004. *Han Zhongguan zhu qian yi zhi* 漢鐘官鑄錢遺址. Beijing: Kexue.

Jiao Nanfeng焦南峰. 2010. "Zongmiao dao, youdao, yiguan dao" 宗庙道游道衣冠道. *Wenwu* (1): 73–77.

Johnson, David. 1981. "Epic and History in Early China: The Matter of Wu Tzu-hsü." *Journal of Asian Studies* 40 (2): 255–71.

Kalinowski, Marc. 1998–99. "The Xingde 刑德 Texts from Mawangdui." *Early China* 23–24: 125–202.

———. 2010. "Divination and Astrology: Received Texts and Excavated Manuscripts." In *China's Early Empires: A Re-appraisal*, edited by Michael Nylan and Michael Loewe, 339–66. Cambridge, UK: Cambridge University Press.

———. 2012–13. "The Notion of '*Shi* 式' and Some Related Terms in Qin-Han Calendrical Astrology." *Early China* 35: 331–60.

Kamada Shigeo 鎌田重雄. 1962. *Shin Kan seiji seido no kenkyū* 秦漢代政治制度の研究. Tokyo: Nihon gakujutsu shinkōkai.

Kamiya Masakazu 紙屋正和. 1974. "Zen Kan shokō ōkoku no kansei—naishi wo chūshin ni shite" 前漢諸候王国の官制—内史を中心について. *Kyūshū daikgaku tōyōshi ronshū* (3): 17–35.

———. 2009. *Kan jidai ni okeru gun ken sei no tenkai* 漢時代における郡県制の展開. Kyoto: Hyōyūshoten.

Kern, Martin. 2001. "Ritual, Text, and the Formation of the Canon: Historical Transitions of *Wen* in Early China." *T'oung Pao* 87 (1–3): 43–91.

———. 2003a. "The 'Biography of Sima Xiangru' and the Question of the *Fu* in Sima Qian's *Shiji*." *Journal of the American Oriental Society* 123 (2): 303–16.

———. 2003b. "Western Han Aesthetics and the Genesis of the *Fu*." *Harvard Journal of Asiatic Studies* 63 (2): 383–437.

———. 2009a. "Bronze Inscriptions, the *Shijing*, and the *Shangshu*: The Evolution of the Ancestral Sacrifice During the Western Zhou." In *Early Chinese Religion: Part One: Shang through Han (1250 BC–220 AD)*, vol. 1, 143–200, edited by John Lagerwey and Marc Kalinowski. Leiden: Brill:

———. 2009b. "Literature: Early China." In *A Scholarly Review of Chinese Studies in North America*, edited by Haihui Zhang, Zhaohui Xue, Shuyong Jiang, and Gary Lance Lugar, 292–316. Ann Arbor, MI: Association for Asian Studies.

———. 2014. "Creating a Book and Performing It: The 'Yao Lüe' Chapter of the *Huainanzi* as a Western Han Fu." In *The* Huainanzi *and Textual Production in Early China*, edited by Sarah A. Queen and Michael Puett, 125–50. Leiden: Brill.

Kinney, Anne Behnke, trans. and ed. 2014. *Exemplary Women of Early China: The* Lienü zhuan *of Liu Xiang*. New York: Columbia University Press.

Klein, Esther. 2010. "The History of a Historian: Perspectives on the Authorial Roles of Sima Qian." Ph.D. dissertation, Princeton University.

Knechtges, David. 1970–71. "Wit, Humor, and Satire in Early Chinese Literature (to A.D. 220)." *Monumenta Serica* 29: 79–98.

———. 1976. *The Han Rhapsody: A Study of the Fu of Yang Hsiung (53 B.C.–A.D. 18)*. Cambridge, UK: Cambridge University Press.

———. 1982. *Wen hsuan, or, Selections of Refined Literature*. Vol. 1: *Rhapsodies on Metropolises and Capitals*. Princeton, NJ: Princeton University Press.

———. 1987. *Wen hsuan, or, Selections of Refined Literature*. Vol. 2: *Rhapsodies on Sacrifices, Hunting, Travel, Sightseeing, Palaces and Halls, Rivers and Seas*. Princeton, NJ: Princeton University Press.

———. 1999. "Criticism of the Court in Han Dynasty Literature." In *Selected Essays on Court Culture in Cross-Cultural Perspective*, edited by Yaofu Lin, 51–77. Taipei: Taiwan University Press.

——— and Eugene Vance, eds. 2005. *Rhetoric and the Discourses of Power in Court Culture: China, Europe, and Japan*. Seattle: University of Washington Press.

Knoblock, John, and Jeffrey Riegel, trans. 2000. *The Annals of Lü Buwei*. Stanford: Stanford University Press.

Kumagai Shigezō 熊谷滋三. 1996. "Zen Kan ni okeru 'Bani kōsha' to 'Kigi bani'" 前漢における「蛮夷降者」と「帰義蛮夷」. *Tōyō bunka kenkyūjo kiyō* 134 (Dec.): 19–71.

———. 2001. "Zen Kan no tenkaku • taikō rei • daikōrō" 前漢の典客•大行令•大鴻臚. *Tōyōshi kenkyū* 59 (4): 69–103.

Lao Gan 勞幹. 1948. "Lun Han dai de neichao yu waichao" 論漢代的內朝與外朝. *Zhongyang yanjiu yuan lishi yuyan yanjiu suo ji kan* (13): 227–67.

Lau, D. C., trans. 1970. *Mencius*. London: Penguin.

Lewis, Mark Edward. 1999a. "The Feng and Shan Sacrifices of Emperor

Wu of the Han." In *State and Court Ritual in China*, edited by Joseph P. McDermott, 50–80. Cambridge, UK: Cambridge University Press.

———. 1999b. *Writing and Authority in Early China*. Albany: State University of New York Press.

———. 2005. *The Construction of Space in Early China*. Albany: State University of New York Press.

———. 2007. *The Early Chinese Empires: Qin and Han*. Cambridge, MA: Belknap Press.

Leys, Simon, trans. and ed. 1997. *The Analects of Confucius*. New York: Norton.

L'Haridon, Beatrice, and Stéphane Feuillas, trans. and annotators. 2012. *Lu Jia, Nouveaux discours*. Paris: Les Belles Lettres.

Li Dalong李大龍. 2014. *Handai Zhongguo bianjiang shi* 漢代中國邊疆史研究. Ha'erbin: Heilongjiang jiao yu chu ban she.

Li, Feng. 2001–2. "Offices in Bronze Inscriptions and Western Zhou Government Administration." *Early China*, 26–27: 1–72.

Li Kaiyuan 李開元. 2000. *Han diguo de jianli yu Liu Bang jituan: Jun gong shouyi jiceng yanjiu* 漢帝國的建立與劉邦集團: 軍功受益階層研究. Beijing: Sanlian.

Li Ling 李零. 2011. "Zhongguo zui zao de 'sheng guan tu': Shuo Kongjiapo Han jian 'rishu' de 'ju guan tu' ji xiangguan cailiao" 中國最早的「升官圖」: 說孔家坡漢簡「日書」的「居官圖」及相關材料. *Wenwu* (5): 68–79.

Li Lingfu李令福. 2009. *Gu du Xi'an chengshi buju ji qi dili jichu* 古都西安城市佈局及其地理基礎. Beijing: Renmin.

Lie nü zhuan zhuzi suoyin 烈女傳逐字索引 1994. (A Concordance to the *Lie nü zhuan*). Edited by Ho Che Wah. Hong Kong: Commercial Press.

Liji jijie 禮記集解. (1989) 2007. Vols. 1–3. Edited and annotated by Sun Xingdan 孫希旦. Beijing: Zhonghua.

Liu Pak-yuen廖伯源. 1983. *Les institutions politiques et la lute pour le pouvoir au milieu de la dynastie des Han antérieurs*. Paris: Collège de France.

———. (1986) 1998. "Xi Han huanggong suwei jingbei za kao" 西漢皇宮宿衛警備雜考. In *Lishi yu zhidu—Han dai zhengzhi zhidu shishi* 歷史與制度一漢代政治制度與試釋, 1–35. Taipei: Taiwan shangwu yinshu guan.

———. 2006. *Shi zhe yu guan zhi yan bian: Qin Han huangdi shi zhe kao lun* 使者與官制演變: 秦漢皇帝使者考論. Taipei: Wen jin chu ban she.

Liu Qingzhu劉慶柱. (1995) 2006. "Han Chang'an cheng Weiyang Gong buju xingzhi chu lun" 漢長安城未央宮佈局形制初論. In *Han Chang'an cheng yizhi yanjiu*漢長安城遺址研究, edited by Zhongguo Shehui Kexue Yuan Kaogu Yanjiusuo Han Chang'an Cheng Gongzuo Dui 中國社會科學院考

古研究所漢長安城工作隊 and Xi'an Shi Han Chang'an Cheng Yizhi Baoguan Suo 西安市漢長安城遺址保管所, 483–95. Beijing: Kexue.

———. 2004. "Xi Han Taihou chui lian ting zheng zhengju que zao—Cong Weiyang gong, Changle gong de kaogu faxian lai kan Xi Han de 'er yuan zheng zhi'" 西漢太后垂簾證據確鑿—從未央宮, 長樂宮的考古發現來看西漢的「二元政治」. *Xinhua wen gao* 9.

———. 2006. "Zhongguo gu dai ducheng yizhi buju xingzhi de kaogu faxian suo fanying de shehui xingtai bianhua yanjiu" 中國古代都城遺址布局形制的考古發現所反映的社會形態變化. *Kao gu xue bao* 3: 281–312.

——— and Li Yufang 李毓芳. 2003. *Han Chang'an cheng* 漢長安城. Beijing: Wenwu.

Liu Rui 劉瑞. 2007. "Xi Han Chang'an cheng de chaoxiang, zhoujian ji buju sixiang" 西漢長安城的朝向, 軸線及佈局思想. *Wen shi* 79 (2): 61–105.

———. 2011. *Han Chang'an cheng de chaoxiang, zhouxian yu nan jiao li zhi jianzhu* 漢長安城的朝向, 軸線與南郊禮制建築. Beijing: Zhonggui she hui ke xue.

——— and Liu Tao 劉濤. 2010. *Xi Han zhuhou wang ling zhidu yanjiu* 西漢諸侯王陵制度研究. Beijing: Zhongguo shehui kexue chuban she.

Liu, Yang. 2012. "City, Palace, and Burial: An Archaeological Perspective on Qin Culture in Shaanxi." In *China's Terracotta Warriors: The First Emperor's Legacy*, edited by Liu Yang, 41–61. Minneapolis: Minneapolis Institute of Arts.

Liu Zhendong 劉振東 and Zhang Jianfeng 張建鋒. 2006. "Xi Han Changle gong yizhi de faxian yu chubu yanjiu" 西漢長樂宮遺址的發祥與初步研究. *Kaogu* (10): 22–29.

Llewellyn-Jones, Lloyd. 2002. "Eunuchs and the Royal Harem in Achaemenid Persia." In *Eunuchs in Antiquity and Beyond*, edited by S. Tougher, 19–49. London: Classical Press of Wales and Duckworth.

———. 2013. *King and Court in Ancient Persia, 559 to 331 BCE*. Edinburgh: Edinburgh University Press.

Lo, Andrew. 2004. "Official Aspirations: Chinese Promotion Games." In *Asian Games: The Art of Contest*, edited by Colin MacKenzie and Irving Finkel, 64–75. New York: Asia Society.

Lo, Vivienne. 2001. "The Influence of Nurturing Life Culture on the Development of Western Han Acumoxa Therapy." In *Innovation in Chinese Medicine*, edited by Elisabeth Hsu, 19–50. Oxford: Oxford University Press.

Loewe, Michael. 1967. *Records of Han Administration*. Vols. 1–2. London: Cambridge University Press.

———. 1974. *Crisis and Conflict in Han China*. London: Allen and Unwyn.

———. 1981. "The Authority of the Emperors of Ch'in and Han." In *State and Law in East Asia: Festschrift Karl Bünger*, edited by Dieter Eikemeier and Herbert Franke, 80–111. Wiesbaden: Harrassowitz.

———. 1986. "The Former Han Dynasty." In *The Cambridge History of China*. Vol. 1: *The Ch'in and Han Empires 221 B.C.–A.D. 220*, edited by Denis Twitchett and Michael Loewe. Cambridge, UK: Cambridge University Press.

———. 1999a. "The Heritage Left to the Empires." In *The Cambridge History of Ancient China*, edited by Michael Loewe and Edward L. Shaughnessy, 967–1032. Cambridge, UK: Cambridge University Press.

———. 1999b. "State Funerals of the Han Empire." *Bulletin of the Museum of Far Eastern Antiquities* (71): 5–72.

———. 2000. *A Biographical Dictionary of the Qin, Former Han, and Xin Periods*. Leiden: Brill.

———. 2004. *The Men Who Governed Han China: Companion to a Biographical Dictionary of the Qin, Former Han, and Xin Periods*. Leiden: Brill.

———. 2008. "The Organs of Han Imperial Government: *Zhongdu guan, duguan, xianguan*, and *xiandao guan*." *Bulletin of the School of Oriental and African Studies* 71 (3): 509–28.

———. 2010a. "The Operation of the Government." In *China's Early Empires: A Re-appraisal*, edited by Michael Nylan and Michael Loewe, 308–19. Cambridge, UK: Cambridge University Press.

———. 2010b. "Social Distinctions, Groups and Privileges." In *China's Early Empires: A Re-appraisal*, edited by Michael Nylan and Michael Loewe, 296–307. Cambridge, UK: Cambridge University Press.

———. 2011. *Dong Zhongshu, a Confucian Heritage and the* Chunqiu fanlu. Leiden: Brill.

———. 2012–13. "Han Yuandi, Reigned 48 to 33 B.C.E., and His Advisors." *Early China* 35–36: 361–93.

———. 2014. "Officials of Western Han and Their Background." *Archiv Orientalni* 82: 381–88.

———. 2015. "Liu Xiang and Liu Xin." In *Chang'an 26 BCE: An Augustan Age in China*, edited by Michael Nylan and Griet Vankeerberghen, 369–90. Seattle: University of Washington Press.

Lü Shihao 呂世浩. 2009. *Cong "Shi ji" dao "Han shu": Zhuanzhe guocheng yu lishi yiyi* 從《史記》到《漢書》: 轉折過程與歷史意義. Taipei: Taiwan daxue chuban zhongxin.

Lüshi chunqiu ji shi 呂氏春秋集釋. 1996. In *Minguo cong shu* 民國叢書. Vol. 11. 5th edition. Shanghai: Shanghai shu dian.

Lu Zhongfa 陸忠發. 2005. "Chaoting ben yi kao" 朝廷本意考. *Yuyan yanjiu* 25 (4): 102–4.

Luo Changpei 羅常培 and Zhou Zumou 周祖謨. 1958. *Han Wei-Jin Nanbeichao yunbu yanbian yanjiu: Diyi fence* 漢魏晉南北朝韻部演變研究: 第一分冊. Beijing: Kexue, 1958.

Luo Qingkang 羅慶康. 1988. "Shuiheng duwei zhidu kao shu" 水横都尉制度考述. *Yiyang shi zhuan xue bao (zhe xue ban)* 益陽師專學報 (哲學版). 1: 13–20.

Lunheng jijie 論衡集解. 1962. Vols. 1–2. Comp. Wang Chong 王充 (27–100? CE). Annotated by Liu Pansui 劉盼遂. Taipei: Shijie shuju, 1962.

Lynn, Richard John, trans. 1994. *The Classic of Changes: A New Translation of the* I Ching *as Interpreted by Wang Bi*. New York: Columbia University Press.

Major, John, Sarah Queen, Andrew Seth Meyer, and Harold D. Roth, trans. and eds. 2010. *The Huainanzi: A Guide to the Theory and Practice of Government in Early Han China*. New York: Columbia University Press.

Martin, John Levi. 2015. "What Is Ideology?" *Sociologia, problemas e prácticas* 77: 9–31.

Meguro Kyōko 目黒杏子. 2011. "Zen Kan Butei no junkō—Saishi to kōtei kenryoku no shiten kara" 前漢武帝の巡幸—祭祀と皇帝権力の視点から. *Shirin* 94 (4): 37–70.

Mengzi ben yi 孟子本意. 1996. In *Minguo cong shu* 民國叢書. Vol. 4. 5th edition. Shanghai: Shanghai shu dian.

Minar, Edward. 2011. "The Life of the Sign: Rule-Following, Practice, and Agreement." In *The Oxford Handbook of Wittgenstein*, edited by Oskari Kuusela and Marie McGinn, 276–93. Oxford: Oxford University Press.

Morgan, Carol. 2004. "The Chinese Game of Shengguan tu." *Journal of the American Oriental Society* 124 (3): 517–32.

Mozi jijie 墨子集解. 1996. In *Minguo cong shu*民國叢書. Vol. 7. 5th edition. Shanghai: Shanghai shu dian.

Nishijima Sadao 西嶋定生. (1965) 1983. "Butei no shi: 「En tetsu ron」 no seiji shiteki haikei" 武帝の死: 「塩鉄論」の史的背景. In *Chūgoku kodai kokka to Higashi Ajia sekai*, 193–233. Tōkyō: Tōkyō daigaku shuppankai. Originally published in *Kodai shi kōza* 22 (1965).

Nissen, Hans J., Peter Damerow, and Robert K. Englund. 1993. *Archaic Bookkeeping: Early Writing and Techniques of Economic Administration in the Ancient Near East*. Translated by Paul Larsen. Chicago: University of Chicago Press.

Nylan, Michael. 1999a. "Calligraphy, the Sacred Text, and the Test of Culture." In *Character and Context in Chinese Calligraphy*, edited by Cary Liu, Dora C. Y. Ching, and Judith G. Smith, 16–77. Princeton, NJ: Princeton University Press.

———. 1999b. "A Problematic Model: The Han 'Orthodox Synthesis,' Then and Now." In *Imagining Boundaries: Changing Coinfucian Doctrines, Texts, and Hermeneutics*, edited by Kai-wing Chow, On-cho Ng, and John B. Henderson, 17–56. Albany: State University of New York Press.

———. 2001. "On the Politics of Pleasure." *Asia Major*, 3rd series, 14 (1): 73–124.

———. 2009. "Classics without Canonization: Learning and Authority in Qin and Han." In *Early Chinese Religion*. Part 1: *Shang through Han (1250 BC–220 AD)*, edited by John Lagerwey and Marc Kalinowski, 721–76. Leiden: Brill.

———. 2011. *Yang Xiong and the Pleasures of Reading and Classical Learning in China*. New Haven, CT: American Oriental Society.

———, trans. 2013. *Exemplary Figures / Fayan*, by Yang Xiong (53 BCE–18 CE). Seattle: University of Washington Press.

———. 2015a. "Assets Accumulating: Sima Qian's Perspective on Moneymaking, Virtue, and History." In *Views from Within, Views from Beyond: Approaches to the* Shiji *as an Early Work of Historiography*, edited by Hans van Ess, Olga Lomová, and Dorothee Schaab-Hanke. Wiesbaden: Harrassowitz Verlag.

———. 2015b. Introduction to *Chang'an 26 BCE: An Augustan Age in China*, edited by Michael Nylan and Griet Vankeerberghen, 3–52. Seattle: University of Washington Press.

———. Forthcoming. "Han View of the Qin Legacy and the Late Western Han 'Classical Turn.'" *Bulletin of the Museum of Far Eastern Antiquities* (79–80).

———, and Griet Vankeerberghen, eds. 2015. *Chang'an 26 BCE: An Augustan Age in China*. Seattle: University of Washington Press.

Okayasu Isamu岡安勇. 1987. Chūgoku ni okeru 'kakurei' no reigū keishiki—Kyōdo kokanja tanku no reigū wo tegakari toshite" 中國古代における客禮 の禮遇形式一匈奴呼韓邪の禮遇を手掛かりとして. *Tōhōgaku* 74 (July): 30–42.

Paterson, Jeremy. 2007. "Friends in High Places: The Creation of the Court of the Roman Emperor." In *The Court and Court Society in Ancient Monarchies*, edited by A. J. S. Spawforth, 121–56. Cambridge, UK: Cambridge University Press.

Peng Hao 彭浩. 1993. "Hubei Jiangling chutu Xi Han jiandu gai shuo" 湖北江陵出土西漢簡牘概說. In *Kankan kenkyū no genjō to tenbō: Kankan kenkyū kokusai shinpojūmu '92 hōkokusho* 漢簡研究の現状と展望: 漢簡研究国際シンポジュウム'92報告書, edited by Ōba Osamu 大庭脩, 166–73. Suita-shi: Kansai daigaku shuppanbu.

———, Chen Wei 陳偉, and Kudō Motoo 工藤元男. 2007. *Er nian lü ling yu zou yan shu: Zhangjiashan er si qi hao Han mu chutu falü wenxian shi du* 二年律令與奏讞書: 張家山二四七號漢墓出土法律文獻釋讀. Shanghai: Shanghai gu ji.

Pierson, Paul. 2004. *Politics in Time: History, Institutions, and Social Analysis*. Princeton, NJ: Princeton University Press.

Pines, Yuri. 2002. "Friends or Foes: Changing Concepts of Ruler-Minister Relations and the Notion of Loyalty in Pre-Imperial China." *Monumenta Serica* 50: 35–74.

———, Gideon Shelach, Lothar von Falkenhausen, and Robin D. S. Yates, eds. 2013. *Birth of an Empire: The State of Qin Revisited*. Berkeley: University of California Press.

Quan Han wen 全漢文. 1961. 63 *juan*. Vol. 1 of *Quan Shanggu Sandai Qin Han Sanguo Liuchao wen* 全上古三代秦漢三國六朝文. Compiled by Yan Kejun 嚴可均 (1762–1843). 746 *juan* (9 vols.). Taipei: Shijie shuju.

Quan Hou Han wen 全後漢文. 1961. 106 *juan*. Vol. 2 of *Quan Shanggu Sandai Qin Han Sanguo Liuchao wen* 全上古三代秦漢三國六朝文. Compiled by Yan Kejun 嚴可均 (1762–1843). 746 *juan* (9 vols.). Taipei: Shijie shuju.

Rawski, Evelyn. 1998. *The Last Emperors: A Social History of Qing Imperial Institutions*. Berkeley: University of California Press.

Richter, Matthias. 2013. *The Embodied Text: Establishing Textual Identity in Early Chinese Manuscripts*. Leiden: Brill.

Roberts, Moss. 2013. "Balancing Power: The Ascent of the Vassal (*Chen*)." *Chinese Studies in History* 46 (4): 6–26.

Robinson, David, ed. 2008. *Culture, Courtiers, and Competition: The Ming Court (1368–1644)*. Cambridge, MA: Harvard University Asia Center.

Rouzer, Paul. 2001. *Articulated Ladies: Gender and the Male Community in Early Chinese Texts*. Cambridge, MA: Harvard University Asia Center.

Sanft, Charles. 2014. *Communication and Cooperation in Early Imperial China*. Albany: State University of New York Press.

Satō Tatsurō 佐藤達郎. 2002. "Kan dai no ko kan shin, yakuchū hen (jō)." 漢代の古官箴、訳注篇 (上). *Ōsaka shōin joshi daigaku ronshū* 大阪樟蔭女子大学論集 39: 11–24.

———. 2003. "Kan dai no ko kan shin, yakuchū hen (chū)." 漢代の古官箴、訳注篇 (中). *Ōsaka shōin joshi daigaku ronshū* 大阪樟蔭女子大学論集 40: 23–34.

———. 2004. "Kan dai no ko kan shin, yakuchū hen (ka)." 漢代の古官箴、訳注篇 (下). *Ōsaka shōin joshi daigaku ronshū* 大阪樟蔭女子大学論集 41: 41–54.

———. 2005. "Kan dai no ko kan shin, ron kō hen. 漢代の古官箴、論考篇. *Ōsaka shōin joshi daigaku ronshū* 大阪樟蔭女子大学論集 42: 11–21.

Schaberg, David. 1997. "Remonstrance in Eastern Zhou Historiography." *Early China* 22: 133–79.

Sewell, William H., Jr. 2005. *Logics of History: Social Theory and Social Transformation*. Chicago: University of Chicago Press.

Shaanxi Sheng Kaogu Yanjiu Suo 陕西省考古研究所, ed. 2004. *Qin du Xianyang kaogu baogao* 秦都咸陽考古報告. Beijing: Kexue.

Shandong Sheng Zibo Shi Bowuguan 山東省淄博市博物館. 1985. "Xi Han Qi wang mu sui zang qi wu keng" 西漢齊王墓隨葬器物坑. *Kaogu xue bao* (2): 223–66.

Shangshu zhuzi suoyin 尚書逐字索引 1995. (A Concordance to the *Shangshu*). Edited by Chan Man Hung. Hong Kong: Commercial Press.

Shiji: *Shiji* 史記. 1959. Compiled by Sima Qian 司馬遷 (145?–86? BCE) et al. 130 *juan* (10 vols.). Beijing: Zhonghua.

Shuihudi Qin Mu Zhujian Zhengli Xiaozu 睡虎地秦墓竹簡整理小組. 1990. *Shuihudi Qin mu zhu jian* 睡虎地秦墓竹簡. Beijing: Wenwu.

Smith, Dennis. 2009. "Norbert Elias and *The Court Society*: From Gallapagos to Versailles via Quai des Orfèvres." Paper presented at Les cours en Europe: Bilan historiographique. Colloque international. Centre de recherché du château de Versailles, France. September 24–26, 2009. Accessed May 15, 2014.https://www.academia.edu/10366074/Norbert_Elias_and_The_Court_Society.

Smith, Rowland. 2007. "The Imperial Court of the Late Roman Empire, c. AD 300–c. AD 450." In *The Court and Court Society in Ancient Monarchies*, edited by A. J. S. Spawforth, 157–232. Cambridge, UK: Cambridge University Press.

Spawforth, A. J. S., ed. 2007. *The Court and Court Society in Ancient Monarchies*. Cambridge, UK: Cambridge University Press.

Sun Xingyan 孫星衍 (1753–1818) and Zhou Tianyou 周天游. (1990) 2008. *Han guan liu zhong* 漢官六種. Beijing: Zhonghua.

Swann, Nancy Lee, trans. and annotator. 1950. *Food and Money in Ancient China: The Earliest Economic History of China to A.D. 25, Hanshu 24, with Related Texts, Hanshu 91 and Shih-chi 129*. Princeton, NJ: Princeton University Press.

Tang Xiaofeng. 2015. "The Evolution of Imperial Urban Form in Western Han Chang'an." In *Chang'an 26 BCE: An Augustan Age in China*, edited by Michael Nylan and Griet Vankeerberghen, 55–74. Seattle: University of Washington Press.

Tatemi Satoshi 楯身智志. 2009. "Kan hatsu kōso koshin I ji ko: Zenkan zenhen ki ni okeru sobyo seido no tenkai to koso koshin rekko no suii" 漢初高祖功臣位次考:前漢前半期　における宗廟制度の展開と高祖功臣列侯の推移. *Tōyō gakuhō* 90 (4): 1–32.

———. 2012. "Zen Kan no sōsei—teishitsu • shokō ōka kankei saikō" 前漢の宗正ー帝室 • 诸侯王家関係再考. *Shigaku zasshi* 121 (3): 1–34.

Tian Tian 田天. 2015a. *Qin Han guojia jisi shi gao* 秦漢國家祭祀史稿. Beijing: Sanlian.

———. 2015b. "The Suburban Sacrifice Reforms and the Evolution of the Imperial Sacrifices." In *Chang'an 26 BCE: An Augustan Age in China*, edited by Michael Nylan and Griet Vankeerberghen, 263–91. Seattle: University of Washington Press.

Twitchett, Dennis. 1992. *The Writing of Official History under the T'ang.* Cambridge, UK: Cambridge University Press.

Van Ess, Hans. 2007. "The Imperial Court in Han China." In *The Court and Court Society in Ancient Monarchies*, edited by A. J. S. Spawforth, 233–66. Cambridge, UK: Cambridge University Press.

———. 2015. "The Late Western Han Historian Chu Shaosun." In *Chang'an 26 BCE: An Augustan Age in China*, edited by Michael Nylan and Griet Vankeerberghen. Seattle: University of Washington Press.

Vankeerberghen, Griet. 2001. *The* Huainanzi *and Liu An's Claim to Moral Authority.* Albany: State University of New York Press.

———. 2015. "Pining for the West: Chang'an in the Life of Kings and Their Families During Chang'an's Reign." In *Chang'an 26 BCE: An Augustan Age in China*, edited by Michael Nylan and Griet Vankeerberghen, 347–66. Seattle: University of Washington Press.

Waley, Arthur, and Joseph Allen, trans. 1996. *The Book of Songs, Shijing: The Ancient Classic of Poetry.* New York: Grove Press.

Wang, Haicheng. 2014. *Writing and the Ancient State: Early China in Comparative Perspective.* Cambridge, UK: Cambridge University Press.

Wang Mingqin王明欽. 2004. "Wangjiatai Qin mu zhu jian gai shu" 王家台秦墓竹簡概述. In *Xin chu jianbo yanjiu*新出簡帛研究, edited by Ai Lan艾蘭 (Sarah Allan) and Xing Wen邢文, 26–49. Beijing: Wenwu.

Wang Shejiao 王社教. 1995. "Xi Han Shanglin yuan de fanwei ji xiangguan wenti" 西漢上林苑德範圍及相關問題. *Zhongguo lishi dili luncong* (3): 223–33.

Wang, Yü-ch'üan. 1949. "An Outline of the Central Government of the Former Han Dynasty." *Harvard Journal of Asiatic Studies* 12 (1–2): 134–87.

Wang Zijin王子今. 2011. "'Han chao' de fasheng: Guojia guannian de lishi kaocha" "漢朝"的發生: 國家概念的歷史考察. In *Qin Han bianjiang yu minzu wenti* 秦漢邊疆與民族問題, 391–405. Beijing: Zhongguo renmin daxue chuban she.

——— and Lü Zongli呂宗力. 2011. "Lun Chang'an 'xiao nü Chen Chigong' da shui e yan shi jian" 論長安'小女陳持弓'大水訛言事件. *Shi xue ji kan* (July, no. 4): 50–55.

Watanabe Masatomo 渡邉将智. 2010. "Go Kan Rakuyōjō ni okeru kōtei •

shokan no seiji kōkan" 後漢洛陽城における皇帝 諸官の政治空間. *Shigaku zasshi* 119 (12): 1–38.

Xiaogan Diqu Di Er Qi Yigong Yinong Wenwu Kaogu Xunlian Ban 孝感地區第二期亦工亦農文物考古訓練班. 1976. "Hubei Yunmeng Shuihudi shiyi hao Qin mu fajue jianbao" 湖北雲夢睡虎地十一號秦墓發掘簡報. *Wenwu* (6): 1–14.

Xin jiao Zizhi tong jian zhu 新校資治通鑑注. 1974. Composed by Sima Guang 司馬光 (1230–1320). Annotated by Hu Sanxing 胡三省 (1230–1320). Collated and compiled by Zhang Yu 章鈺 (1865–1937). 294 *juan* (15 vols.). Taipei: Shijie shuju.

Xinyu zhuzi suoyin 新語逐字索引 1995. (A Concordance to the *Xinyu*). Edited by Chan Man Hung. Hong Kong: Commercial Press.

Xu Fuguan 徐復觀. (1978) 2001. *Liang Han sixiang shi* 兩漢思想史. Vol. 1. Shanghai: Huadong shifan daxue.

Xu Weimin 徐衛民. 1991. "Xi Han Shanglin yuan gong dian tai guan kao" 西漢上林苑宮殿台觀考. *Wen bo* 4: 34–41.

———. 2011. *Qin Han ducheng yu ziran huanjing guanxi yanjiu* 秦漢都城與自然環境關係研究. Beijing: Kexue.

Xunzi jian shi 荀子柬釋. 1996. In *Minguo cong shu* 民國叢書. Vol. 4. 5th edition. Shanghai: Shanghai shu dian.

Yakuchū Seikei Zakki, Dokudan 訳注西京雜記、独断. 2000. Edited and annotated by Fukui Shigemasa 福井重雅. Tōkyō: Tōhō shoten.

Yan Buke 閻步克. 2009. *Cong jue benwei dao guan benwei: Qin Han guanliao pinwei jiegou yanjiu* 從爵本位到官本位:秦漢官僚品位結構研究. Beijing: Sanlian.

Yan Changgui 晏昌貴. 2008. "Kongjiapo Han jian 'ri shu' tian lao pian jian zhen" 孔家坡漢簡《日書》天牢篇箋證. Paper presented at the International Forum on Bamboo and Silk Documents, University of Chicago. Accessed February 12, 2017. http://cccp.uchicago.edu/archive/2008_IFBSD/Yan_Changgui_2008_IFBSD.pdf.

Yan Kejun, ed. 1999. *Quan Han wen*. 54 *juan*. Beijing: Shang wu yin shu guan.

Yao Shengmin 姚生民. 2002. "Yunyang gong • Linguang gong • Ganquan gong" 雲陽宮•林光宮•甘泉宮. *Wenbo* (4): 50–54.

Yi Ping 易平. 1989. "'Shi ji • jiang xiang biao' daoshu yi li kao bian" 《史記 • 將相表》倒書義例考辨. *Anhui shi daxue bao (zhexue shehui kexue ban)* 3a.

Yoneda Kenshi 米田健志. 2000. "Nihon ni okeru Kandai kanryō sei kenkyū" 日本における漢代官僚制研究. *Chūgoku shigaku* 10 (Dec): 167–88.

Yoshinami Takashi 好並隆司. 1968. "Zen Kan go han ki ni okeru kotei shihai to kanryō sō no dōkō" 前漢後半期における皇帝と官僚の動向. *Tōyō shi kenkyū* 26 (4): 138–58.

———. 1976. Kandai kōtei shihai chitsujo no keisei" 漢代皇帝支配秩序の形成. *Tōyōshi kenkyū* 35 (2): 39–70.

———. 2003. "Chōkasan Kan kan no ritsu bun ni okeru 'kan kōtei' ni tsuite" 張家山漢簡の律文における⊠宦皇帝⊠について. *Beppu daigakuin kiyō* (3): 31–37.

You Yifei 游逸飛. 2013. "Gong zhi tian xia' qian xi—Zhanguo zhi Han chu de jun zhi bian ge" 「共治天下」前夕——戰國至漢初的郡制變革. Ph.D. dissertation, National Taiwan University.

Yu, Ying-shih. 1967. *Trade and Expansion in Han China: A Study in the Structure of Sino-Barbarian Economic Relations*. Berkeley: University of California Press.

Zhang Zhenze 張震澤, ed. and annotator. 1993. *Yang Xiong ji jiao zhu* 揚雄集校注. Shanghai: Shanghai guji.

Zhangjiashan Ersiqi Hao Han Mu Zhujian Zhengli Xiao Zu 張家山二四七號漢墓竹簡整理小組. 2006. *Zhangjiashan Han mu zhu jian (Er si qi hao mu): (Shiwen xiu ding ben)* 張家山漢墓竹簡 (二四七號墓) : (釋文修訂本). Beijing: Wenwu.

Zhao, Dingxin. 2015. "The Han Bureaucracy: Its Origin, Nature, and Development." In *State Power in Ancient China and Rome*, edited by Walter Scheidel, 56–89. Oxford: Oxford University Press.

Zhongguo Shehui Kexue Yuan Kaogu Yanjiusuo 中國社會科學院考古研究所. 1996. *Han Chang'an cheng Weiyang gong: 1980–1989 nian kao gu fa jue bao gao*漢長安城未央宮 : 1980–1989年考古發掘報告. Beijing: Zhongguo da bai ke quan shu.

———. 2006. "Xi'an shi Han Chang'an cheng Changle gong si hao jianzhu yizhi" 西安市漢長安城長樂宮四號建築遺址. *Kaogu* (10): 30–39.

———. 2010. *Zhongguo kaogu xue: Qin Han juan* 中國考古學: 秦漢卷. Beijing: Zhongguo shehui kexue chubanshe.

———. 2011. "Xi'an shi Han Chang'an cheng Changle gong liu hao jianzhu yizhi" 西安市漢長安城長樂宮六號建築遺址. *Kaogu* (6): 11–25.

Zhongguo Shehui Kexue Yuan Kaogu Yanjiusuo and Nihon Nara Kokuritsu Bunkazai Kenkyūjo 日本奈良国立文化財研究所. 2007. *Han Chang'an cheng Gui gong: 1996–2001 nian kao gu fa jue bao gao* 漢長安城桂宮: 1996–2001年考古發掘報告.

Zhu Zongbin 祝總斌. 1990. *Liang Han Wei Jin Nanbei chao zaixiang zhidu yanjiu* 兩漢魏晉南北朝宰相制度研究. Beijing: Zhongguo shehui kexue.

Zikpi, Monica. 2014. "The Afterlives of Qu Yuan." Ph.D. dissertation. University of Oregon.

Zufferey, Nicolas. 2003. *To the Origins of Confucianism: The* Ru *in Pre-Qin Times and During the Early Han Dynasty*. Bern: Peter Lang.

INDEX

CPSIA information can be obtained
at www.ICGtesting.com
Printed in the USA
BVOW08*2322161217
502953BV00004B/14/P